Modern Cost-Benefit Methods

Modern Cost–Benefit Methods

An Introduction to Financial, Economic and
Social Appraisal of Development Projects

George Irvin

with the assistance of Richard Brown

BOOKS
10 East 53d St., New York 10022
(a division of Harper & Row Publishers, Inc.)

First published in Great Britain 1978 by
The Macmillan Press Ltd

Published in the U.S.A. 1978 by
HARPER & ROW PUBLISHERS, INC.
BARNES AND NOBLE IMPORT DIVISION

Printed in Great Britain

Library of Congress Cataloging in Publication Data

Irvin, George
    Modern cost-benefit methods.

    Bibliography: p.
    Includes index.
    1. Cost effectiveness. 2. Externalities (Economics)
3. Capital investments. I. Title.
HD47.I78   1978   658.'552   78 – 2718
ISBN 0 – 06 – 493236 – 2

CONTENTS

ACKNOWLEDGEMENTS

I should like to thank a number of people who have made valuable contributions to the book in its present form. First and foremost, I am indebted to my colleague Richard Brown who contributed major parts of Chapter II as well as helping with some of the worked examples in the text and much of the material contained in Appendix A. Pedro Misle Benitez also provided help with worked examples, some of which are drawn from his own Manual on project appraisal used for internal teaching purposes at the Institute of Social Studies. Members of the Institute's staff who provided useful comments on the first draft include Aurora Carreon, Kurt Martin and Paul van der Wel.

I am also indebted to a number of others for comments and suggestions which I have endeavoured to incorporate in the present text; notably Andrew Barnett, Valpy FitzGerald, Stephen Guisinger, John MacArthur, David Pearce, Maurice Scott and John White.

On the production side, particular thanks are due to Jean Sanders, the Institute's Publications Officer, as well as to Kristi Cruzat, Henny Kouwenhoven and Netty Born who saw the manuscript through various stages of typing.

The usual absolution regarding errors and omissions applies.

INTRODUCTION

For some years now, one of my obligations has been to give a series of lectures on social cost-benefit analysis. My first lecture normally includes an example of a project to build a bridge which displaces an existing ferry, an example pirated from the Introduction to Richard Layard's book which he took from someone else. In any event, the salient point is that the 'bridge and ferry' lecture in its earliest form distinguished between financial appraisal, in which only toll charges were counted as a benefit, and 'social appraisal' which required explaining such concepts as willingness to pay, consumer surplus, externalities and so forth. As one might expect, building the bridge always turned out to be financially unsound but socially warranted. Since then, however, the bridge and ferry lecture has evolved considerably. There are now at least four different ways of appraising the project: private financial, Government financial, economic and social. Notions of consumer surplus and the like have been supplemented by more advanced technical razzle-dazzle; calculations of accounting ratios, consumption conversion factors, income distribution weights and the like currently extend to several blackboards. Not surprisingly, all the methods yield different answers. To make matters worse, students who once listened attentively asking occasional questions about the meaning of this or that calculation now seem more concerned with the political implications of pursuing trade efficiency and distributional objectives and the role of the public sector within dependent capitalist economies. An ex-student of mine sat in on this year's bridge and ferry lecture and remarked that life was simpler in the old days.

Partly for this reason, the present work is a somewhat unorthodox mixture of didactic exposition, basic theory and political commentary, sacrificing a degree of rigour and elegance in the process. The general structure adopted for the book, as the title suggests, broadly divides the field into sections on methods of financial, economic, and social analysis, moving gradually from elementary discounting techniques with which most readers may be presumed familiar to more complex principles and procedures many of which are still the subject of disagreement in the literature. Unlike traditional cost-benefit texts, welfare theory is here largely eschewed, the salient assumption being that the strategic role of the public sector in setting the rate of accumulation and ensuring equitable distribution through direct intervention in economic

activity is now so widely accepted — at least in the development literature if
not in practice — that the debate as to whether atomistically conceived
individual preferences can ever be efficiently aggregated, through the market
or otherwise, is now little more than an intellectual *curiosum*. In this sense
cost-benefit analysis is not, as is sometimes suggested, the application of welfare economics, but its successor. Its merit is to successfully conceptualise a
hierarchy of price systems in which ruling market prices are accorded lowest
status, and the generalised use of social accounting prices is seen as an ultimate objective. By implication, cost-benefit analysis could be argued to be
least appropriate in the case of a predominantly capitalist economy, and most
appropriate for an advanced socialist economy (in which enterprises enjoy a
large measure of autonomy in investment decisions) though such an inference
is rarely drawn in the present literature.

Although the book is intended for a wider audience than that of specialists
in the subject, notably planners as well as those academics (professional
economists or otherwise) who wish to catch up with recent developments in a
rapidly expanding field, it focuses predominantly on theory and application
of what is termed the 'new methodology', or synthesis of thought which has
emerged since the publication of the OECD *Manual* nearly a decade ago. Accordingly, the first three chapters may be treated as optional reading since
these deal with basic discounting and investment criteria, investment appraisal
under risk and uncertainty, and the elements of financial accounting. The
inclusion of the latter, though somewhat unconventional, is intended to help
clarify what is for most economists as obscure an area as is social cost benefit
to the business school graduate. The section on discounting and investment
criteria sets out what are now broadly accepted conventions basic to all forms
of investment appraisal, while the material on risk and uncertainty analysis
includes a brief review of elementary statistical principles. Together, these
constitute a necessary point of departure for the introductory reader, while
those already familiar with the subject matter may find it helpful to briefly
review the ground or else move directly to the following chapters.

Chapters IV through VII deal with 'economic' evaluation or, broadly, with
the theoretical justification and methodology for transforming ruling market
prices into what are sometimes called shadow prices but which in this book
are termed economic accounting prices. Here, current orthodoxy dis-
tinguishes between two levels of market price 'distortion', the first arising
from protectionist policies in the trade sector working their way through to
price relatives in all domestic markets including that for factors, and the
second arising from non-trade induced factor market distortions; viz. labour's
opportunity cost and the opportunity cost of public funds.

Chapter IV opens with a summary of developments in cost-benefit theory
stressing the rise of the new (post-1968) methodology from the fusion of dif-

ferent currents of thought, notably the neo-classical theory of public finance which is largely concerned with developed capitalist economies, and the post-war development literature with its strong classical emphasis. This is followed by a critical review of the 'trade efficiencv' debate which suggests that while the pursuit of comparative advantage raises many more questions than it answers (viz. assessing comparative advantage in the longer term and mini-mising adverse effects of trade dependency), the adoption of world prices — the Little-Mirrlees proposal — decisively breaks the nexus between production decisions and domestic market forces, hence opening the way to a new round of debate about the role of the public sector in planning the trade and non-trade sectors. Finally, the major features of the Little-Mirrlees, Squire-van der Tak and Marglin-Sen-DasGupta approaches are summarised.

Chapters V and VI deal with the economic pricing of traded and non-traded goods respectively and are essentially a didactic exposition of the synthesis of approaches proposed by Little and Mirrlees and Squire and van der Tak (LMST). Concepts of alternative *numéraires*, trade distortions, shadow exchange rates, and consumption conversion factors are explained in detail and the UNIDO approach is seen to be a special (second best) case of currently accepted practice. Iterative calculations of accounting ratios for traded and non-traded goods are illustrated by means of numerical examples, the latter being shown to involve problems of principle where non-traded goods are project outputs. The valuation of potentially traded goods is related in the conventional manner to expectations about changes in future trade policies. Concluding sections cover the calculation of elasticities where changed policies are accompanied by devaluation and show the symmetry be-tween the general equilibrium exchange rate approach and the project specific decomposition and conversion approach, and a discussion of 'optimal tax/ tariff' strategy and cartelisation is included.

The economic valuation of factors in terms of opportunity cost is dealt with in Chapter VII, the separation of 'economic' and 'social' parameters (Chapter VIII) being deemed useful for reasons of exposition. This allows an explicit distinction to be made between 'second best' economic valuation (that is to say, where 'social' objectives are ignored) and first best valuation in which economic and social prices coincide because additions to government savings are treated at par with additions to consumption for all income groups or regions. The treatment of labour's foregone output requires an excursion into aspects of labour market theory and alternative positions are reviewed in brief. In discussing capital, attention is first drawn to some wellknown definitional problems, and simple elements of theory are introduced to dis-tinguish notions of time preference, marginal productivity of public and private funds, and the opportunity cost of public finance. The SOC vs. STP debate is introduced as a prelude to the modern 'social' pricing approach, the former (SOC) position being shown to be consistent with an essentially conservative view of the role of the public sector and the latter (STP) emphasising Government's role as having ultimate responsibility for determining the rate of accumulation. Since both positions are normative, it can be argued that for the purposes of 'second best' economic valuation the appropriate discount rate is simply whatever rate rations projects in a manner which uses up available public capital. If such a discount rate cannot easily be determined by trial and error, investment ranking criteria (PV/K) may need to be employed in the initial instance. The chapter concludes with a brief section on measuring the effective cost of overseas public borrowing.

The final chapter deals with social pricing parameters. The Little and Mirrlees (LM) and Squire and van der Tak (ST) consumption weighting procedures are discussed and illustrated, there being some slight difference of approach between the two. The logic of the social wage rate (SWR) is examined and possible refinements noted; the discussion then relates the SWR to choice of techniques and, ultimately, to the choice of sectoral investment strategy. Continuing on the lines of Chapter VII, the ideal public sector discount rate for consumption (CRI), the social discount rate for investment (SARI) and the conditions under which these coincide are discussed in more detail. A section then follows on the relationship between the use of distribution weights at micro-level and welfare assumption implicit in orthodox National Income accounting conventions (which is perhaps the substantive point of *Redistribution with Growth*), arguing the need for consistency between planning prices at different levels. The chapter closes with a critical examination of the role of the State implicitly assumed in much of the cost-benefit literature, the salient argument being that effective realisation of trade efficiency, distribution and growth objectives which are the central concern of the new cost-benefit synthesis, far from having to be incorporated into project evaluation criteria because of constraints on other areas of State power, imply a major extension of public control over key 'surplus generating' activities.

In the accompanying appendices, besides a standard set of discount tables, the reader will find a set of questions and numerical examples accompanied by a limited set of sample answers. These are grouped according to chapter and are intended to make the book more generally useful as an aid to teaching. Finally, one should mention at least some of the things which have been left out. No discussion appears, for instance, of the particular problems associated with the evaluation of sectorally specific projects (viz. industry, agriculture and transport) other than incidentally in some of the textual examples. Nor has it been attempted to deal with a variety of questions which complement project analysis, such as optimal size of plant, optimal location theory, regional investment balance and so on. Perhaps the most important omission in this respect is to have treated macro-planning issues in cursory fashion and ignored macro-planning techniques altogether, particularly with respect to how these are used to identify candidate projects. In a different vein, the book is open to the criticism that in having attempted to relate technique to broad political issues, justice has been done to neither. Suffice it to say that I am aware of these limitations and can only hope that these will provide an incentive to readers to take up where I have left off.

Institute of Social Studies   George Irvin
The Hague, March 1977

I

PRINCIPLES OF PROJECT APPRAISAL AND SELECTION

1.01 *Stages of Project Planning*

Economists often speak of something called the 'project cycle' by which is meant the various stages of information gathering and decision making which take place between a project's inception and completion. One may list these in roughly the following manner:

1. identification;
2. pre-feasibility;
3. feasibility (technical, financial, economic);
4. pre-investment;
5. investment.

Such a characterisation, based on categories typically used by administrators and consultants, suggests neat dividing lines between stages in project evaluation. In reality, these divisions are somewhat artificial, but do serve to emphasise the need to think of project planning as a *process* of decision making taking place over time. Broadly speaking, what is important about this process is that it should begin with the identification of a number of alternatives, using existing information and gathering new data in such a way as to limit alternatives under consideration to those few which are most promising. In short, the project evaluation process is essentially one of elimination. While the planner naturally hopes that the best alternative will emerge, hence contributing to maximising welfare, he will be pleased if the process produces something less than that: i.e. minimises the incidence of 'white elephants'.

Much therefore depends on what happens at the beginning of the process, or project identification stage. In theory, the identification of projects should be an integral function of the planning process. Hence, a growth rate for the economy may be projected over the next five year period which, according to how income is distributed, will give rise to a pattern of final demand for food, clothing, houses, and so on. To satisfy extra consumption at the margin, it

will be necessary to produce more of each commodity domestically, or increase imports or both. More production will, in turn, require increased
supplies of intermediate inputs as well as more capital goods which, again, can
be met from domestic production or imports. By calculating the direct and
indirect needs of every sector, estimating the effects upon trade and upon the
allocation of skilled manpower and other resources, and re-adjusting initial
assumptions about the growth of incomes, savings, etc. a feasible and consistent set of output targets can be built up on a sector by sector basis. It is
such sectoral information that is at the basis of project identification; i.e. it is
the extra 50,000 KW of required electric generating capacity or Rs. 50
millions of extra textile demand which signals the need for investment. With
sectoral targets known, regional investment plans may then begin to emerge.
For some types of investment, the region may be predetermined (as for
instance where only one major river exists on which to place a hydroelectric
dam); in other cases, there may be significant scope as to choice of region,
and working out the regional distribution of demand and supply in the form
of a regional development plan integrated into an overall plan framework may
be required.

Such a characterisation of project identification does not of course hold
true for all countries, or even for most. Few Western non-socialist countries
have, until recently at least, planned their economies in this way. Important
investment decisions are generally taken in the private sector under the
guidance of the 'invisible hand' of market forces, for better or worse. Socialist
countries, on the other hand, plan and control the allocation of resources almost exclusively through the public sector, relying for the most part on the
elaboration of consistent physical output targets (material balances). Less
developed countries (hereafter LDCs) vary enormously as to the scope and
sophistication of planning. In one sense this is not unusual, as one would
expect quite different forms of planning to be used in, say, India and Sierre
Leone. In another sense, it has become part of the conventional wisdom that
almost every LDC should have a development plan irrespective of the political
regime under which it operates. Since some countries operate under regimes
which are dedicated to the virtues of free enterprise, it is not surprising that
some development plans should be 'paper plans', either in the sense of expressing pious hopes that planned output targets will be reached largely
through the efforts of the private sector without willing the means to ensure
that the private sector can be made to comply, or else in announcing gran-
diose targets for the public sector which cannot be realised simply because
available public resources are limited. More on this type of thing later though.

Ideally, identification of investment projects emerges from the planning
process. If the planning process is very sophisticated, projects may emerge at
a relatively high degree of definition with respect to scale, location, type of

output, etc. In most cases, however, the projects suggested by plans are fairly unspecific – that is to say, there will still be a number of alternatives to be examined before a final decision is reached. In some cases, projects will emerge for reasons which have little to do with the plan but which serve the interests of particular business groups and politicians. Generally, the experienced project economist will be familiar with the need to take account of a project's 'political history' as one component in overall evaluation. A variant of 'political planning' familiar in countries highly dependent on external finance is the case where the public sector investment priorities are determined almost entirely on the basis of which international agency is thought to be lending for what purpose in the current period. Hence one has a situation in which the Planning Office no longer exists as an agency for improving the allocation of domestic resources but rather as a 'shop window' for attracting external finance.

Pre-feasibility and feasibility studies differ essentially with respect to the amount of work required in order to determine whether a project looks viable. For some types of projects, fairly simple analyses – perhaps a short market study and some rough projections and costings – are all that is needed to determine that *no* possible version of the project is likely to be successful. For more complex projects, typically in agriculture and for certain types of infrastructural investment, a good deal of work will be needed to determine whether the project is viable, or more precisely to determine which one of many potential *packages* of resources will make most sense. At this stage, a team of specialists covering a range of disciplines (typically engineers, scientists, economists, and more recently sociologists) will need to work together. A recurrent problem in such situations is that of drawing up appropriate *terms of reference*, and while no simple *pro forma* exists for this exercise, it will be important to bear in mind that consultants (whether domestic or foreign) will need both some indication of planners' perceptions of the nature of project potential as well as clear guidelines concerning what to investigate and how to consult with Government officials about their progress.

A related problem at feasibility stage concerns the role of the economist. While the economist in principle has a central role in performing the calculations which narrow down the range of project options to the few which are most promising, all too often he is used merely to provide elaborate justification for a set of decisions already taken at technical design stage. A typical example is that of a dam project where the choice of dam site will need to be considered in the light of the effect of alternative locations on regional economic activity as a whole and not merely taken on the basis of optimal engineering criteria.[1]

1   See Joy (1968).

As part of the final feasibility report, the economist will normally present cost-benefit calculations summarising the project's viability and efficiency with respect to the economy-wide use of resources. The distinction between various cost-benefit approaches, and particularly the set of techniques which have come to be grouped under the rubric of *social* cost-benefit analysis is the central subject of what follows. At this early stage in the discussion, though, it will be useful to repeat the warning, however obvious it may seem, that evaluation is basically an exercise in predicting physical quantities and prices, and hence subject to margins of error which arise both from the nature of the data base being used and from the effect of unforeseen circumstances.

The further stages of the project cycle which follow feasibility are not really within the scope of the present volume, but a few remarks will be appropriate. After feasibility, planners will be concerned with two types of things: firstly, mobilising the necessary financial resources for the project (which is discussed briefly in a later section of evaluating aid offers), and secondly, mobilising the expertise necessary for successful construction and operation of the project. It is at this stage that many of the operational decisions are taken: viz. recruitment of management and technicians, supervision during construction, and implementation of ancillary programmes necessary to ensure the supply of inputs. There is evidence to show that this may indeed be the most critical stage in determining project success or failure.[1] While some of this work can successfully be 'contracted out', as for example by having the original consulting engineers supervise contract tender and construction,[2] other aspects will need to be placed under the direct responsibility of the Planning Office, the relevant Ministry, or the appropriately created authority. Unfortunately, this area of project planning is typically relegated to the area of 'public administration' and hence deemed of marginal interest to the economics profession.

1.02 *Alternatives, Enumeration and Quantification*

Once a project has evolved to a point where it becomes relevant to carry out full economic appraisal, it will be useful to think of the problem in terms of a number of broadly defined headings.

To begin with, the analyst will need to have a clear picture of the nature of the alternatives to be studied. Is it one project that is to be evaluated, or several alternatives? Are these best defined with respect to technology, size,

1 See Hirschman (1967).
2 Such a practice is not entirely without risk; it effectively encourages consulting engineers to 'pass' a project at feasibility stage in order to reap the very generous rewards associated with supervision.

or perhaps the way in which the total project is phased through time? Determining the *relevant* alternatives can be a critical problem, though perhaps the one least mentioned in the literature since it is typically assumed that such matters will be settled at terms of reference stage and be part of the economists' brief. In practice this is rarely the case, and one needs to emphasise that appraisal and design are part of a single planning process.

An obvious corollary is that there are always at least two alternatives in a project appraisal. Even where only a single version of a project is being considered, the implicit alternative is *not to do* the project and a careful analysis of the 'without' situation is needed if the incremental effects of the project are to be assessed. It is this increment which one is attempting to identify and quantify.

Having determined relevant alternatives, the analyst is now concerned with calculating costs and benefits. Here it will be useful to distinguish between the *enumeration* of costs and benefits and their *quantification*. By enumeration is meant the determination of costs and benefits relevant to the particular type of analysis being carried out, bearing in mind that these will differ according to the point of view from which profitability is being considered. To take a simple example, suppose one is evaluating the construction of a new port facility. From the point of view of the port authority, the benefits are the receipts from berthing and handling charges, while the costs are those associated with the maintenance of port facilities together with any debt financing charges including taxes and levies. Treasury officials, however, will be concerned with how far direct and indirect receipts from the port (including such items as increased tax revenue from expanded economic activity) cover Government's outlays (including capital expenditure and possibly recurrent expenditure). The economic planner will be concerned with how far the new facility generates extra net benefits for the economy; viz. how far there is a costs saving to existing port users, to new port users, and how far these can be captured in the form of increased port revenue, lower freight charges on imports and exports, etc. In addition, the port may have important effects on local service activity, or stimulate industry and agriculture in a variety of indirect ways which will need to be studied carefully. What is to count as a cost or a benefit will depend upon which of these various viewpoints is being considered. It will be seen that this has a bearing on the notion of 'primary' and 'secondary' net benefits. Primary benefits and costs refer to project outputs and inputs.[1] Secondary costs and benefits exist where a project enables more efficient use of resources to be made elsewhere

1 As will be seen subsequently, how benefits are distributed and what weight is to be given to extra income in the hands of different recipients is the subject of 'social' cost-benefit analysis.

in the economy, or leads to extra claims on resources elsewhere. Tracing the total impact of a project on the economy in some cases can be exceedingly difficult, either because these cannot be readily indentified (where the port facility generates extra employment in the services sector) or because they cannot easily be priced (as where, say, new port traffic increases water pollution). The 'tracing through' of secondary impacts is the proper subject of economic analysis where, as will be seen, direct and indirect foreign exchange impacts are important. Suffice it to say that when evaluating a project, defining the *effective scope* or boundary of project activity is a key question, and how this boundary is drawn will depend upon the point of view from which the project is being appraised.

Since costs and benefits of a project occur in the future, accurate prediction is a prerequisite for *quantification* of both physical quantities and prices. Typically, problems of prediction will tend to be more difficult on the output side of a project, though the nature of such problems will differ according to the type of project in question. In the case of an industrial manufacturing project, for example, it is usual to carry out a market study to determine expected demand and price of the product, this (together with technical and cost information) being used to indicate the size of plant required. How quickly full capacity operation will be reached once the plant is completed may then be a matter of engineering judgement (assuming that no bottlenecks exist on the supply side). But in the case of, say, an irrigation project where new crops are being introduced into existing farming systems, the rate of buildup of output depends both on the rate at which farmers take up new cropping opportunities and the rate of growth of yield achieved. These in turn will depend on non-engineering aspects of project design, such as the provision of adequate credit facilities, as well as on supply-response factors which may by their very nature be difficult to predict.

Like the quantification of physical output, the quantification of prices will need to be based on accurate prediction. For the purposes of financial analysis, one will be concerned with domestic market prices. Two broad questions may be distinguished here: firstly, how far is the project itself likely to have an impact on prices (i.e. are project sales or purchases non-marginal) and, if such an impact exists, how does one take it into account?; i.e. the consumer surplus problem. Secondly, how are prices themselves likely to move in the future under the influence of other factors? This question is one of price forecasting *per se*. Inflation is one aspect of the problem since one wants to know how prices of inputs and outputs will be changing relative to each other in relation to some base year; hence it is general practice to express all prices in constant terms. Likely movements in constant prices over time can then be analysed either by use of behaviouristic models of price formation or, more usually, by the analysis of trend data (see Chapter III).

The same principles apply in the case of economic analysis. Unlike financial analysis, which is concerned with the profitability of the project at market prices, economic analysis is concerned with the determination of that set of prices which best reflects 'net efficiency' benefits to the nation. It is now broadly accepted that the 'efficiency' measure of a project output turns on the question of its actual or potential value as an import or export; similarly, the opportunity cost of any input is related to the question of its potential contribution to (or claim on) foreign exchange. World price relatives rather than domestic price relatives are thus appropriate for assessing the economic efficiency of public projects. Beyond the question of 'efficiency' is that of 'equity' — the distributional impact of a project both on the global savings-consumption balance of the economy and its impact on the current distribution of personal incomes. A further set of adjustments to prices may therefore be needed if the welfare implications of a project are to be properly assessed, and this explains the use of the word 'social' in the term 'social cost-benefit analysis' (SCBA).

Financial, economic and social evaluation are aspects of project appraisal and constitute the central subject matter of the chapters which follow. Appraisal, though, is only one part of the project planning cycle. Crucial though it may be, since it provides the basis on which the 'accept/reject' decision is taken, a carefully researched and professionally executed project appraisal is only useful if the right alternatives have been identified and if the various steps from identification to implementation are carried out as part of an integrated planning process. The economist who invests time and effort in understanding the complexities of modern project appraisal methodology only to find that public sector planning is largely a matter of window dressing and that the public sector plays a marginal role in development is, to put it bluntly, wasting his time.

1.03 *Cash Flows*

Whether one is calculating a financial or an economic rate of return, a key part of the analysis will be to work out the actual flows of income and expenditure. The basic principle of the 'cash flow', as the term suggests, is that income (inflow) and expenditure (outflow) should be counted only at the time they actually occur. Hence concepts such as that of 'depreciation' and 'sinking funds' are not required.

Consider the hypothetical example of a fertiliser plant having an operating life of 10 years and requiring an initial capital investment of 20 million dinars. It is assumed that the plant will take one year to build (year 0 below) and commence full capacity operations at the beginning of year 1, operations ceasing and equipment being scrapped with no salvage value at the end of year 10. The price of fertiliser (ex-factory) is D.1400 per ton and the capacity of the plant 10,000 tons per annum. Fixed operating expenses amount to D.1 million per annum while unit costs of manufacture are D.900 per ton. Hence total costs starting in year 1 are D.10 million per year [(D.1 m.) + (D.900 x 10,000); and sales revenue is D.14 million. The total cost stream is subtracted from the total revenue stream to obtain the net financial cash flow.[1]

Figure 1.1   *Cash Flow for Fertiliser Project*
             (in millions of Dinars)

Year	Costs	Revenue	Cash flow
0	-20.0	-	-20.0
1	-10.0	14.0	4.0
2	-10.0	14.0	4.0
3	-10.0	14.0	4.0
4	-10.0	14.0	4.0
5	-10.0	14.0	4.0
6	-10.0	14.0	4.0
7	-10.0	14.0	4.0
8	-10.0	14.0	4.0
9	-10.0	14.0	4.0
10	-10.0	14.0	4.0

In practice, the composition of costs will be a good deal more complex, as we discuss in a separate section. Some general principles to bear in mind, though, are the following. *Costs* are typically broken down into investment and operating cost components. Investment costs cover capital expenditure items such as plant and machinery together with costs of site preparation and construction. Operating costs (incurred only once the project is underway) are normally divided into variable and fixed components, the former covering such things as raw material and labour inputs required for manufacture, which will vary directly with the volume of production, while the latter will include maintenance, administration and managerial charges, etc. which will be relatively fixed with respect to the volume of production (but may vary with scale of operation). At the early stages of evaluation, one will usually be able to work with rules of thumb for estimating costs and returns to different scales of operation – viz. 'Unit operating costs vary proportionately to output, but for a doubling of output volume, investment and fixed operating

1   Where one is working with market prices, the cash flow stream is referred to as the Financial Cash Flow. Where market prices are adjusted to reflect national efficiency and equity objectives, one may speak of the Economic Net Benefit Stream and Social Net Benefit Stream respectively.

costs go up by only 50 percent...' — but at later stages it may be necessary to consider these in much more detail.

For financial analysis carried out from the point of view of the project entity, tax and subsidy elements in cost (and revenue) components will be left in the calculation. Where one is calculating the post-tax return on investment, quite detailed accounting projects may be required in order to assess company tax liability (showing such things as debt repayment, investment allowances and depreciation schedules). For financial analysis from a national point of view, tax and subsidy elements will normally be netted out of the calculations (since these are transfer payments to and from Government). Depreciation will also be omitted, this being no more than an accounting device for putting aside funds to replace the capital stock. Real or imputed interest payments should be excluded too since the analysis serves to establish (among other things) whether the real return on capital borrowed is higher than its cost (interest), a point which will be illustrated in the chapter on accounting conventions.

Where detailed economic analysis is required (along lines described in later sections of this book), the cost breakdowns used for standard accounting purposes are typically insufficient. Here one will need to reclassify all project inputs and outputs into traded and non-traded goods and basic factors of production, including labour which will need to be broken down into several components. This often constitutes a serious problem for the project evaluator, particularly in the case of capital items. Engineering costing conventions are usually based on historical cost data which are apt to include undifferentiated items such as transport and installation charges and contingency allowances. In determining the cost of lining a canal, for example, the engineering volume of the feasibility study will typically cite a figure of X thousand dollars per kilometer, no indication being given of how this figure is made up. In general, there is no guarantee that the economist will find cost data in a form (or at a level of aggregation) suited to the several forms of analysis which he will need to carry out.

A point which sometimes causes concern is the question of how to calculate the life of a project (10 years in the above example). Machines, unlike men, have no natural life span; they can be maintained almost indefinitely, though at a cost. The economic life of a machine is determined by the fact that the older it gets, the more it will cost to maintain, and hence there comes a point when borrowing money to replace it is cheaper than repairing it. The calculation of economic life can be complicated by rapid technological change, for not only will the capital and operating costs of potential replacement machines be changing, but so too will technical specifications, affecting the nature of the output and the efficiency with which inputs are transformed. Fortunately, determining whether a given bundle of equipment has an economic life of 20 or 30 years will make little difference to the calculations of net economic profitability where the discount rate used is set realistically. For example, using a 10% discount rate means that a payment of $100 in 20 years' time has a present value of only $14, and a similar payment in 30 years' time has a present value of only about $6. But it is useful to bear in mind that the lower the discount rate used, the more sensitive will results be to changes in the assumption made with respect to economic life.

1.04 *Discounting and the Investment Decision*

Having established the financial or net economic flows, as in Figure 1.1, the problem is to express these in terms of a common measure; i.e. to derive a *present value* by discounting all items in the net cash flow back to year 0. The need for such a procedure will be apparent if one considers the following simple argument.

Suppose one is offered the choice between receiving £100 today and receiving the same sum in a year's time. Clearly it will be rational to prefer receiving the money today for several possible reasons. To begin with, one may expect inflation to reduce the real value of £100 in a year's time. Where there is no inflationary effect (say where the offer is made in real terms), it would still be preferable to take the money today and invest it at some rate of interest, r, hence receiving a total sum of £100 (1 + r) at the end of the year. Even if no investment opportunities are available, such as might be true on a desert island, one might reason that £100 today would still be preferable on the grounds that there is a finite risk of not being around to collect the money next year. Moreover, it is sometimes argued that even where inflation, investment opportunities, and risk are ignored, there is something called 'pure time preference' which would lead one to prefer the immediate offer; i.e. that there is a natural inclination to prefer 'jam today' to 'jam tomorrow'.[1]

For all these reasons, one says that there is a positive *rate of discount* which leads us to place a lower present value on a given sum of money the further in the future one expects it to accrue. Suppose that it is 1980 and one wants to know the present value (P_0) of £100 received in a year's time; if the relevant discount rate is denoted by r, then:

$$P_{0\ 1980} = £100_{1981} / (1 + r) \tag{1.1}$$

1 While the notion of individual 'pure time preference' is a useful expositional device, the more general notion of social time preference determined from the aggregation of individual preferences is regarded by many as misleading, particularly when used in the context of the neo-classical treatment of factor rewards where interest is regarded as a 'reward for waiting'.

or if r = 10%, then:

$$P_{o\ 1980} = £100/ (1 + 0.10) = £90.91$$

In other words, £100 received in a year's time has a present value of £90.91. If one wanted to work out the present value of £100 received in 1982, it will be apparent that $£100_{1982}$ will be worth £100/ (1 + r) in 1981 which in turn will be worth £100/ $(1 + r)^2$ in 1980. Writing P_o for the present value and P_1, P_2 ..., P_t for the stream of payments accruing from years 1 to T, the general form of the discounting expression becomes:

$$P_o = P_1/(1 + r)^1 + P_2/(1 + r)^2 + ... P_T/(1 + r)^T \qquad (1.2)$$

or more compactly:[1]

$$P_o = \sum_{t=0}^{T} P_t/(1 + r)^t \qquad (1.3)$$

What is important to remember about the above formula is that the use of a single discounting parameter, r, assumes that the time value of benefits falls *at a constant rate*; were this not so, the whole exercise would become rather more complicated.[2]

For private companies, or even public corporations carrying out financial analysis, the discount rate used is normally the interest rate at which bank

1 'r' is, of course, an annual rate of interest. However, compounding can in principle take place quarterly, monthly, weekly, etc. such that at the limit where compounding takes place instantaneously at a nominal interest rate, r, over some time period, t, the expression $(1+r)^{-t}$ is replaced by the expression e^{-rt} where e is the base (2.71828) of the natural system of logarithms.

2 To show that the use of the discount rate, r, assumes that the time value of benefits falls at a constant rate over time, suppose the set of payments (P_1, P_2 ... P_T) to be multiplied by a set of weights (w_1, w_2 ... w_T) where $1 > w_1 > w_2 ... > w_T$. For any pair of consecutive weights (w_t, w_{t+1}), let the rate of fall in value be a constant, r. Then:

$$(w_t - w_{t+1})/w_{t+1} = r$$

hence,

$$(w_t/w_{t+1}) - 1 = r$$

or,

$$w_{t+1}/w_t = 1/(1+r)$$

loans are available, or where the enterprise's own funds are being used, the rate which banks would pay on the deposit of such funds — their 'opportunity cost'. The important point is that own funds are not 'free'. In the case of public investment criteria, the discount rate is set by the central planning authority, but may similarly be related to the alternative use of funds where public authorities are seen as competing with the private sector for finance.

Having set the discount rate, it follows that an investment project will be deemed acceptable if the sum of the discounted net benefits (benefits minus costs) is positive. This sum is sometimes called the Present Net Worth (PNW) or Net Present Value (NPV) of the project, and the corresponding investment decision rule can be abbreviated to 'accept if':

$$NPV > 0$$

One may also do the calculation in separate parts by discounting the benefits (B) and the costs (C) individually, in which case the rule becomes that the discounted benefits should exceed the discounted costs:

$$B > C$$
$$NPV = B - C > 0$$

The application of discounting can be briefly illustrated by considering the fertiliser investment example given above. Suppose a loan is available for financing the project bearing 10 percent interest. Recalling that the net cash flow for the project showed a figure of -20.0 millions in the base year and $+4.0$ m. in each successive year and looking at expression (1.2) above, we may write:

$$P_o = -20/(1 + .10)^0 + 4/(1 + .10)^1 + 4/(1 + .10)^2 + \dots \dots \tag{1.4}$$

Spelling out the whole of the above expression is a bit awkward, not to say raising 1.10 to successive powers. The exercise is more easily shown in tabular form (Figure 1.2). Note that the column labelled 'discount factors for 10%' consists of a set of numbers corresponding to the values of the expression $1/1.10^n$ for $n = 0, 1, 2 \dots 10$; these values may be found in any standard set of discount tables (see Appendix B).

Since discounting the cash flow at 10 percent produces a positive NPV of 4.57 million dinars, we conclude that the project should be undertaken. However, suppose that the cost of capital were to rise to 20 percent; in this event, the NPV of the project is negative (-3.21 m. dinars) as shown in the extreme righthand column of Figure 1.2, and the project would have to be rejected.

Figure 1.2 *Discounted Cash Flow for Fertiliser Project* (m. dinars)

Year	Cash Flow	Discount Factors for 10%	Discounted Cash Flow (10%)	Discount Factors for 20%	Discounted Cash Flow (20%)
0	-20.00	1.000	-20.00	1.000	-20.00
1	4.00	0.909	3.64	0.833	3.33
2	4.00	0.826	3.30	0.694	2.78
3	4.00	0.751	3.00	0.579	2.32
4	4.00	0.683	2.73	0.482	1.93
5	4.00	0.621	2.48	0.402	1.61
6	4.00	0.564	2.26	0.335	1.34
7	4.00	0.513	2.05	0.279	1.12
8	4.00	0.467	1.87	0.233	0.93
9	4.00	0.424	1.70	0.194	0.78
10	4.00	0.386	1.54	0.162	0.65
NPV			4.57		-3.21

1.05 *Inflation*

An important question to consider when discounting the net cash flow of a
project is whether revenues and costs have been given in current prices. It is
sometimes argued that the effects of inflation can be ignored as long as inflation acts in the same way on revenue and costs since, in this event, the
effects cancel each other out. This argument is misleading as simple arithmetic will show. Suppose that both revenues and costs in the above case are
inflating at an annual rate of 10 percent. The difference between them (cash
flow) will also be growing at 10 percent annually.; hence if we apply a 20 percent discount rate to the net cash flow in current prices, the NPV turns out
to be the same as that derived in Figure 1.2 for the cash flow at 10 percent.
In short, one must either estimate the rate of inflation (assuming it to be
identical for costs and revenue) and add it to the appropriate discount rate,
or one must express all flows in constant prices before discounting. In general, it will be preferable to do the latter since it is not usually the case that
costs and revenues will be affected identically by inflation.

1.06 *The Internal Rate of Return (IRR)*

It will be apparent that there is some discount rate which will result in an
NPV of exactly zero for the above project. Formally, it is the solution to the
following expression where the internal rate of return is denoted by R:[1] :[1]

$$NPV = \sum_{t=0}^{T} P_t/(1 + R)^t = 0 \qquad\qquad \dots\dots (1.5)$$

By trying a number of different discount rates between 10 and 20 percent,
we can ascertain the IRR of the project, which in the present case turns out
to be fractionally above 15 percent. A useful way of deriving an approximate
solution is to plot the NPVs corresponding to several discount rates, taking
care that these are chosen in such a way as to define the desired curve over
the relevant range. Figure 1.3 illustrates the application of this principle to
the case of the fertiliser project.

This graph, sometimes called the NPV curve, is particularly useful because
it summarises the required information at a glance. Three points are usually
sufficient to produce a reasonable approximation of the desired relationship,
but clearly the more points are plotted, the better the approximation to the
'true' underlying NPV curve will be.

---

1   In socialist economies, the IRR is sometimes referred to as the 'efficiency index' of a
project and this is contrasted with the planners' discount rate or 'test discount rate'.

Figure 1.3   *The NPV Curve Showing NPV of Project of Different Discount Rates*

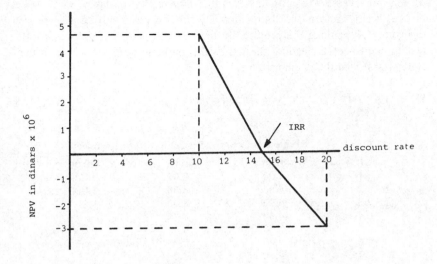

The decision rule corresponding to the IRR is 'accept the project if the IRR is greater than the cost of capital' $(R > C)$. In the present case, the NPV and IRR criteria give the same results since, just as the project was accepted on NPV grounds where the discount rate chosen was 10 percent (and rejected for 20 percent), one would accept the project on IRR grounds if the cost of capital was 10 percent and reject it for 20 percent.

In general:

when $NPV > 0$ then $R > r$
          $NPV = 0$ then $R = r$
          $NPV < 0$ then $R < r$.

1.07 *NPV or IRR?*

The widespread use of the IRR in project appraisal reports is conventionally justified on the grounds that, being a 'pure number', it is more useful in allowing projects of different size to be compared directly, and also because it is claimed that it eliminates the need for choosing a discount rate. While the latter argument is obviously invalid (since the IRR decision rule 'accept if $R > r$' requires r to be known), the former point needs to be considered in more detail.

Suppose that planners are considering three projects designated A, B and C. Assume that project A has a cash flow identical to that given in the above example while B's cost and revenue figures are exactly double but B has a life of only nine years. Project C involves the same capital outlay as A (D.20 m.) but yields a net return of D.14 m. annually for two years only. As can be seen in Figure 1.4, ranking the projects by their NPVs (using a 10% discount rate) results in project B heading the list, while ranking them according to their IRRs would lead the planners to prefer C.

Figure 1.4 *NPVs and IRRs of Three Projects*

		Cash flows	
Year	Project A	Project B	Project C
0	–20.00	–40.00	–20.00
1	4.00	8.00	14.00
2	4.00	8.00	14.00
3	4.00	8.00	-
4	4.00	8.00	-
5	4.00	8.00	-
6	4.00	8.00	-
7	4.00	8.00	-
8	4.00	8.00	-
9	4.00	8.00	-
10	4.00	-	-
NPV at 10%	4.57	6.08	4.36
IRR	15.1%	13.7%	25.8%

There is an apparent difficulty here since the preference ordering of the projects varies according to the criterion adopted. However, this is only a difficulty insofar as one is ranking projects. If all of the above projects can be undertaken, then both NPV and IRR give the same accept-reject decision; in this case, there is no need to rank projects and one should accept all three. However, there are two possible reasons why all the above projects cannot be undertaken. One is that capital funds may be limited — in this case, the real problem is that the discount rate has not been set correctly. The other problem may be that two or more of the three projects are mutually exclusive (dealt with in section 1.08 below).

Suppose for example that A and B represented alternative processes for fertiliser production. Proponents of version B would point to its higher NPV while those favouring version A might argue that the IRR was the relevant basis for decision making. Resolving the problem depends on understanding a key principle underlying the choice of the discount rate. It is sometimes argued that as long as capital funds are 'unlimited' and the projects are not mutually exclusive, NPV is the relevant criterion. But the function of the discount rate is to ration capital in such a manner as eventually to pass just sufficient projects as will use up available investment resources. Hence the important question is not whether NPV or IRR is to be preferred as a criterion, but whether planners have set the discount rate correctly.

For the sake of argument, assume that the total investment budget is 80 million dinars and that the above projects constitute an exhaustive list of all feasible projects in the economy. In this case planners could do all three projects. However, suppose the budget were only D.40 million, implying that either B could be undertaken, or alternatively A and C. Planners would clearly do better to choose A and C yielding a total NPV of D. 8.93 million (4.57 + 4.36) rather than B which yields only D. 6.08 million at a 10 percent discount rate. It should be apparent, however, that in this situation 10 percent is not an appropriate discount rate since it effectively 'passes' all three projects, more than can be accommodated given the capital constraint. Raising the discount rate to 20 percent would, on the other hand, leave us with surplus investment funds since projects A and B would have negative NPVs at this rate and would therefore be rejected. Only if the rate is set fractionally below 15.1 percent (15 percent for convenience) will the right number of projects be accepted as is confirmed by performing the relevant calculations:

Project:	A	B	C
NPV 15%	0.08	−1.84	2.76
NPV 10%	4.57	6.08	4.36
NPV 20%	−3.23	−7.75	1.39

The argument is summarised diagrammatically in Figure 1.5 below.

A further though somewhat formal point about the IRR is that it is possible for there to exist more than one value of R which will satisfy expression (1.5) above. This will occur where a project's cash flow changes signs more than once. Consider the example of a person who is considering taking out a 20 year lease on a piece of land which is expected to yield a net revenue of 100 pesos per annum for four years, but which will require 1500 pesos of major drainage investment in year 5 increasing the cash yield to 200 pesos annually thereafter.

Year	Cash Flow	Discount Rate	NPV
1–4	+100	20%	+30
5	−1500	30%	−11
6–20	+200	40%	− 4
		45%	+ 6

Figure 1.5 *NPV Curves for Projects A, B and C*

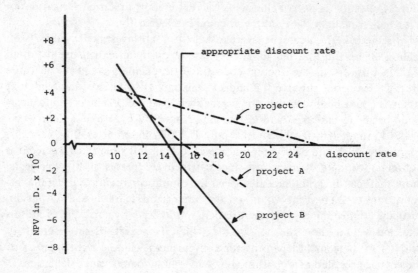

Figure 1.6 *Drainage Scheme Having Multiple IRRs*

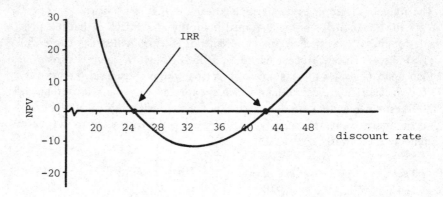

As will be seen from Figure 1.6, the resulting NPV curve is perverse. Two IRRs exist, appearing to imply that he should take out the lease if the opportunity cost of his money is either below 25 percent or above 42 percent. While such examples are relatively rare in practice, the illustration constitutes further evidence for preferring the NPV curve approach, in which full information is shown, to the 'single point' IRR criterion.

1.08 *Other Investment Criteria*

Besides NPV and IRR, a number of other measures of investment performance are in common use and deserve mention.

The most common of these is the *payback period* criterion, which is widely used in commercial enterprises as a rough guide to assessing the relative desirability of two or more projects. As the name suggests, the rule leads one to choose that project which recovers its capital costs in the shortest period (and is hence sometimes referred to as the *capital recovery* criterion). Applying the principle to the set of projects described above (Figure 1.4), it will be seen that project C is preferred since it pays for itself in 1.4 years (20 ÷ 14), while projects A and B both have recovery periods of exactly 5 years and one should therefore be indifferent between them. Although the calculation is normally performed by dividing the capital cost by the cumulative sum of the undiscounted net cash flow, a 'discounted payback period' (DPP) is occasionally encountered. Using a 10 percent discount rate for DPP would lead to longer payback periods in the three cases, though the ranking results would be unaltered. In essence, the difficulty with the use of this criterion (in either form) arises from the fact that all net benefits accruing after the payback year are ignored, and thus a bias exists against long-lived projects having a low initial yield which only gradually builds up to a maximum.

Similar problems are encountered when using another crude index of investment efficiency popular amongst economic planners called the *output-capital ratio*. This is defined as the average (undiscounted) value-added produced per unit of capital expenditure. Here the problem is that no account is taken of the efficiency of the use of factors other than capital with a resulting bias in favour of those projects using, say, relatively large amounts of land and/or labour in place of capital.

A criterion occasionally used as a 'discounting' version of the above is the *present value over capital* or PV/K ratio (sometimes called the benefit-cost ratio). PV/K compares the discounted net revenue stream with the discounted capital costs; hence, the numerator (PV) does not include initial capital costs and may be thought of as a gross rather than a net present value. The corresponding decision rule requires one to accept the project if PV/K > 1. Since for any project having a positive NPV, PV/K will be greater than unity, it follows that all projects passed by NPV will also be passed by PV/K. However, the PV/K criterion may sometimes be useful as a capital rationing device where the discount rate has not been set in such a way as to exhaust available public funds.

1.09 *Mutually Exclusive Projects*

The PV/K criterion has popularly been used to choose between mutually exclusive projects; for example, alternative versions of the same project. Returning to the earlier example, suppose that the appropriate discount rate is 10 percent and that one is being asked to choose between versions A and B of the fertiliser project. B has the larger NPV but A has the larger PV/K (Figure 1.7). This result follows from the fact that the size of the project will affect

Figure 1.7 *Mutually Exclusive Alternatives for Fertiliser Production Ranked Using PV/K and NPV Criteria*

Year	Version A		Version B		'Version (B-A)'	
	K-Cost	Revenue	K-Cost	Revenue	K-Cost	Revenue
0	20.00	-	40.00	-	20.00	-
1		4.00		8.00		4.00
2		4.00		8.00		4.00
3		4.00		8.00		4.00
4		4.00		8.00		4.00
5		4.00		8.00		4.00
6		4.00		8.00		4.00
7		4.00		8.00		4.00
8		4.00		8.00		4.00
9		4.00		8.00		4.00
10		4.00		-		-4.00
PV 10%	20.00	24.57	40.00	46.08	20.00	21.49
PV/K	1.23		1.15		-	
NPV	4.57		6.08		1.45	

the absolute magnitude of its NPV, the larger NPV associated with version B reflecting its much greater capital cost and net revenues. While one might be tempted to use PV/K as the appropriate criterion, the proper way of approaching the problem is to consider the choice as being not between A and B, but between A and the extra bit of investment which would, so to speak, transform A into B. This incremental project can be thought of as (B - A) and the returns to it can be calculated by subtracting the respective net revenue streams. The resulting NPV for version (B - A) is shown in the extreme right hand column of Figure 1.7 and is positive. Hence it will be profitable to do the 'incremental project' in addition to doing project A, which is another way of saying that version B should be adopted. While this may seem a round-about way of arriving at the result, it is in fact the correct way and avoids the misleading choice of version A which use of PV/K would have favoured.[1]

1.10 *Summary*

We have seen that there are a variety of conventions governing the evaluation of investment projects which cover both what items are to be counted as costs and benefits, how they are to be quantified and — what has been the main concern of the present Chapter — the form in which an index of invest-ment profitability should be presented. While some of the cruder investment criteria, such as the payback period, are at times useful for 'back of the envelope' type assessments, the discounted cash flow approach is now more or less universal in application. Central to the understanding of the use of dis-counting is a conceptual grasp of the rationale underlying the choice of dis-count rate. For the purposes of determining whether a single project should or should not be undertaken, it has been shown that the NPV and IRR criteria give the same results, but that in ranking several projects, ranking order will not always be invariate with respect to the discount rate and that the IRR can sometimes be misleading. Since the 'equilibrium' discount rate may not always be known to the project analyst, it will usually be advisable to calculate the NPV for different rates (NPV curve). Finally, where one is concerned with choosing amongst mutually exclusive project alternatives, use of the incremental NPV will be appropriate.

1.11 *Further Reading*

An introduction to the principles of DCF is to be found in any one of a num-ber of textbooks on contemporary capital budgeting methods of which the best known are Merrett and Sykes (1966) and Bierman and Smidt (1971). A useful summary discussion of discounting methods, investment criteria and capital rationing problems is also provided in Chapter 19 of Baumol (1972), while Part IV of Mishan (1972) contains a good discussion of the comparative

1   It might be noted that the same result would have been obtained by calculating the IRR of the incremental project which, as the reader will see, must be greater than 10 percent.

merits of IRR, NPV and PV/K criteria. Logical objections to the IRR are covered by Hirshleifer (1958) and Feldstein and Flemming (1964). Additionally, the practitioner will find it useful to have a more comprehensive set of discount tables than those given at the back of the present book, and Lawson and Windle (1974) is one of the better sets available.

II

BASIC CONVENTIONS OF FINANCIAL ACCOUNTING

2.01 Principles of Financial Accounting

The section which follows is designed to help develop a general understanding of the main accounting conventions used in assessing the financial profitability of a firm. These constitute, so to speak, the main building blocks of private profitability accounting. The hypothetical examples used are necessarily simplified; in reality, company accounts are very much more complex. Moreover, from the point of view of the economist (as opposed to that of the accountant) it will be necessary to bear in mind that 'private' and 'national' financial profitability are distinct concepts. It is important to understand at the outset how firms (private or public) typically organise their accounts for two main reasons. First, a project analyst will need to use private (or public) financial records to extract the required data for economic and social accounting. Secondly, it will often be important to assess financial profitability of a project from several viewpoints before assessing its economic or social profitability. In the case of most projects, the economist will need to carry out separate analyses from the point of view of the firm, the government executing agency (if there is one) and perhaps too look at the project's overall implications for Government finance (including loan repayments, direct and indirect subsidies and tax payments, etc).

In assessing an enterprise's current and future financial position, financial analysis relies upon three main statements:
1. the Income and Expenditure Statement;
2. the Balance Sheet;
3. the Source and Applications of Funds Statement.

The Income and Expenditure Statement summarises recurrent receipts and expenditures over the financial year, and will normally show how these are divided between the manufacturing and trading operations of the firm. The Balance Sheet is not a statement of flows; rather, it is concerned with the firm's net asset position at the end of the financial year. The Sources and Applications of Funds Statement re-arranges elements of the current and capital accounts to show how assets (including operating profit flows) are used to finance liabilities (including debt servicing).

2.02 The Income and Expenditure Statement

The prime question for the firm is whether it has been able to cover its expenses and still realise a profit in the current year, as well as whether it will be able to continue doing so in the future. In practice one will usually be looking at income and expenditure accounts for several recent years in order to project these. Here the economist will need to develop a 'feel' for using this sort of information as a guide to identifying those aspects of firm policy which may critically affect profitability. For example, one will want to know whether receipts from sales have been received promptly and all income properly due to the firm is being paid in; whether prices have been set at the right level and costs are realistic; whether there is sufficient working capital, and so on.

Income and Expenditure Accounts are generally divided into Manufacturing, Trading and Profit and Loss Statements, sometimes accompanied by an Appropriation Account. The division is functional to identifying expenditures and receipts associated with each stage of company operations, companies themselves sometimes having separate manufacturing and trading divisions. From the economist's point of view, the main use of this form of presentation is in facilitating the distinction between costs which vary proportionally with the volume of output (such as raw materials and to a lesser extent labour) and costs which are relatively fixed (such as services and administration).

To illustrate the main principles involved, consider the example of a hypothetical shoe manufacturing operation which has just finished drawing up accounts for its first year of business. Fleet Footwear (East Africa) Ltd. was started on 1 January 1978 to manufacture plastic sandals for a growing urban market on a total investment of Shillings 33,000, two-thirds of the sum coming in the form of Government and bank loans bearing 10 percent interest, and the balance being Mr. Fleet's own venture capital (including Sh. 1000 working capital). At that time, he reckoned on manufacturing 20,000 pairs annually at a wholesale price of Sh. 1.00 per pair (gross revenue Sh. 20,000) and incurring annual costs of Sh. 12,500 thus netting Sh. 7,500, or an average annual return of 23 percent (7,500/33,000) on total capital.

Initial back-of-the-envelope calculations were as follows:[1]

---

[1] Had an IRR been calculated on the basis of these figures (assuming zero scrap value of fixed assets at the end of the 10 year period), a figure of just over 18% would have been derived. It should be apparent that the 23% figure shown above makes no allowance for the value of receipts accruing at different points in time.

	Shillings
Gross returns	20,000
Cost	
purchased inputs	5,000
wages	2,500
salaries	2,000
office expenses	1,000
other	2,000
Total	12,500

$$\frac{Net\ return}{Capital\ Investment} = \frac{7,500}{33,000} = 23\%$$

On 31 December 1978, having completed the end of a year's operations, Mr. Fleet with the help of his part-time accountant now finds the situation to be somewhat different, net operating profit being Sh. 5,500. Figure 2.1 shows the firm's Income and Expenditure Statement for the period in question. By convention, the two sides of the account must balance since all claims against revenue must be accounted for. Hence, in the topmost (manufacturing) account, after allowing for any differences in stocks (raw materials and work in progress) at the opening and close of the financial year, the sum of all expenditure on raw materials, labour and capital consumption must by definition be equal to the right-hand entry for cost of manufactured goods.

Note that depreciation has been entered as a cost additional to maintenance in this account although, unlike other expenses, it is not a financial transaction between the firm and the outside world. Rather, it represents a sum notionally set aside to allow for the eventual replacement of fixed assets such as machines which will eventually wear out. This has the advantage of allowing the firm to apply the retained portion of profits to financing net investment rather than replacement investment; it also has the advantage of reducing tax liability since firms are normally taxed on the basis of profit net of depreciation charges. It should be noted in this respect that there are various methods of depreciating an asset, the three most common being the Straight-Line, Declining-Balance, and Sum-of-the-Year's-Digits methods.

To illustrate each of these methods consider the example of a machine costing £15,000 with an estimated life of five years and salvage value of zero. The Straight-Line method spreads the depreciation charges over the estimated life of the asset in equal yearly instalments of £3,000. The book value of the machine therefore declines by £3,000 each year and is zero at the end of the fifth year. Using the Declining-Balance or Sum-of-the-Year's-Digits methods, on the other hand, the earlier years of the machine's life bear higher depreciation charges than the later years. The Declining Balance method applies a fixed percentage to the book value of the machine each year – 20 percent per annum in the case of a machine with a five-year life, implying depreciation

Figure 2.1

Fleet Footwear Ltd.
Income and Expenditure Statement for the Year Ending 31 December 1978

Expenditure			Income	
Manufacturing Account				
Opening Stock		0	Closing Stock (raw materials	
Purchased Inputs		5000	and work in progress)	100
Factory Overheads		6000		
Wages	2500		Balance (cost of goods	
Maintenance	1300		produced)	10900
Depreciation	2200			
		11000		11000
Trading Account				
Opening Stock		0	Closing stock (finished	
Cost of goods produced		10900	goods)	100
Trading (gross) profit		11200	Sales revenue	22000
		22100		22100
Profit and Loss Acount				
Salaries		2000	Trading profit	11200
Office expenses		1000		
Interest on debt		2200		
Other		500		
Operating (net) profit		5500		
		11200		11200
Appropriation Account				
Taxation		1600	Operating profit	5500
Retained earnings		3900		
		5500		5500

charges of £3,000 in the first year; £2,400 (20% of £12,000) in the second
year; £1,920 (20% of £9,600) in the third year, and so on. It should be noted
that the depreciation charge decreases each year by a smaller amount and that
there is a residual book value at the end of the machine's life. With the Sum-
of-the-Year's-Digits method, however, although the earlier years still bear
relatively higher depreciation charges, the amount by which these fall during
the machine's life is constant and there is no residual book value at the end.
To calculate the depreciation charges for the first year, the formula $\frac{2D}{n+1}$ is
used, where D is the initial cost of the machine (£15,000) and n is its expected life in years (5). Using this formula, the first year's depreciation charge
is: $\frac{2D}{n+1} = \frac{2 \times 15000}{5+1} = \frac{30000}{6} = £5,000.$

The amount by which this depreciation charge declines each year is given by the formula $\frac{2\,D}{n(n+1)}$, which in the example is:

$$\frac{2\,D}{n(n+1)} = \frac{2 \times 15000}{5 \times 6} = \frac{30000}{30} = £1000.$$

The depreciation for the second year is £4,000 (£5,000 – £1,000); for the third year, £3,000; and so on.

Each of these methods is illustrated graphically in Figure 2.2.

Figure 2.2

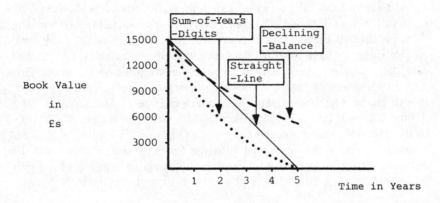

In deriving a net cash flow, depreciation is *not* treated as a cost, implying that the method of depreciation can have no *direct* effect on the firm's financial profitability. However, as firms are taxed on the basis of net profit after allowing for depreciation charges, the method of depreciation can still affect the firm's net cash flow *indirectly* through the effect that it has on taxation.[1]

'Cost of Manufactured Goods' derived from the manufacturing account is then carried over to the Trading Account as a cost which, together with other selling expenses and net inventory changes in finished goods, is set off against gross revenue from sales. The difference is the 'Trading' or 'Gross' Profit which is Sh. 11,200 for Fleet Footwear Ltd.

In addition to manufacturing and trading expenses, a firm will have other administrative and financial expenses such as salaries, office expenses and interest on debt which must be set against trading profit. Note that interest

1 For a good discussion of the different methods of depreciation and measurements of the indirect effect of depreciation charges on the firm's net cash flow, see Bierman and Smidt (1971) Chs. 7 and 13.

on debt is a financial expense borne as a result of the operation and therefore enters into the calculation of operating profit. Amortization (repayment of principal), on the other hand, is not an expense but rather a change of the company's indebtedness and does not therefore enter into this calculation.[1] The Profit and Loss Account shows a net firm operating profit of Sh. 5,500. Finally the Appropriation Account shows how the operating profit is distributed between claims (tax, dividends, reserves, etc.), the residual or Retained Earnings (Sh. 3,900) being available for the firm's expansion.

If on the basis of these accounts, Mr. Fleet were to attempt to measure the profitability of the firm by taking the ratio of retained earnings, or of net operating profit, to initial capital expenditure, he would be dismayed by figures derived of 12% and 17% respectively, in contrast to the 23% resulting from his original calculations. However, these results are not directly comparable since the figures include debt service, depreciation and (in the former case) tax. A proper assessment of the situation from his own point of view would require adding back debt service and depreciation to operating profit, though subtracting tax, to get a net annual revenue of Sh. 8,300 (5500 + 2200 + 2200 – 1600 = 8300) which, as a 25% return on the Sh. 33,000 originally invested, suggests that Fleet Footwear has done rather better than expected. An economist concerned with the financial rate of return for the enterprise might project this sum, assuming all things to remain constant, over the ten-year period of expected plant life in order to derive an NPV or an

---

1   Whether to treat interest and amortization as a cost in deriving a net cash flow for financial evaluation purposes is a question which often bothers students. The general rule in deriving an NPV (or IRR) is to exclude interest and amortization from the calculation if one has included the capital borrowed in the net cash flow since debt service charges are an annualisation of this capital.

An example will help clarify the point. Suppose a firm invests in a machine costing £10,000 and yielding an annual return (exclusive of debt service and depreciation) of £2,000 per annum. Further assume the cost of capital borrowed for this purpose to be 10 percent, and the machine to have a ten year life and zero scrap value. One way to determine the profitability of the investment is to discount the net revenue stream (£2,000 per annum for 10 years) at 10 percent (discount factor = 6.1446) which yields a present value of £12,289; subtracting the capital cost from this sum gives an NPV of £2,289.

Alternatively, since the net revenue is constant over time, we can annualise the capital outlay (£10,000 divided by 6.1446 = £1,627) and compare this to the annual net revenue (£2,000) giving an annual net *profit* of.£373. It will be apparent that an NPV of £2,289 is equivalent to a ten year stream of profits of £373 per annum since £373 x 6.1446 = £2,289. But annualising the outlay of borrowed funds is in principle (though not always in practice) the same as calculating interest and amortization. Suppose the terms of the loan to be that the full principal is only paid back in the 10th year. Thus, £1,000 in interest is paid by the firm each year and, in addition, it must set aside an annual sum that will grow to £10,000 in 10 years' time. This sum is calculated with the help of tables (sinking fund) and is £627 p.a., making a total of £1,627.

IRR. With slight adjustments, the same type of calculation could be done to determine the project's profitability from a national financial point of view. The calculations would be as shown in Figure 2.3.

Figure 2.3 *Preliminary Financial Analysis*

	Firm's Financial Analysis	National Financial Analysis
Year 0	– 33,000	– 23,000
Year 1-10	+ 8,300	+ 8,900
Year 11	+ 10,000	-
NPV (10%)	+ 21,505	+ 31,687
IRR	22.6%	37%

In the firm's financial analysis, investment costs would consist of the initial capital outlay on plant, buildings, land and working capital. Land would have a resale value (Sh. 10,000) assumed to be more than its cost, while the remaining items might readily be assumed to have zero scrap value. The return would be the annual net revenue figure of Sh. 8,300. In the national financial analysis, tax (Sh. 1,600) would need to be added to this figure. Land, however, might not be treated as having an initial financial cost but, rather, its return in its next-best use or opportunity cost at market prices (assumed to be Sh. 1,000 per annum) would be deducted from revenue, giving an annual net revenue of Sh. 8,900 for the ten year period. Before drawing conclusions though, it will be useful to examine the firm's Balance Sheet at the end of the first year's trading to determine the structure of its liabilities and assets.

2.03 *The Balance Sheet*

Whereas an Income and Expenditure Statement shows the composition of items determining profit over a given period, a Balance Sheet lists assets and liabilities actually owned and owed on a particular day. Critical examination of past balance sheets together with projected balance sheets over the project implementation period will be important in order to judge whether the capital structure of the project entity is viable and what impact the proposed project can be expected to have upon it.

Figure 2.4 shows the Balance Sheet for the firm in the present example on 31 December 1978. By convention, liabilities and assets normally appear in descending order of liquidity; i.e. current liabilities are what the firm owes to others and must pay in the short term while current assets are either fully liquid (cash) or payments due to the firm in the near future. Stocks (inventories) are usually included as current *assets* since it is reasonable to suppose

Figure 2.4   *Fleet Footwear Ltd.*
                    Balance Sheet as at 31 December 1978

Liabilities			Assets		
1. *Equity*			1. *Fixed Assets*		
Capital		11000	Land (at cost)		10000
Retained Earnings		3900	Buildings and		
			plant at cost	22000	
2. *Debentures*			*Tax* depreciation	2200	19800
10 year Govt. loan	20000				
Less repayment	1400	18600	2. *Current Assets*		
2 year bank loan		2000	Stocks		200
			Debtors		3200
3. *Current Liabilities*			Cash		4100
Creditors		200			
Tax due		1600			
		37300			37300

that unsold goods or raw materials can be turned into cash reasonably quickly. Non-current assets include items such as land, buildings and plant which cannot readily be sold (without jeopardising the firm's operations). Similarly, liabilities such as debt are due only at some fixed future date while holders of equity may never hope to get their money back except by selling their shares to others. Note, too, that fixed assets are normally shown net of depreciation (i.e. their Book Value).

While Fleet Footwear's profit position for the year's operations appears to be satisfactory it does not necessarily follow that the firm's 'liquidity' and 'solvency' position is also sound. Liquidity refers to the ability of the firm to meet its current liabilities; and solvency, to its ability to meet its total external liabilities, the determination of which requires careful analysis of items in the balance sheet.

The first test of liquidity is the ratio between current assets and current liabilities, usually referred to as the 'current ratio'. Where current assets fail to cover current liabilities the firm is illiquid and is likely to find itself with a serious cash flow problem. From Figure 2.4 it is apparent that Fleet Foot-wear's current assets exceed current liabilities by a comfortable margin, the current ratio being 4 : 1. However, while cash is immediately available and most debtors can be expected to pay within the normal credit period, stocks are less liquid in that the firm must wait until they are processed into final output before they can be converted into cash or debtors. For this reason it is perhaps better to compare current assets *excluding* stocks, with current liabilities when determining a firm's liquidity position. This ratio is commonly referred to as the 'acid test' or 'quick assets ratio' which, in the case of Fleet Footwear, is also about 4 : 1 — a more than adequate margin. Another point worth consideration is that while accounts due (debtors) would normally be expected to be settled within three months from the date of purchase, should for any reason a large number of clients default on their accounts, it is possible that a firm would find itself with a serious cash flow problem, despite its having a sound quick assets ratio. Again it is apparent that default on the part of Fleet Footwear's debtors would not seriously affect the firm's liquidity position. Where a firm does find itself with a liquidity or cash flow problem and is unable to meet its current commitments it would either have to put off its creditors or resort to short term borrowing, which is what is meant by the expression 'trading on goodwill'. Any surplus of current assets over current liabilities, on the other hand, is normally referred to as 'working capital'. This is needed to finance recurrent commitments falling due in the near future, such as raw material purchases and wages, as well as unforeseen expenses. Fleet Footwear's balance sheet indicates a working capital of Sh. 5,700.

The test of solvency is the ratio between the total assets of the firm and its external liabilities. If the former fail to cover the latter, the firm is 'insolvent'. The degree of solvency is usually measured by taking the difference between total assets and external liabilities and expressing this as a percentage of total assets. Applying this measure to Fleet Footwear's balance sheet gives a 'solvency ratio' (or 'degree of solvency') of 40 percent; i.e. (37300 - 22400)/ 37300.

Another point worth notice is that while the major part of the firm's debt capital is in the form of a long-term (10-year) Government loan, Sh. 2,000 is in the form of short-term (2-year) bank loan which must be repaid at the end of next year. However, Fleet Footwear has made no provision for this repayment during the current year and may find itself in difficulty when the loan falls due. As far as the ten-year loan of Sh. 20,000 is concerned, it should be noted that a first repayment instalment of Sh. 1,400 has been made during the current year. Unless future instalments (or the annual provision for repayment) are increased substantially, the firm may again find itself in difficulty if the full amount of the loan is to be repaid by the end of the tenth year and provisions for refinancing this debt cannot be arranged.

2.04 *Sources and Applications of Funds*

The Sources and Applications of Funds Statement links the Balance Sheet with the flow of income and expenditure. Since funds may come either from firm operating profits or from increased capital account liabilities, and may be applied either to meeting financial expenses or increasing assets, the Statement incorporates elements of both accounts. Like the previous statements, it balances by definition.

The structure of the statement is illustrated in Figure 2.5 by reference to the present example. The first two columns cover the year in which the initial investment takes place and operations begin while the final column records liquidation of the project during the eleventh year. At the beginning of 1978 (year 0) sources of funds are limited to the capital market and applied almost wholly to increasing fixed assets (plant, buildings, etc.), Sh. 1,000 of the total going towards initial working capital shown here as an entry in the 'cash balance' row.

Figure 2.5   *Fleet Footwear Ltd.*
                  Source and Applications of Funds Statement

Sources:	0	1	...	11
Operating Profit before tax and interest	-	7700		-
Depreciation	-	2200		-
New borrowing	22000	-		-
New equity	11000	-		- 10000
	33000	9900		- 10000
Applications:				
Fixed Assets	32000	-		- 10000
Buildings and Plant	22000	-		-
Land	10000	-		- 10000
Current Assets	1000	4700		-
Cash	1000	3100		
Debtors minus creditors	-	1400		-
Stocks	-	200		-
Debt Service	-	3600		-
Interest	-	2200		-
Loan repayment	-	1400		-
Reserve	-	1600		-
	33000	9900		- 10000

At the end of the first year's operations (year 1) no new borrowing has taken place, funds coming entirely from within the firm itself, from profits and provision for depreciation. Note that one is not here concerned with the financing of the firm's operations but only with the sources and uses of its operating profit, which is defined in this case as *exclusive* of interest on debt. To this depreciation must be added as this is not a cash payment to anyone outside the firm but merely an internal accounting device to provide for the eventual replacement of fixed assets. This sum is therefore available as a source of cash funds.

Total internal sources of funds in year 1 thus amount to Sh. 9900 and are applied to meeting tax and debt service obligations as well as to financing net stockbuilding (inventory accumulation) and holding increased short term debts to the firm in the form of payments outstanding. The residual is re-flected in the cash balance, the 'balancing' function of which will be apparent if one considers that a decrease in payments outstanding (customers suddenly paying their bills) will result in an increased cash balance.

The Sources and Applications of Funds Statement is particularly useful to the project analyst concerned with projecting net financial flows through time and thus diagnosing possible shortfalls in working capital which will need to be financed from external sources. Equally, projected over the full life of the project, it provides the information necessary for calculating the financial rate of return since it groups both initial capital expenditure and the flow of financial profit together with particular claims on that profit which may need to be deducted. This contrasts with the Income and Expenditure Statement which records revenues and firm operating costs in order to *derive* profit, capital expenditure being shown indirectly via annual capital consumption and debt services charges. The usefulness of the Sources and Applications Statement as a basis for deriving financial profitability in the present case will be apparent by checking Figure 2.5 against the calculations given earlier in Figure 2.3.

2.05 *Integrated Documentation System for Financial Accounting*

Having reviewed the basic principles and conventions on which enterprise ac-counts are based, it will be helpful to briefly consider the example of a modern standardised documentation system suitable for dealing with the sort of complexities which emerge in attempting to analyse real projects. The standardised tables given below are based on an 'Integrated Documentation System'[1] and consist of three tables, the Financial Income Statement (FIS), the Financial Balance Sheet (FBS) and the Financial Cash Flow (FCF), which while differing in format from the statements shown in the earlier part of the present Chapter are based on the same principles. Although no universally accepted layout exists for setting out project data, this system has the merit of providing a readily recognisable set of headings which allow most enterprise accounts to be translated into a form suitable for both financial and economic analysis using DCF methods. It also incorporates con-ventions for itemising each heading in such a way as to facilitate cross ref-erence to supporting documentation.

Figure 2.6 shows a sample Financial Income Statement for another hypothetical project. Instead of being arranged in balance sheet form, it lists

1 See J.R. Hansen, 'A Guide to the UNIDO Guidelines', IBRD (31 July 1975), Chapter 3, which in turn is based on the work of Powelson (1968).

items vertically, starting with the project's revenue from sales, and going on to show operating expenses, operating profit and the various claims upon profit. Years are shown from left to right, and it is thus possible to trace the evolution of sales revenue, costs, profit and claims on profit through time over the (3 year) life of the project. Major items and their detailed breakdown are indicated by use of digital subdivisions; viz. item 4 shows total operating expenses while 4.2.2 is skilled labour and 4.2.2.1 might be machine operators. Supporting documentation for particular sections of the table might consist of, say, sales projections by type of market, raw material requirements breakdowns showing domestic purchases and imports, and so on. An example of such documentation referring to those sections of the FIS indicated with an asterisk is given in Figure 2.7.

Figure 2.8 shows the annual balance sheet projections over the hypothetical project's lifetime. From this statement one can readily trace the evolution of project liabilities and assets, noting such things as changes in the current ratio, the evolution of the project's debt structure, how assets are being depreciated, etc.

Finally, Figure 2.9 shows the project's projected financial cash flow position (Sources and Application of Funds). For convenience, a distinction has been made between Net Operating Flows, Non-Operating Financing Flows, and Net Financing Flows. The items included in the calculation of the Net Operating Flows result from the firm's productive operations, and from Figure 2.9 it is evident that this flow consists of the difference between the firm's operating profit (before interest and tax) plus depreciation and its net asset formation through time. It is from this flow that the pre-tax financial IRR or NPV of the firm's operations as a whole are calculated.

Non-operating financing flows include all the financial transactions relating to the external financing of the firm, the servicing of debt and the various claims on the firm's profit. This separation and breakdown of external financing flows enables a comparison to be made between internal (operating) and external (equity and debt) sources of finance over the years. From Figure 2.9 it can easily be seen that in the initial year, since there are no operating profits, operations are financed entirely by new equity and borrowing (items 2.1.1 and 2.1.2), while in subsequent years finance comes mainly from operating profits (item 1.1) and is applied to such items as debt service and external claims on profit (item 2.2). In addition this separation of cash flows relating to financing transactions facilitates calculation of the financial return on the equity component of the firm's funds and determination of how this will vary with changes in the debt component and its servicing.[1] It should

1   Although debt servicing is not included in the calculation of the net operating flow, interest charges on outstanding debt are normally included as expenses for tax assessment purposes. A change in the structure and/or conditions of the firm's debt finance and the servicing of this will therefore influence the post-tax financial return on the net operating flow.

Figure 2.6 *Sample Financial Income Statement*

Item	Year		
	1	2	3
1. Cost of Goods Produced	4800	12000	14800
1.1 Sales at Factor Cost*	4050	11925	15570
1.2 Inventory (Stock) Changes	+750	+75	− 770
2. Material Inputs*	2400	6000	7400
3. Gross Profit	2400	6000	7400
4. Operating Expenses*	2400	4400	5000
4.1 Utilities and Services	400	1000	1200
4.2 Labour	800	1800	2200
4.2.1 Unskilled	400	920	1120
4.2.2 Skilled	400	880	1080
4.3 Capital Consumption	1200	1600	1600
5. Operating Profit	0	1600	2400
6. Interest Payments	160	120	280
7. Net operating Profit Before Tax	− 160	1480	2120
8. Company Tax	-	160	200
9. Profit After Tax	− 160	1320	1920
9.1 Dividends	-	-	360
9.2 Retained Earnings	− 160	1320	1560

* Items for which supporting documentation appears in Figure 2.7.

Figure 2.7 *Sample Supporting Documentation For FIS*

Item	Year		
	1	2	3
Sales Projections			
1.1 Projected Sales (Factor Cost)	4050	11925	15570
1.1.1 Industrial Sector	3038	8944	11678
1.1.1.1 Unit Value (Sh/lb)	2.0	2.2	2.4
1.1.1.2 Quantity	1519	4065	4866
1.1.2 Household Sector	1012	2981	3892
1.1.2.1 Unit Value (Sh/lb)	1.0	1.1	1.2
1.1.2.2. Quantity	1012	2710	3244
Material Requirements			
2. Material Inputs	2400	6000	7400
2.1 Domestic	240	600	740
2.2 Imported	2160	5400	6660
2.2.1 Copper	1200	3000	3700
2.2.2 Aluminium	960	2400	2960
Operating Expenses Details			
4. Operating Expenses	2400	4400	5000
4.1 Utilities and Services	400	1000	1200
4.1.1 Utilities	40	80	120
4.2.1 Services	360	920	1080
4.2 Labour	800	1800	2200
4.2.1 Unskilled	400	920	1120
4.2.2 Skilled	400	880	1080
4.3 Capital Consumption	1200	1600	1600
4.3.1 Depreciation	800	1200	1200
4.3.2 Repairs and Maintenance	400	400	400

Figure 2.8 *Sample Financial Balance Sheet*

Item	Year			
	0	1	2	3
1. *Assets*	5600	6400	8400	8360
1.1 Current Assets	1600	3200	6400	7200
1.1.1 Cash	400	800	1200	1200
1.1.2 Receivables	-	400	2000	2800
1.1.3 Inventories	1200	2000	3200	3200
1.2 Fixed Assets	4000	3200	2000	800
1.2.1 At Cost	4000	4000	4000	4000
1.2.2 Accum. Depreciation	0	800	2000	3200
1.3 Other (Securities, etc.)	-	-	-	360
2. *Liabilities and Net Worth*	5600	6400	8400	8360
2.1 Liabilities	2800	3760	4440	2840
2.1.1 Current liabilities	1200	2160	2840	1240
2.1.1.1 Creditors	1200	2160	2840	1240
2.1.2 Long Term Debt	1600	1600	1600	1600
2.2 Net Worth	2800	2640	3960	5520
2.2.1 Equity	2800	2800	2800	2800
2.2.2 Retained Earnings	-	- 160	1160	2720

Figure 2.9 *Sample Financial Cash Flow*

Item	Year				
	0	1	2	3	31a
1. *Net Operating Flows*[b]	-4400	160	280	1200	6760
1.1 Sources	0	800	2800	3600	0
1.1.1 Operating Profit (BIT)	0	0	1600	2400	0
1.1.2 Depreciation	0	800	1200	1200	0
1.2 Applications	4400	640	2520	2400	-6760
1.2.1 Net Current Assets[c]	400	640	2520	2400	-5960
1.2.2 Fixed Assets	4000	0	0	0	-800
2. *Non-Operating Financial Flows*	4400	-160	-280	-1200	-1600
2.1 Sources	4400	0	0	0	0
2.1.1 New Borrowing	1600	0	0	0	0
2.1.2 New Equity	2800	0	0	0	0
2.2 Applications	0	160	280	1200	1600
2.2.1 Debt Service	0	160	120	280	1600
2.2.1.1 Interest	0	160	120	280	0
2.2.1.2 Principal	0	0	0	0	1600
2.2.2 Taxes	0	0	160	200	0
2.2.3 Dividends	0	0	0	360	0
2.2.4 Securities	0	0	0	360	0
3. *Net Financing Flows*[d]	0	0	0	0	5160

a. This column records liquidation of project at end of year 3.
b. This row contains the cash flow required for calculating the project's financial rate of return.
c. Change in current assets minus current liabilities.
d. Net financing flows = net operating flows *plus* non-operating financial flows.

also be noted that in all years, apart from the financial year in which the firm's operations are liquidated, the Net Financing Flow is zero.

2.06 *Use of the System for Financial and Economic Analysis*

It should now be clear how the three above statements, the FIS, FBS and FCF, fit together. Building up the FIS from basic data, as suggested from the supporting documentation, will constitute the bulk of the analyst's task, and more is said about techniques of projection in the following Chapter. Similarly, the FBS will need to be built up from projections of fixed and working capital, and in both cases the detailed data on prices of the various elements entering these statements will prove crucial at a later stage when economic and social cost-benefit analysis is carried out. For the moment, though, our concern is with financial analysis of the project and, here, it is the FCF (which summarises the key elements of the two other statements) which is most important.

Since the firm is concerned with how internal and external funds are obtained and used to maintain current and fixed asset formation, the FCF will be concerned with money flows; i.e. with flows at current market prices. Hence the projected rates of inflation for revenues and cost items enter into the construction of the statement. This can either be allowed for by incorporating an 'inflation premium' in the discount rate, or more satisfactorily, by adjusting the FCF statement to show all flows at constant market prices relative to the appropriate base year.

Calculation of the financial profitability of the project is determined by discounting the net cash flow at a rate reflecting the opportunity cost of funds. At the right side of the table in Figure 2.10, NPVs at four discount rates have been calculated in order to present the results in graphical form (NPV curves). Three curves are shown, representing pre-tax and post-tax financial profitability of the project as a whole, and post-tax financial return on equity funds.

Looking at the post-tax NPV curve for the project as a whole, the condition for accepting it on financial grounds will be that it should show a positive NPV at the appropriate opportunity cost of funds. Hence, if this was judged to be 20 percent the project would be acceptable while a 25 percent figure would result in a negative decision. Note, however, that once the opportunity cost of funds exceeds the cost of debt finance (11 percent), the post-tax NPV of the net flow on equity funds becomes greater than the post-tax NPV of the net operating flow; the former is still positive at a 25 percent figure and only becomes negative at a 28 percent discount rate. This is important because if the project were considered desirable from an *economic*

Figure 2.10 *Financial Profitability Calculations*

	0	1	2	3	3'	0%	10%	20%	25%
			YEAR				NPV		
Net Operating Flow	−4400	+160	+280	+1200	+6760	4000	1955	536	−17
TAX	0	0	−160	−200	0				
Net Operating Flow after Tax	−4400	+160	+120	+1000	+6760	3640	1672	310	−222
Borrowing and Debt Service	−1600	−160	−120	−280	−1600				
Net Flow on Equity Funds	−2800	0	0	+720	+5160	3080	1616	604	211

NPV CURVES

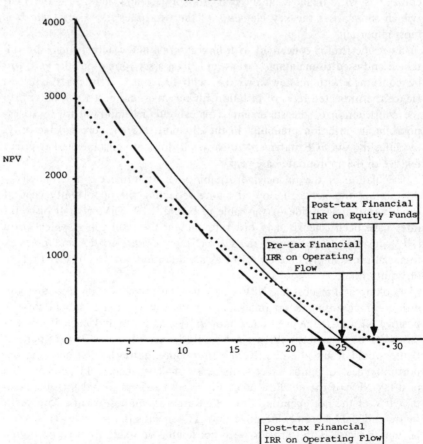

and *social* point of view, private investors would be willing to undertake the investment in circumstances when the financial NPV for the operation as a whole was negative. Note, however, that at 28 percent the level of taxation becomes critical in determining the project's return to equity and it might be necessary to introduce special tax or debt financing concessions in order to induce private investors to undertake the project. Calculating the economic and social rate of return to the project, however, is a subject which is dealt with in subsequent chapters.

2.07 *Further Reading*

A straightforward introduction to financial accounting conventions which the reader may find useful is Powell (1970). A detailed treatment of accounting practices applicable to industrial projects appears in Vol. I of Little & Mirlees (1972), while a lucid account of cash flow budgeting techniques is to be found in Part I of Bierman & Smidt (1971). The Spanish speaking reader may find it worthwhile to consult ILPES (1973) which is essentially a guide to project presentation. Price Gittinger (1972), besides covering the general methodological problems associated with the appraisal of agricultural projects, also contains a useful introduction to accounting conventions and layout. Finally, an introduction to the principles of an integrated documentation system is to be found in the early sections of Hansen (1973), which in turn is based on the work of Powelson (1969).

III

PROBABILITIES, PROJECTIONS, AND INVESTMENT

3.01 *Project Appraisal and Forecasting*

Whether one is appraising a project from a financial point of view or using the most recent SCBA techniques, project appraisal remains in essence an exercise in using limited information to make predictions about the future, contrasting the 'with' and 'without' project situations. Since a typical project will involve one or more outputs and a whole series of inputs, the net revenue (or net benefit) stream which eventually emerges will be the result of a string of calculations based on projected physical quantities and prices. To a limited extent, the confidence which is placed in the net revenue forecast will rely on assuming that overestimates in one place will be offset by underestimates elsewhere. But it would be unwise to rely excessively on such reasoning. For one thing, it will be helpful to distinguish those key variables which have most influence on the results, typically the larger cost and revenue items, particularly those appearing in the initial years of the cash flow. If variations in these values are all independent of each other, and are themselves 'normally distributed', one set of conclusions about the confidence to be placed in the resulting net revenue stream may be warranted while if these are interdependent and non-normally distributed quite another conclusion may emerge. Hence carrying out a project appraisal must be underpinned by a knowledge of the elements of statistical theory.

In what follows, a distinction is first drawn between the definitional relationship in which project appraisal variates stand to each other, and the underlying behavioural relationships which describe the values assumed by particular variates. Typically one works with limited information, the extent and reliability of the information in hand determining how far key behavioural relationships can be specified and tested.[1] Concepts of risk and un-

---

1 Indeed the typical project appraisal report usually contains one or two price forecasts made on the basis of extrapolating past trends, and quantity forecasts based on technical judgements, sophisticated treatment of risk or uncertainty being reserved for special types of projects such as flood control investment in which making any decision at all requires the explicit calculation of probabilities.

certainty are then examined and, concentrating on the former, the next part of the chapter sets out the basic elements of probability theory illustrating the importance of so doing by the use of examples. Short cut (three point) distributions are discussed, and problems of aggregating probability distributions are examined. The latter sections of the chapter consider different decision rules applicable to risk and uncertainty situations, and in the final section basic forecasting methods are examined in more detail.

3.02 *Risk and Uncertainty*

It will be useful to begin by noting the distinction between a 'definition' and a 'functional relationship'. The statement 'current sales revenue equals sales volumes times price', or

$$R_t = V_t . P_t$$

is true by definition. However, the proposition that current sales volume is a function of current price and the current level of consumers' income, or,

$$V_t = f(P_t, Y_t)$$

states a relationship which, when further specified, can be tested for empirical validity by the use of appropriate statistical techniques. The statements encountered in the previous chapter were almost entirely definitions. In the second part of the current chapter one shall be concerned more with underlying functional relationships. But before looking at some of the functional relationships which will be important for project evaluation purposes, it will be worthwhile reviewing certain basic principles of statistical analysis necessary to a proper understanding of the material which follows.

Consider the definition,

$$NPV = \sum_{t}^{T} P_t(1 + r)^{-t}$$

which is simply the expression for discounted cash flow. Calculating the profit stream, $P_{t=1...T}$, will involve predicting values for each of the various elements entering into the definition of profit: viz. volume of output sold, selling price, required investment, labour costs per unit, maintenance costs of machines, and so forth. Of these various elements, some will be possible to determine with little trouble while others may require the use of elaborate statistical techniques. Equally, the degree of sophistication used in prediction will obviously depend on how sensitive project profitability is to changes in the value of a particular element. One would not for instance spend much time on predicting the expected price of an input accounting for a tiny fraction of total cost. The degree of confidence to be associated with such predictions will in turn depend on the nature and quality of data available to the analyst as well as the extent to which factors that determine changes in these variables — the underlying functional relationships — are properly understood.

When one speaks of the NPV of a project, one must bear in mind that this is only one value amongst all possible values of NPV outcomes. Clearly, some outcomes will be more likely than others; formally, one may speak about a probability distribution of outcomes, or P (NPV), being 'jointly determined' by the probability distributions of all the various constituent elements entering the definition of NPV. Good probabilistic information will enable P (NPV) to be determined with reasonable accuracy, thus making it possible to say that there is 'such and such' a risk of attaining (or not attaining) a certain figure. This is what is meant by formally defining 'risk' as 'quantifiable uncertainty'.[1] Clearly, the less one knows about possible outcomes, the more one is 'uncertain' about what is likely to happen. Hence it will be useful to think of certainty and uncertainty as defining the extreme points of a continuum, the object being to remove as much 'uncertainty' as possible from the problem of quantifying risk through further research and the application of appropriate statistical techniques.

3.03 *Probability Distributions and their Characteristics*

A probability distribution, $P(x)$, is merely an enumeration of the various values (x_i) which a variable (x) may assume accompanied by an indication of the probability of occurrence of each value (p_i). The mean of this distribution is called the *expected value* of the variate (a variable having a probability distribution is called a variate) and is defined as: $E(x) = \Sigma \ p_i x_i$. Visualised in graphical form, a distribution may be 'stepped' (where a limited number of discrete outcomes are possible) or 'continuous'. The shape of the distribution may be 'skew' (one tail is elongated) or symmetrical. Probability distributions are characterised by various parameters, the most important of which are the measures of central tendency and dispersion. To derive the characteristics of the distribution of the variate with respect to a given population, we must normally sample that population; viz., to determine the distribution of annual earnings amongst families in a certain region of the U.K., one might collect a sample of 1000 observations. Hence one must distinguish between population characteristics and sample statistics.

1   This definition was first advanced by Knight (1921).

Measures of central tendency provide information about the centre of a sample and some commonly used measures are: the *arithmetic mean* (the sum of the values of the observations divided by the number of observations), the *mode* (the most frequently observed value of the variable) and the *median* (the middle value of the ranked observations). An important characteristic of the Normal Distribution is that all these measures of central tendency coincide.

Measures of dispersion may be absolute or relative, and indicate the extent to which observations deviate around the central tendency. The *variance*, the *standard deviation* (square root of the variance) and the *range* are measures of absolute dispersion while the *coefficient of variation* (standard deviation divided by the arithmetic mean) is a useful measure of relative dispersion.

The Gaussian or Normal Distribution (the familiar smooth bell curve shape), sometimes attributed to the English mathematician De Moivre (1733), is particularly useful for two reasons. First, one can easily determine the probability that an observation will lie within a given distance of the mean. As shown in Figure 3.1, approximately 68 percent of observations will lie between ± 1 standard deviation, 94 percent will lie within a range of ± 2 standard deviations, and 100 percent between ± 3 s.ds. (Standard normal tables relate percentage of the area under the curve to distance from the arithmetic mean in detail.) But more important is the fact that any empirically derived distribution (or what is called a *sample* distribution to distinguish it from a theoretical distribution derived mathematically) will approximate a normal

Figure 3.1 *The Normal Distribution*

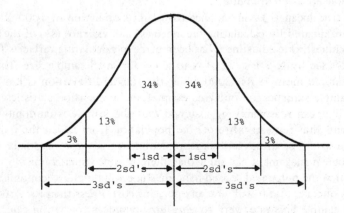

distribution, the degree of approximation increasing with sample size (Central Limit Theorem). In practice, most samples having in excess of 20 observations will approximate a normal curve if the variate is distributed reasonably normally, while for a skew distribution suitable transformations can be used. For small samples, a modified normal distribution known as *Student's t-distribution* can be used.

3.04 *Deriving Probability Distributions: An Example*

To illustrate the application of some of these principles in practice, imagine the case of an Indian firm which is considering whether or not to purchase a second-hand machine of given specification and vintage. Because the machine in question is several years old, its operating costs are substantially greater than those of the current model, and it is this stream of extra annual costs incurred over its operating life which will need to be compared to the capital cost savings in order to determine whether the older machine is preferred to the new model. The management has calculated that if extra running costs of the second-hand machine exceed those of the new one by Rs. 2800 per annum, the proposition is uneconomical. From the machine manufacturer's records it has been established that 1000 machines were produced in all; unfortunately, only 12 of these can be traced to their present owners. Hence, the operating cost characteristics of the entire population of second-hand machines (from which the one in question is assumed to be drawn 'at random') will need to be estimated from the characteristics of a sample population numbering only a dozen. Estimates of extra annual operating costs for the sample are given in Figure 3.2.

The true mean (μ) and variance (σ) of the population of 1000 machines are approximated by calculating the mean ($\bar{x}$) and variance (s^2) of the sample (12 machines). One adjustment has been made in calculating variance, $(x - \bar{x})^2$ being divided by N-1 instead of N to allow for small sample size. The computed sample mean is Rs. 2000 while the standard deviation is Rs. 770. If these sample statistics are unbiased estimates of population statistics, that is to say if it can reasonably be assumed that the sample is randomly drawn from (and thus representative of) the population from which the purchased machine would be drawn and measurement errors are also randomly distributed, then management can infer that there is approximately an 85 percent chance that the purchased second-hand machine will be more economical than the new one; i.e. that it will have an operating cost of less than Rs. 2800.

This sample illustrates very roughly how sample information can be used to derive a probability distribution of possible outcomes (though futher adjustments could be made here; viz. using a Student's t-distribution).

Figure 3.2 *Estimates of Operating Costs of Second-Hand Machines*
       (All figures in Rs. x 10^2)

No.	X	$\bar{X}$	$(X - \bar{X})$	$(X - \bar{X})^2$
1	21	20	1	1
2	10	20	-10	100
3	16	20	- 4	16
4	23	20	3	9
5	21	20	1	1
6	14	20	- 6	36
7	30	20	10	100
8	18	20	- 2	4
9	27	20	7	49
10	20	20	0	0
11	7	20	-13	169
12	33	20	13	169
total	240			654

$$\bar{X} = \Sigma X/_N = 240/_{12} = 20 \quad (= \text{Rs. 2000})$$

$$s^2 = \Sigma(X-\bar{X})^2 /_{N-1} = 654/_{11} = 59.5$$

$$S = \sqrt{s^2} = 7.7 \, (= \text{Rs. 770})$$

3.05 *Three Point Distributions*

In some cases, even the limited information presented above might not be available. A typical situation is where only high (H), low (L) and best guess (B) estimates can be made. A very useful device is the use of some form of three-point distribution such as the 'triangular' and the 'Beta' distributions. Suppose that instead of obtaining the above sample information, management had only been able to obtain the manufacturer's opinion that operating costs were unlikely to be above Rs. 3500 at worst, or below Rs. 500 at best, their own best estimate being Rs. 2000.

Statistics for the *triangular* distribution are:

$$\bar{x} = \frac{H + 2B + L}{4} \quad \text{or} \quad \bar{x} = \frac{3500 + 4000 + 500}{4} = 2000$$

$$s = \frac{H - L}{4} \quad \text{or} \quad s = \frac{3500 - 500}{4} = 750$$

In the case of the *Beta* distribution, more weight is given to the central value in relation to the extreme point values. Hence we have:

$$\bar{x} = \frac{H + 4B + L}{6} \quad \text{or} \quad \bar{x} = \frac{3500 + 8000 + 500}{6} = 2000$$

$$s = \frac{H - L}{6} \quad \text{or} \quad s = \frac{3500 - 500}{6} = 500$$

Comparing these results to those obtained above (Figure 3.2), it will be seen that the estimates of mean value ($\bar{x}$) coincide while those for standard deviation are smaller, particularly in the case of the Beta distribution. The coincidence of mean estimates and the fact that extreme values chosen are equidistant from the best estimates (B) suggests that the manufacturers assumed a normal distribution. However, the fact that the standard deviation estimated from the Beta distribution is smaller than that estimated from the triangular distribution reflects the smaller weight given to extreme point values in the case of the Beta distribution. Choice of which of these three-point distributions to use when one is working with limited information (uncertainty) will clearly depend on the analyst's judgement of how far high and low estimates encompass the entire range of possible outcomes; i.e. judgments of the form 'Is the high (low) estimate merely an infrequent occurrence or an extremely exceptional occurrence?' In general, though, such approximations can be extremely useful provided that the general characteristics of the underlying population distribution are understood and proper caution is exercised in applying the results derived.

3.06 *Aggregating Probability Distributions*

At the beginning of this Chapter, it was noted that the probability distribution of a project's NPV is determined by the distributions associated with the various elements entering its definition. This raises the problem of aggregating probability distributions.

It is important in this connection to distinguish between distributions generated by correlated and uncorrelated variates. To illustrate this distinction, let us continue with the story of the second-hand machine, the operating costs (C_t) and associated probabilities for which have been determined. Management now wants to determine the gross operating profit of the machine (P_t) which is defined as the value of output produced (V_t) minus operating costs (C_t), or:

$$P_t = V_t - C_t$$

In determining V_t, it is first assumed that price is fixed. However, operating costs vary according to the volume of output. That is to say, when the machine is running smoothly and producing at rated capacity, operating costs are relatively low, but if serious breakdowns occur output volume falls and operating costs rise. Hence the variables C_t and V_t do not vary independently of each other.

Figure 3.3 illustrates this situation. Discrete distributions are shown for each of the variates. As long as operating costs are Rs. 2000 or less, the value of output is Rs. 10,000, but where costs rise above this figure, the volume

Figure 3.3 *Joint Probability Distribution Correlated Variables*
   (All figures in Rs. x 10^2)

f Frequency	C_t Operating Cost	V_t Values Output	P_t Gross Profit
10%	10 (1)	100 (10)	90 (9)
20%	15 (3)	100 (20)	85 (17)
40%	20 (8)	100 (40)	80 (32)
20%	25 (5)	80 (16)	55 (11)
10%	30 (3)	60 (6)	30 (3)
100%	(20)	(92)	(72)

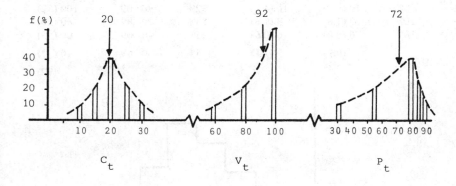

(and hence the value) of total output falls. Note that while the distribution of C_t is normal, that of V_t is highly skew; hence the resulting skew distribution of P_t is jointly determined by those of the defining variables. Note too that the modal value of P_t (Rs. 8000 expected in 40 percent of cases) and the mean expected value (Rs. 7000) are different. The mean is calculated in this case by multiplying the profit estimates times their associated probabilities and summing the values (as shown by the figures in brackets). It would have been misleading to take the most frequently occurring outcome (modal value) as a guide to profitability since what one is concerned to estimate is that figure which. best represents profit 'taking the good years with the bad'. Finally, were full probabilistic information not available in the above form, the reader can check for himself that using Rs. 9000, Rs. 8000 and Rs. 3000 as H, B, and L estimates for a Beta distribution would result in very nearly the same mean value as that derived above.

Another example of a jointly determined distribution is shown in Figure 3.4. Here, the value of output (V_t) has been disaggregated into its price and quantity elements, or:

$$V_t = P_t.Q_t$$

and price is now assumed to be a variate of known distribution and to vary

Figure 3.4 *Joint Probability Distribution Non-Correlated Variables*
            (All figures in Rs. x 10^2)

Frequency f	tons Output Volume Q_t	Price P_t	Frequency f	Class Intervals	Value Output V_t
10%	10 (1)	14 (1.4)	7%	130-149	140 (10)
20%	10 (2)	12 (2.4)	16%	110-129	120 (19)
40%	10 (4)	10 (4)	32%	90-109	100 (32)
20%	8 (1.6)	8 (1.6)	25%	70- 89	80 (20)
10%	6 (0.6)	6 (0.6)	15%	50- 69	60 (9)
	(9.2)	(10)	5%	30- 49	40 (2)
					(92)

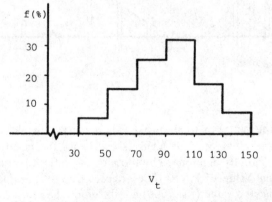

independently of quantity produced by the firm. Calculating the possible values of V_t and associated probabilities is now more difficult. Since a price of Rs. 600 per ton will only occur in 10 percent of cases, and in only 10 percent of *these* cases will output volume be 6 tons, a total output value of

Rs. 3600 will have only a 1 percent chance of occurrence. By multiplying all values for P_t and Q_t pairwise, grouping them in class intervals, and noting the number of observations in each, a distribution for the variate V_t can be determined as shown in the histogram in Figure 3.4.

Once again, it is to be noted that the mode and mean of $P(V_t)$ differ, and that the mean of $P(V_t)$ can be calculated directly from knowledge of $E(Q_t)$ and $E(P_t)$. However, the main point to note is that even though the distribution of one of the variates is highly skew, the resulting distribution of V_t is nearly normal. This is because variations in P_t and Q_t are assumed independent. The point has important implications for the characteristics of the distribution of the NPV variate in most project appraisals since, if most variates entering the definition of NPV can be assumed independent of each other and if there are a large number of such variates, then, whatever the shape of the distributions of these primary variates, P(NPV) can in most cases be assumed to approximate a normal curve.

3.07 *Use of Probabilistic Information in Project Appraisal*

Having distinguished between correlated and non-correlated variables and noted the importance of these in the aggregation of probabilities, one may turn to the wider issue of how probabilistic information can be used in project appraisal. One must begin here by noting that, in many project appraisal exercises, information of the sort described above typically gets lost. At the crudest level, a single estimate of NPV (or IRR) will be presented on the basis of which the decision maker will be asked to accept or reject a project. What such a number represents is typically unclear. Is it a mean expected value of possible outcomes, a maximum likelihood estimate, or simply the result of a string of arithmetic computations? Have sophisticated statistical methods been used to establish some project parameters but others merely been guessed at? Nor will it be enough to trust in the common sense of the appraiser and hope for a 'reasonable' result. The common sense of one appraiser might indicate using conservative estimates for key parameters in all cases, while another might argue that optimistic assessments are justified, if only to offset the conservative bias of the engineer or the agronomist. The treatment of risk clearly needs to be handled systematically, if only to establish common standards which make one project appraiser's NPV consistent with another.

The basic choice to be made is between presenting a single point estimate of profitability (a central tendency measure) and presenting central tendency *and* dispersion estimates derived from probabilistic information. Several of the traditional methods of handling risk are best understood in such a light. For example, one popular method of treating a 'high risk' project is to include a 'risk premium' in the discount rate. This effectively adjusts the estimate of central tendency downwards according to some (often entirely subjective) estimate of dispersion. It is an unsatisfactory method, partly because it combines two bits of information which should properly be separated, but also because it introduces a separate source of bias, notably the implicit assumption that risk is a compounding function of time, and hence discriminates against those projects having long gestation periods.

Another method popularly thought of as allowing for risk is the use of 'sensitivity analysis'. This consists essentially of varying key parameter values, usually one at a time but sometimes in combination, and assessing the effect of such changes on the central tendency estimate of profitability. This can be useful if information about key parameters is such that some common yardstick can be used to assess how far each parameter should be varied; for example, each parameter might be varied by ± 1 standard deviation. Unfortunately, it is more common to vary primary parameters by a fixed percentage (viz. 10 percent) which tells us nothing useful about the measurement of dispersion associated with P (NPV), although varying each parameter separately may tell us something useful about which of these is most critical in *explaining* dispersion.

Far more satisfactory is to use available probabilistic information to approximate P (NPV) directly. This can be done in principle by aggregating distributional information for primary variates numerically, but as should be clear from the example in Figure 3.4 such a procedure would be impossibly laborious when applied to a real project, the number of required compu-

Figure 3.5 *Choosing between Projects Having Different Probability Distributions of NPV*

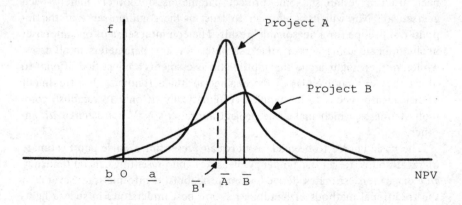

tations rising as an exponential function of the number of independent variates. Fortunately, there are computer routines available which simulate numerical solutions by repeatedly sampling the population of possible values for basic variates and calculating a large number of NPVs, hence producing an approximation of the required distribution.

A clearer idea of the significance of handling risk in different ways may be gained by referring to Figure 3.5. Two projects are shown, A and B, the latter having a higher mean NPV ($\bar{B} > \bar{A}$) but also being 'riskier' in the sense that dispersion about the mean is greater. (Note that the minimum possible NPV for B, shown at point b, is negative; i.e. the project could make a loss.) Adding a premium to the discount rate to allow for extra risk in the case of B would cause the value of the NPV to fall to $\bar{B}'$, project A being chosen in preference. Performing sensitivity analysis in the form of recalculating the NPVs using pessimistic extreme point values for all underlying parameters would determine the lowest possible outcomes of the two projects (a, b) and provide information supplementing the original calculations ($\bar{A}$, $\bar{B}$). Finally, the P(NPV)s could be calculated numerically, resulting in the curves shown; more plausibly, the curves could be approximated using simulation methods.

3.08 *Choice under Risk and Uncertainty*

While the above discussion suggests that much can be done by way of systematically organising and using probabilistic information in project evaluation, nothing has so far been said about how to *choose* between projects under these conditions. In fact, the literature on this subject is considerable, and little more will be attempted here than to outline the relevant concepts involved.

Imagine for the moment that the situation depicted in Figure 3.5 involved having only four bits of information about projects A and B., notably points $\bar{A}$, $\bar{B}$, a and b, and that no associated probabilities are given. Such a situation would be one of uncertainty, there being no way of telling, should project A be chosen, which of the two NPVs, $\bar{A}$ or a, would be most likely. (In light of the above comments about appraisal practices, the example is not so far-fetched as it may seem.) Indeed, one can imagine real situations in which this might apply as, for example, if project outcomes were conditional on alternative states of nature which were in essence unpredictable; viz. a fishmeal project on the west coast of South America depending upon future shifts in the Humbolt current. To facilitate the illustration, the outcomes $\bar{A}$, $\bar{B}$, etc. will be assigned numerical values as shown in Figure 3.6.

Suppose that projects A and B represent two different versions of an investment proposal for the construction of a fishmeal processing plant. Ver-

Figure 3.6   *Decision Making Under Uncertainty. Alternative NPVs of Fish-meal Project* (Figures in Pesos x 10^3)

	Without Fish	With Fish
Project A	20 (a)	100 ($\bar{A}$)
Project B	–10 (b)	150 ($\bar{B}$)

sion B is relatively more capital intensive than A, and thus turns out to be more economical in those years when the fish catch is plentiful and a high volume of throughput can be maintained. Under such conditions, the mean NPV of version B is pesos 150,000 while that of A is only P. 100,000. However, in years where the catch is relatively meagre (the 'without fish' situation) version A still manages to realise a small positive return and has an NPV of P. 20,000 while version B shows a negative NPV (P.-10,000).

Several decision criteria applicable to choice under uncertainty have been developed in the context of games theory, the two best known being the *maximin-returns* principle and the *minimax-regret* principle. The former suggests that alternatives should be evaluated on the basis of the largest minimum return (maxi-min) which can be secured should things go wrong. On this basis one would be led to choose project A which guarantees a minimum return of 20,000 Pesos in the event of an unfavourable shift in current. Obviously, this is an exceedingly conservative principle since it focuses entirely on minimising losses in an unfavourable situation and ignores the gains to be secured from the choice of version B should the fish be running. On the other hand, the *minimax-regret* principle takes into account both potential gains and potential losses under alternative states of nature. Thus, in the present case, choice of project B would entail the 'regret' of incurring an extra loss of 30,000 Pesos [20-(-10)] in the 'without fish' situation while choice of project A would entail the 'regret' of sacrificing a potential extra gain of 50,000 pesos [150 – 100] in the 'with fish' situation. If no probabilities can be attached to these alternative states of nature, one must implicitly assume them equally probable, and thus choose B since this choice entails minimising 'regret'.

Turning now to choice in a situation where probabilities *can* be assigned to alternative outcomes (choice under risk as opposed to choice under uncertainty), let us suppose that the 'with fish' situation has a 90 percent chance of occurrence while the alternative state has a 10 percent chance. In this case, one rule which might be adopted is to choose that version having the highest *mean expected value* of NPV, or version B:

Version A : 0.1 (20) + 0.9 (100) = 92
Version B : 0.1 (–10) + 0.9 (150) = 134

This rule can obviously be generalised to cover situations where there are more than two discrete outcomes, as depicted in the continuous probability distributions shown in Figure 3.5.

There are situations, however, when the expected value rule cannot serve as a guide to choice, as for example when two versions of a project have the same E (NPV) but different variance, or when the rule may prove unacceptable as a guide to choice as can be shown in certain types of insurance situations. More powerful tools for analysing choice are provided by using information on both central tendency *and* dispersion, as best illustrated by the diagram shown in Figure 3.7 commonly referred to as the 'gambler's indifference map'.

Figure 3.7 *The Gambler's Indifference Map*

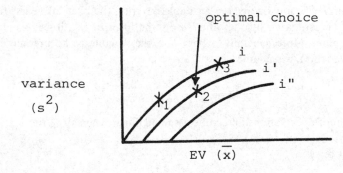

Here, expected value information is given along the horizontal axis while variance information appears on the vertical axis. Knowledge of P (NPV) for each of a set of projects allows any project to be represented on the graph as a single point (shown above as an 'X') once the mean and variance of NPV have been computed. Choice now depends upon the extent of the decision maker's aversion to risk which can be conceptualised in the form of a family of indifference curves, or 'map', and knowledge of which is gained by supposing him to select combinations of points between which he is indifferent (viz. projects X_1 and X_3). While the decision maker will be indifferent amongst all projects lying along any one curve, such as curve i, he will prefer projects lying on a higher value curve (i">i'>i) since moving from left to right along the horizontal axis will entail reaching a higher EV for a given amount of variance. Hence, in the above case, project X_2 will be the optimal choice.

3.09 *Time Series Analysis*

Much of the present chapter has focused on basic principles governing the
deviation and use of probabilistic information in the context of project
appraisal. It will be appropriate to conclude by briefly considering problems
of prediction *per se*; that is, how historical information may be used to make
inferences about what is likely to happen in future. Here one enters the realm
of functional relationships which deal with questions of the form 'How far
are changes in one variable, the dependent variable, caused by changes in
some other variables or set of variables, the independent variable(s)?'. A
proper understanding of causality underlying a given relationship will be
critical both to the interpretation of statistical results and to the choice of the
tools of analysis themselves.

The simplest and most widely used prediction technique involves looking
at historical data for a given variable and inferring from past behaviour what
future behaviour will be. Hence if one wishes to predict, let us say, the value
of GNP in 1990 and figures are available covering the past 20 years, future
GNP can be estimated by hypothesising some form of relationship between
GNP and time. More generally, where Y is the variable to be predicted (dependent variable), we assume:

$$Y = f(x), \quad \text{where } x = \text{time.}$$

If the form of the relationship can be assumed linear, we may write:

$$Y = a + bx$$

where a is the y-intercept and b the slope.[1] Then, by determining values for
the parameters a and b, values of Y (GNP) can be predicted corresponding to
desired future values of x (time). To determine the values of a and b one
typically uses statistical techniques (simple regression analysis) making assumptions about the characteristics of the data with which one is working,
the most important of which is that observations are independent of one another.

Figure 3.8 illustrates the computation of a trend line by the use of simple
regression techniques. In the example given, one is concerned to predict the
world price of wheat in 1973 using seven observations covering the years
1961-1967. In the right hand column, the price of wheat (US$ per tonne) is

---

1 Where the underlying relationship is non-linear, it may be transformed into a linear
function for regression purposes by the use of logarithms. For example, the non-linear
function $y = ax^b$ can be written $\log y = \log a + b.\log x$ and the least square estimation
equations amended accordingly. A variety of such log transformations exist for forecasting purposes (semi-log, double log, log-inverse, etc.).

Figure 3.8 *Forecasting Trend in World Wheat Price*

Year	Price of Wheat ($ per tonne)	IBRD Index (1967=100)	Y Wheat at 1967 constant prices	x Year
1961	64.6	93	69.5	0
1962	66.4	94	70.6	1
1963	69.0	94	73.4	2
1964	67.3	95	70.8	3
1965	68.0	98	69.4	4
1966	71.1	99	71.8	5
1967	65.6	100	65.6	6

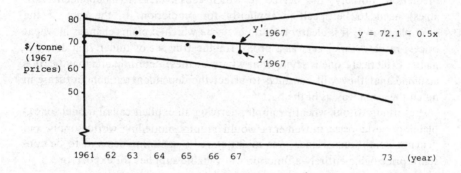

shown at current prices, and an index of world commodity prices is used to transform the series into constant 1967 prices (column Y). Y is then regressed on X, the normal equations[1] for estimating a and b being:

(I) ΣY $= na + b\,(\Sigma X)$
(II) ΣXY $= a(\Sigma X) + b(\Sigma X^2)$
where n   = number of observations

and hence the method of obtaining the desired parameters is called the 'least squares' method. In the above case, the estimated trend line is $Y = 72.1 - 0.5X$,

1   The straight line which is given by the solution of these two equations has the important property of minimising the sum of the squares of the differences between the observed Ys and the corresponding point on the regression line (Y'); viz. the 1967 observation. Formally this property may be written:
   Min $\Sigma(Y - Y')^2$

and the predicted value of Y in 1973[1] is obtained simply by substituting the number of the year (12) for X and solving, which gives us \$66.10. One could also estimate confidence intervals (at say, 95 percent probability) for predictions, as shown by the curves above and below the trend line in the diagram. Finally, one would normally estimate the degree to which variation in the variable Y is explained by variation in X (the coefficient of determination, R^2) as well as test whether the estimated slope coefficient, b, is significant.

3.10 *Explicit Causal Models*

The use of regression analysis in the context of the above problem serves to highlight an important question about the use of functional relationships in prediction, notably, the degree to which causal factors (independent variables) need to be specified explicitly for prediction. In the case of the example shown, it is clearly not 'time' *per se* which explains changes in wheat prices; rather, 'time' acts as a proxy for the true set of underlying determinants. Effectively one is saying that whatever these determinants may be, it is assumed that they will continue to affect the dependent variable in future in much the same way as in the past.[2]

Returning to our wheat example, deriving an explicit causal model for explaining world price movements would require modelling world supply and demand conditions. Hence, one might start by assuming demand to be constant, price being entirely a function of available supplies for export, or:

$$P_t = f(X_t)$$

One could then plot prices against available exports by year, observing how good a 'fit' was obtained. Or again, one might use the difference between world export supply and import demand as the determinant of price:

$$P_t = f(X_t - M_t)$$

Clearly, the more explanatory variables are introduced, the more explicit the nature of the causal relationships becomes, and the more information is needed. It is then the chosen set of explanatory variables which needs to be forecast; i.e. to predict the price of wheat in 1980, one needs first to predict the level of available exports and import demand in 1980, these depending in

1   It may be noted that the actual price for wheat obtaining in 1973, at 1967 prices, was \$71.20.
2   Further aspects of time series analysis not covered here concern the decomposition of such series into 'explainable' seasonal, cyclical, trend and random components, the underlying causes of each can then be examined in turn.

turn on the successful specification of models predicting their behaviour. For example, import demand may be a function of income in importing countries (Y_t^m) and price (P_t), and export supply a function of income in exporting countries (Y_t^x) and price (P_t); hence the following system of equations:

$$P_t = f(X_t - M_t)$$
$$X_t = g(Y_t^x, P_t)$$
$$M_t = h(Y_t^m, P_t)$$

which in this case would need to be solved simultaneously.

While statistical techniques exist for dealing with more than one explanatory variable (multiple regression), as indeed for dealing with the very much more complex problems encountered in analysing systems of interdependent relationships such as that outlined above, this is properly the area of the statistician and not of the project analyst. Nevertheless, it should be clear from the above discussion that the ability to determine, interpret and apply probabilistic information is a key part of the economist's task. Properly used, the tools of statistical analysis and probability theory have an important role to play in understanding and improving project planning and evaluation.

3.11 *Further Reading*

For the reader who wishes to review basic statistical principles a variety of introductory textbooks are available of which the simplest probably remains Moroney (1962), although others which might be mentioned are Wonnacott & Wonnacott (1972), Hoel (1965), Yamane (1964) and Yeomans (1968). OECD (1969) and UNIDO (1972) both contain sections on risk and uncertainty. Useful material on probabilistic analysis of projects under conditions of limited information is provided by Reutlinger (1970) and Pouliquen (1970). Both deal with the theory and provide several illustrative case studies, the latter being oriented towards risk appraisal while the former is concerned with uncertainty. The simplest introduction to games theoretical concepts is probably still Dorfman (1962), which incidently covers some of the more general points on project appraisal decision rules under risk and uncertainty very compactly. Further discussion of games theoretical approaches is to be found in Raiffa (1970).

A useful introduction to market analysis and forecasting methods is provided by Ferber and Verdoorn (1969) while Labys (1975) contains a more advanced discussion of commodity price forecasting. Such techniques are also covered at an elementary level with specific reference to development projects by UNO (1958). On the purely empirical side, there is a wealth of material in this field published at regular intervals by various national and international agencies as well as by groups of commodity producers, specialist brokers, etc.. IBRD publishes annual price forecasts for selected commodity groups as well as a general commodity price index and agricultural commodities are covered in detail by FAO and USDA publications.

IV

SCBA: HISTORICAL AND ANALYTICAL PRINCIPLES

4.01 *Public Sector Investment Planning*

Previous chapters have been concerned with the basic tools required for investment appraisal. The elements of discounting, the concepts of an appropriate decision criterion, elementary accounting conventions and the relevant statistical concepts required for prediction are all areas with which the investment analyst needs to be familiar whether one is concerned with private or public profitability calculations. At this juncture, however, the reader is asked to take something of a major jump — from the field of the purely technical into that of the more theoretically oriented aspects of investment analysis in the public sector which come under the general rubric of social cost-benefit analysis (SCBA).

The term 'social cost-benefit analysis' has come to mean a variety of different things to different people, so much so that a bewildering assortment of books exists on the subject some of which bear little more than titular relation to each other. In principle, SCBA is concerned with the theory and application of criteria for investment decision making in the public sector. In the early days of the subject, what served to distinguish the public sector investment decision as a field worthy of study in its own right was the 'non-commercial' nature of investment projects typically undertaken by public authorities, which in turn meant that special methods of appraisal were needed in order to determine their economic soundness. Hence, just as there are sociologists specialising in the study of deviant behaviour, there were economists specialising in the measurement of externalities, the valuation of collective goods, and other *curiosa* the theoretical ramifications of which came to constitute a form of *ex-post* justification for limited types of state intervention.

More recently, the scope of SCBA has been widened to include public investment appraisal in the Third World. With the increase in project aid flows and associated technical assistance which took place throughout the 1950s and 1960s, agencies through which such funds were channelled found it in-

creasingly important to lay down standards of appraisal determining economic viability, particularly in the field of infrastructure investment (power,
transport, etc.) to which the bulk of such aid was being applied. The result
was an increase in demand for appraisal methodologies and practitioners,
initially met by economists trained in developed countries and later supplemented by Third World graduates. Such graduates would not have found
very much in the early SCBA literature of practical guidance (apart from a
few books on water resource economics). At the same time, an accumulating
literature on development suggested the need for an economic calculus
applicable to investment planning which eschewed much of the rhetoric of
perfect markets and provided tools of analysis more in tune with the stuff of
reality. These new constructs, when they did eventually appear, came as
much from the field of operations research as from economics proper as the
term 'shadow price' suggests. A major breakthrough was undoubtedly the
publication of the OECD *Manual* in 1968, for although its authors would
see themselves as well within the mainstream of neo-classical tradition, it can
be argued that many of the assumptions upon which their analytical framework subsequently developed are more consistent with a socialist view of the
State as prime organiser of investment activity than with the classic liberal
stance.

   The essence of the Little and Mirrlees (LM) proposal was that world prices
be taken as shadow prices for all goods and services, those commodities not
entering trade being broken down into their equivalent traded components
and thus all production eventually being valued in terms of its balance of payments impact. On this view, trade efficiency becomes the central concern of
the planner. The initial methodology also contained a novel approach to the
valuation of investible surplus in hands of Government relative to capitalist
profits and workers' wages where the rate of accumulation was thought to be
too low, and this 'distributional' element has subsequently been extended
to include adjustments for realising greater equity in the personal income
distribution. These two dimensions of distribution form the 'social' basis of
the new SCBA methodology. While Professor Little himself appears initially
to have viewed the political implications of the method as involving little
more than enhancing the 'traditional' role of Government as regulator of
commercial policy (viz. the plea for 'rational' trade policies), the central
contribution of the method is as much in the questions it raises as in those it
answers. For once one passes from the neo-classical characterisation of
distortions as temporary departures from equilibrium in an economy where
the public sector has marginal influence on the structure of investment, to
one in which distortions are ubiquitous and have become the central concern
of a powerful planning office, it is but a short step to asking what the ideal
scope of public sector control over the allocation of resources should be. The

elevation of trade efficiency and distribution to the centre of the stage opens a Pandora's box of questions. To what extent can the gains from trade, once identified, be captured; what are the costs associated with opening an economy to trade, and hence to foreign capital and foreign consumption patterns, and how can they be minimised; why should Government hope to raise the global savings ratio, or realise a more equitable distribution of income, through the project selection mechanism alone; and so on. In this sense, the new SCBA methodology, while remaining impeccably neo-classical in its language of analysis, has taken a major and perhaps irreversible step away from the neo-classical view of the role of the State in planning.

It will perhaps be argued that such a step is more in the nature of a catching-up than an advance; much of the mainstream macro-planning and growth literature has for some time been predicated on assumptions radically at variance with 19th century liberalism. However one takes this argument, one point would seem to be crucial. The experience of the past two decades has suggested that planning at the level of macro-aggregates has in many countries produced little in the way of concrete results. It is one thing, after all, to produce elaborate plans based on sophisticated prediction and optimisation techniques but quite another thing to implement them. Micro-planning focuses on the point of implementation, the investment decision itself, and thus the question of who takes the investment decision, who appropriates the surplus, and which sectors are most crucial in the economy, cannot be avoided.

4.02 *Historical Aspects*

The first systematic attempts to develop SCBA are associated with work which took place in the field of water resource development in the United States in the 1930s, and which was later codified in the form of a manual prepared for the Federal Inter-Agency River Basin Committee (1950). Although concepts such as public goods and externalities were already familiar to economists, the acknowledgement of public sector investment criteria as a field meriting special study reflects the changing attitudes of the period towards the role of Government in managing the economy. To be sure, few Western governments used direct public sector investment as a major tool of economic management, and even in those sectors where governments created nationalised industries few projects were appraised in other than the conventional ways. The application of SCBA in advanced capitalist economies has been, and continues to be, restricted to those special cases where for one reason or another major investment decisions undertaken by public authorities cannot be justified on conventional financial grounds alone.

By contrast, the volume of academic literature on the theory of public investment decisions grew enormously in the 1950s and 1960s, and an important new element at the end of the period was the increased interest expressed in applying these methods to planning in the Third World. This
change in orientation is best illustrated by the attention given to publications by OECD (1968) and UNIDO (1972). Equally, the major multilateral
aid agencies (most particularly the World Bank) and some of the bilateral
agencies[1] have reinforced the trend by the adoption of increasingly sophisticated methodological requirements in assessing the suitability of projects.

One needs to understand the sudden surge of interest in SCBA as emerging
from the fusion of a number of influences amongst which developments in
the academic literature is only one. By the mid-1960s, a good deal of scepti-
cism was being voiced about the results of the many national development
plans and programmes launched in the previous decade. While it is true that
some of these were little more than 'paper plans', it is equally the case that
even in those countries where planning was being taken seriously, the realisation of planned investment targets appeared to be seriously constrained by
the availability and quality of resources devoted to project level planning.
Thus, for example, Streeten (1968), criticising India's excessive reliance on
heavy industrial projects to promote development, noted the need for 'small
scale local analysis' in planning, while in a different context Waterston (1965)
remarked that 'the shortage of good, well-prepared projects is now widely
recognised as a major impediment to the execution of plans for development'.
The view that the relative importance accorded to macro- and micro-level
planning might need to be significantly altered was underpinned by widespread concern about the wisdom of basing developmental strategy too
narrowly upon the growth of a manufacturing sector encouraged by over-
valued domestic currencies and increasingly complex tariff and quota restrictions. A pertinent and widely cited example was that of Pakistan where
Soligo and Stern (1965) showed that value-added in domestic manufacturing
when measured at world prices was actually negative. More general arguments
along these lines together with supporting empirical evidence from experience
elsewhere have been provided, amongst others, by Balassa (1971) and Little,
Scitovsky and Scott (1970).

To the changing climate of development opinion one must add the role of
the aid agencies, particularly that of the multilateral donors which over the
decade have disbursed an increasing proportion of total official development

1   Bilateral agencies expressing an early interest in the new methodology were ODM in
the U.K. and KfW in West Germany. Both investigated the feasibility of applying the
principles set out in the OECD *Manual*; it was not until after the publication of the
UNIDO *Guidelines* that the World Bank appears to have taken a serious interest in the
debate.

assistance and which are predominantly project oriented. The conventional rationale is that control of aid on a project basis is instrumental in guaranteeing a more efficient pattern of resource use, recipients having to provide elaborate justification for monies borrowed in the form of economic feasibility studies conforming to standards imposed by the donor. While it is true that commercial credit sources have expanded in parallel to official development assistance, likely beneficiaries of the former are those countries having the resources and credit-worthiness enabling them to use the commercial market effectively, and it is probably true that least-developed countries are now more dependent than ever on official aid sources. Moreover, with increasing attention being given to industrial and agricultural lending by such agencies as the World Bank, one may argue that not only are appraisal standards tightening, but their application is increasingly focused on critical sectors in the most dependent countries.

4.03 *The Literature of the 1960s*

Early work in SCBA was chiefly concerned with establishing the scope of benefits and costs to be taken into account, popularising the discounted cash flow method and related decision rules, and valuing particular types of costs and benefits not readily priced by the market. Such work rested firmly on the neo-classical notion of consumer sovereignty, 'willingness to pay' being the ultimate yardstick of welfare and the market being assumed to function efficiently so long as competitive conditions prevailed. For applications of SCBA to certain types of non-marketed goods and services, one might cite the work of Harrison and Quarmby (1969) on time saving, Mishan (1971) on human life, and Blaug (1968) on education, the latter being a particularly striking example of the application of orthodox market efficiency assumptions to determining rates of return in a non-conventional market situation.

A key issue of debate in the mainstream literature was the problem of choosing an appropriate discount rate given the reduced credibility of neo-classical interest rate theory in the light of Keynesian influence. Notable contributors to this debate include Marglin (1963a), Lind (1964) and Harberger (1969), and the issues have been well summarised by Feldstein (1964, 1973). Ignoring a more formal set of questions falling within the domain of welfare economics and concerning the 'existence' of a social welfare function, one might well claim that this was effectively *all* that happened in SCBA during the two decades prior to 1970. The genesis of what is now emerging as the 'new' SCBA, applicable to planning in the Third World, lies more in certain key areas of development economics than in traditional SCBA literature. Such areas include work on labour market theory and its relevance to capital accumulation of which the best known example is Lewis (1954); the conceptualisation of these relationships in the context of choice of techniques (COT) associated with Sen (1960); a rather different though related class of debates about national investment criteria associated with Kahn (1951), Chenery (1953) and Galenson and Leibenstein (1955); and work carried out on the theory and practice of protectionism, examples of which have been cited above. One might note in passing that even in the early 1970s standard SCBA 'textbooks' omitted virtually any mention of development related issues, examples being DasGupta and Pearce (1972), and Mishan (1972).

4.04 *The New Methodologies*

The publication of the OECD *Manual* (1968) created something of a stir amongst academics and planners. Although nominally intended as a manual for the evaluation of industrial projects in LDCs, the work rested on rigorous and novelly presented theoretical foundations lying within the mainstream of the neo-classical tradition. The planning implications of the Little-Mirrlees (LM) method, if prophetic to some, seemed demonic to others, for what was essentially argued was that if project level decisions could be got right, the rest could largely take care of itself, and that the way to make successful project decisions was to use world prices as the basis for evaluating all project inputs and outputs. The existence of goods and services in consumption or production which were non-traded (or partially traded) was neatly taken care of by the proposal to break these down into their tradeable components; 'free foreign exchange in the hands of Government' was recommended as *numeraire* rather than consumption, or traditionally 'domestic value'. The method incorporated related adjustments for taking care of domestic factor market distortions. The task of evaluation, it was argued, should be given to a powerful central office of project evaluation whose responsibility would extend to all (important) public sector projects.

The debate was fully joined with the appearance, in 1972, of the UNIDO *Guidelines* (1972). Superficially, this seemed to follow along more orthodox lines, though it did stress one area largely ignored by the Little-Mirrlees *Manual*, that of weighting intra-temporal consumption gains and losses. Although much disagreement over the relative merits of the *Guidelines* and the *Manual* was voiced in academic literature, some of its acrimonious,[1] a certain amount of artful juggling particularly with respect to Shadow Exchange Rate derivation and consumption weighting procedures has since produced a rec-

1 See *Bulletin of the Oxford Institute of Economics and Statistics* (BOUIES), February 1972.

onciliation of the two positions variously described by Lal (1974), Balassa (1974), and most recently by Squire and van der Tak (1975). In effect, with agreement about the nature of the summetry between the LM and UNIDO methodologies and with the adoption of compromise terminological conventions provided by Squire and van der Tak (ST), one can usefully speak of a unified project appraisal methodology as having emerged, hereafter refered to as the LMST (Little-Mirrlees, Squire and van der Tak) methodology.

The new methodology differs from the older version of SCBA in a number of crucial respects. The most important are: (i) productive efficiency for all traded goods is taken as determined independently of the domestic consumption pattern; (ii) interpersonal utility comparisons are firmly re-established via the principle of social valuation of consumption benefits to different groups; and, (iii) the present method, by articulating crucial macro-planning variables in micro-level selection criteria, lays claim to playing a central role in the overall planning process.

In a neo-classical world, domestic price is presumed to reflect marginal utility of consumption on the one hand, and marginal production cost on the other. The legitimacy of such an assumption is conditional upon certain well-known conditions being satisfied; viz. homogeneous goods, perfect knowledge, the absence of externalities, the acceptance of the ruling pattern of income distribution, and the assumption that consumers are the best judges of their own welfare. That some, or all, of these conditions may not hold is widely recognised, particularly in the case of LDCs where income disparities are likely to be very wide, markets poorly articulated, and choice information at a premium. Nevertheless, it has usually been convenient to justify valuation decisions 'as if' such conditions did hold. The new methodology escapes this trap by concerning itself with productive efficiency in trade, all inputs and outputs being valued at world prices which are formed *independently* of whatever imperfections may prevail in the domestic market. The existence of inputs and outputs which are not fully traded complicates the argument somewhat but is not decisive. Either such goods are treated as non-traded and broken down into their traded components, or if it can be assumed that they will be traded in future, they are then treated as traded goods.[1] Similarly, where a country can affect the world market price of a good, the marginal import cost or export revenue figure (and not the *ex ante cif* or *fob* price) is taken as the basis for valuation. The treatment of resource allocation decisions as having their ultimate impact on trade — whether directly or indirectly — remains the cornerstone of the procedure. Obviously,

---

1 The problem of valuing non-traded goods, particularly where these are project outputs, reintroduces certain difficulties in this respect discussed more fully in Chapter VI.

use of world prices as the benchmark of efficiency in production has its rationale in the neo-classical doctrine of comparative advantage, but it does not follow that to use the methodology is to espouse free trade. For one thing, the neo-classical doctrine incorporates well-known *provisos* covering infant industries and other externalities. For another, adopting the new methodology merely means that a country will plan its production pattern in a manner most efficient in the light of its *planned trade policies*, it being feasible to weigh up the gains and losses resulting from alternative trade patterns (including pure autarky) accordingly. In fact, it can reasonably be argued that the method is particularly suited for use in a fully centrally planned economy, as indeed is the case in some socialist countries where in the absence of 'free market' prices, world prices are used as a basis for investment decision making.

Beyond the question of the valuation of commodities (the pure 'efficiency' aspect of the argument) there is the question of how different aggregate bundles of commodities constituting extra consumption for different groups at different moments in time are to be weighed relative to each other. In the original OECD *Manual*, the problem of equity amongst contemporaries received little attention apart from the suggestion that capitalist's consumption might be accorded a zero weight. (*Per contra*, distributional equity between generations in the form of determining the relative marginal value of investment and consumption received much attention.) The more comprehensive treatment of this subject which appeared in the UNIDO *Guidelines*, together with more recent work by Little-Mirrlees, has served to elevate the problem of intra-temporal distribution (between members of the present generation) to a position of central importance. On purely logical grounds, the use of intra-temporal consumption weights is merely a consistent extension of the notion of 'pure time preference', or as Little-Mirrlees have noted:

[If] the main reason for discounting future consumption was the expectation that consumption per head would be higher in the future...it is clearly only logical to attach less weight to the consumption of a rich man today than to a poor man today.[1]

The divorce of production and consumption decisions, together with the articulation of distributional objectives in the logic of shadow pricing, serves to strengthen the implicit claim that the new methodology can be applied to determining the total number of projects and their sectoral allocation for the economy as a whole, unlike older SCBA methods which are useful for selecting the most suitable projects in a single sector. Indeed, the *Manual* was explicit in contrasting one view of planning based on 'hunches, dogmas, doctrines, or strategies...of no general value' with its own view based on the

1   Little-Mirrlees (1974), p.52.

primary of project evaluation techniques allowing for a rational 'division of investments between sectors'.[1]

Major planning responsibility would, in this view, devolve upon a Central Office of Project Evaluation (COPE) which — unlike its *Guidelines* counterpart which merely works out values for key parameters implicit in Government policy — has the power to set all key parameter values. These powers may be characterised as depending on decisions taken with respect to three areas of policy, as the above discussion suggests. The first is how far Government values the gains from following a 'comparative advantage' growth path relative to the possible costs of opening the economy (or benefits from closing it). Second is a set of judgements about the relative importance of equity and growth. And the third, and most crucial, concerns the role of the public sector in determining the first two. The growth versus equity choice is used to set all remaining parameters once goods and services are taken care of by the first decision (which determines what is to be priced directly in terms of border prices and what is to be decomposed). How valuable Government judges workers' consumption relative to the *numeraire* (available Government investment funds) determines the public sector wage bill via setting of the shadow wage rate and, residually, the resources available for investment — implicitly the value of future versus present consumption. (This exercise can of course be done the other way round starting with the desired rate of investment.) And this is where the third choice comes in, since the rate at which more growth or more equity, or both, is *actually* achieved through project selection will depend critically on the role of the public sector in total investment activity.

At this stage, however, the reader may feel that the discussion is running ahead a bit too quickly, and so we now turn to a more detailed exposition of the fundamentals of the new project appraisal methodology which takes up the remainder of the present Chapter.

4.05 *Efficiency Pricing and the Rationale of the New Methodology*

Consider the basis of the distinction between efficiency pricing and social pricing. The analytical limitations of this distinction are well established within the mainstream of neo-classical thought since, as every student of welfare economics will know, an efficient price set can only be postulated in relation to a given distribution of income. Hence, to say that a given set of price relatives is 'efficient' is to imply that, all other things being equal, the ruling distribution of income is in some sense 'preferred'. This is clearly a

1   OECD (1968), Vol. II, pp. 58-59.

very strong assumption, and is unlikely to prove acceptable in most developed countries, still less in a majority of less-developed countries where income is distributed in a highly inequitable manner. What then is the economist to do, since resources and their different uses must be priced in some way regardless of whether the allocative function is performed predominantly by the market or predominantly by the central planning authority. The neo-classical answer would seem to require the determination of that set of prices which is efficient in relation to some distribution of income which can be agreed upon as being 'preferred', although rules for reaching such agreement within a non-dictatorial framework have given rise to a notorious *impasse* in the welfare economics sphere.[1]

The introduction of international trade possibilities into such a framework alters the position in a critical respect. In a perfectly closed economy, the function of the price mechanism is to allocate resources towards such uses as will meet the present and future needs of consumers. Hence, the signals thrown up in an economy where income is distributed in a highly unequal fashion may differ significantly from allocative signals emerging in a highly egalitarian economy (as reflected in the relative profitability of manufacturing, say, luxury motor cars and bicycles). In a fully open economy, the domestic pattern of production is, in principle at least, no longer determined by the domestic distribution of income and consequent pattern of consumption. Rather, production is determined by trade possibilities, and judicious pursuit of the gains from trade in theory enable total consumption of every good to exceed what would have been the case in the non-trade (autarky) situation. Figure 4.1 illustrates the essential principle.

Figure 4.1 *The Gains from Trade*

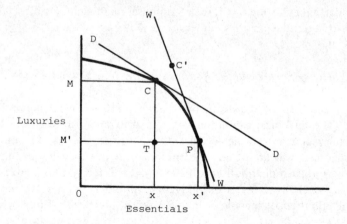

1   See Arrow (1963) as well as the many contributions which have followed, well summarised recently in Mayston (1974).

Imagine a country producing two types of goods, essentials and luxuries. Assume initially that neither good enters into trade, that the domestic price relative of the goods is given by the line DD, and that the country's resources can be used to produce any combination of essentials and luxuries described by the production frontier (heavy curve). In such a situation, production and consumption take place at the same point (C), OM luxuries and OX essentials being produced and consumed. However, if one now imagines trade possibilities to exist at a world price ratio of WW, 'capturing the gains from trade' will imply shifting production from C to P, or producing XX' more essentials and MM' fewer luxuries domestically. Since the extra essentials produced can be turned into more luxuries through trading than by producing domestically – i.e. the slope of WW or rate of transformation in trade is greater than the rate of transformation in domestic production shown along the corresponding segment of the production frontier – consumption under trade can take place at a point (C') which exceeds the initial consumption position (C) in respect of both types of goods. More generally, consumption can take place anywhere along the world price line (WW) according to how income is distributed and hence what pattern of consumer demand prevails. The key point is that the pattern of production is determined by ruling world prices alone while consumption is determined by the domestic income distribution.

With consumption and production decisions divorced in this manner, efficiency and distributional dimensions are separated. (There are a number of problems about whether such separation exists in practice, but these are discussed at a later stage.) The hypothetical country in the above example can produce at point P whether it is capitalist or socialist, its political complexion being reflected in its consumption (import) pattern. With efficiency prices given by the world market, further 'social adjustments' to planning prices – that is, adjustments reflecting distributional priorities – are then required to the extent that it is thought necessary to effect redistribution through the mechanism of investment selection rather than through fiscal or direct controls on wages and profits.

Such are the essentials of theory underlying the new methodology, familiar to some readers no doubt, but worth reviewing because they lie at the core of the discussion. Before proceeding to a more detailed discussion of the mechanics of the new methodology, though, it is worth briefly considering some of the objections which exist to using world prices as the relevant datum on which to base domestic production decisions in the manner suggested above.

4.06 *Problems of Pursuing Comparative Advantage*

A first argument is that world prices are themselves 'inefficient' both in the sense of being formed in markets which bear little resemblance to the classical market-place characterised by large numbers of informed buyers and sellers selling homogeneous products, and also in the sense of reflecting a highly inequitable world distribution of income. That world prices reflect the influences of a variety of institutions and practices — product differentiation, transfer pricing, discriminatory trade practices, etc. — which are inconsistent with the norms of welfare maximisation applied on a global scale is obviously true. From the single country point of view, however, such considerations are beside the point since a country is presumed to be concerned with maximising its own potential gains from trade, and not with that of optimising the allocation of world resources. Hence, in socialist countries and capitalist countries alike, decisions are taken about whether (non-strategic) commodities should best be produced domestically or imported using expected future world prices as reference datum. That a different set of world price relatives may be desirable — for example, an increase in the price of certain primary commodities relative to manufactures — is an important but separate question.

A more difficult argument is that which states that by pursuing the gains from trade in the short term, a country may jeopardise its long term development prospects. In its most general form, this is an argument about externalities in production and in consumption. The most familiar example of production externalities is the 'infant industry' argument which essentially puts the view that skills, technological know-how and markets can only be acquired slowly and, hence, protection will be required in the early years of industrial development if comparative advantage in the longer term is to be gained in those lines which ultimately have the highest payoff. Conversely, myopic concentration on short-term comparative advantage may result in the 'internalisation' of the wrong types of externalities. As Hirschman (1969) has suggested, few countries are likely to welcome the suggestion that they should indefinitely continue to exploit a comparative resource advantage in illiterate peasants and exploited workers. The consumption version of the argument, again broadly paraphrased, states that a country opening its doors to trade must be prepared not only to take in foreign goods, but foreign tastes, technology and political influences of a sort which ultimately heighten income disparities and distort the pattern of domestic industrialisation. Put most succinctly, the argument states that trade dependence brings economic and political dependence, the costs of which may far outweigh the formal gains from trade described by the theory.

Finally, there is the argument about long term movements in the commodity terms of trade. This says very broadly that prices of the sorts of commodities in which the poorest countries tend to have a comparative advantage, particularly agricultural commodities such as food and fibres, have failed to keep up over the years with prices of industrial manufactures, particularly the sorts of producer goods which LDCs need in order to carry out industrial expansion. While there has been a good deal of disagreement about the statistical evidence supporting this proposition, the underlying explanation offered (first associated with the work of Singer and Prebisch) is twofold. Firstly, it is argued that the income elasticity of demand for primary commodities is typically lower than for industrial manufactures; hence as world incomes rise, demand for the latter has tended to rise more rapidly than for the former with consequent effects on their relative world prices (terms of trade). Secondly, at a rather more sophisticated level, it is claimed that although technological innovation has enabled both categories of commodities to be produced more efficiently, the superior bargaining power of capitalists and workers in developed countries has enabled a larger proportion of the resulting benefit to be captured in the form of higher profits and/or real wages. In short, pursuit of comparative advantage in those commodities whose real purchasing power is declining relative to developed country manufactures may lead, in Bhagwati's phrase, to 'immiserizing growth'.

Figure 4.2 summarises these points in diagrammatical form. Imagine two countries with initially identical resource endowments, technologies and tastes, which produce, consume and trade two categories of goods: 'high technology' and 'low technology' goods. Both start with production possibility frontiers given by the heavy curve T_1T_1 and face identical world prices shown by the lines labelled W_1W_1. Tariffs on high technology goods in both cases result in domestic prices of DD. Country A maintains its tariff and initially produces and consumes at point C. Country B, eschewing protection, produces at P_1 and is able to consume at C_1 through trade thus appearing to be better off than A. Pursuit of comparative advantage in the case of B means, however, that in the long term B's production frontier evolve in a highly skewed manner (as described by the curve T_2T_2 in the lower diagram). Its capacity to produce low-technology goods greatly increases but its corresponding high-technology capacity actually falls. World prices may, in the meantime, move in favour of high-technology goods with the result that production at P_2 can be used to purchase only C_2 consumption; i.e. country B means, however, that in the long term B's production frontier evolves in a pursued a more balanced growth pattern under protection. At the new set of world prices, W_2W_2, it is able to produce at P_2 and by exporting high-technology goods ends up consuming at C_2. Also note that A, by remaining relatively 'closed' in the initial period, has developed a growth path of consumption which is less high-technology oriented than that of B.

How far this cautionary tale is useful in analysing the relative merits of protectionist and free trade strategies actually pursued by different countries

Figure 4.2 *Dynamic Gains from Trade*

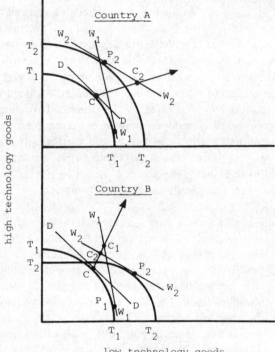

is of course debatable. Some countries have been highly successful in making the best of comparative advantage under conditions of free trade and there are many countries in which protectionist policies have been ill-conceived and damaging. In essence, though, to interpret the story as being about the relative merits of free trade is misleading. What is at issue in this case is, firstly, how far ruling world prices can be taken as indicative of long run comparative advantage, and secondly, how the gains from trade are best captured while minimising deleterious side-effects. The former is an empirical question. The latter is in part a question of strategy and in part one of political economy.

Clearly, it is not in all cases a precondition of securing productive efficiency in the tradable goods sector that protection be removed (or be made uniform). Removing or rationalising tariffs is merely a way of pursuing the trade efficiency objective by improving market price signals and will be necessary only to the extent that key investment decisions are based on such signals. In many countries, protectionist policies have built up in piecemeal fashion to satisfy one or another political interest or to secure additional government revenue, and a major overhaul of the structure might be no bad thing. Tariffs and quotas, taxes and subsidies have distributional as well as allocative effects, and if Government can control resource allocation by other means – for example by licencing, or ultimately by direct ownership of industry and planning of investment decisions – controls on trade may be justified on distributional grounds. One can just as readily envisage the conditions for trade efficiency being met in a centrally planned economy using world prices as its planning prices, as in a free-market free-trade situation such as described in the textbooks.[1] In short, the gains-from-trade story is compatible with the operation of a diverse range of commercial policies under different types of political regime.

4.07 *Essentials of the New Methodology: Efficiency Pricing*

The essential distinction between conventional methods of project appraisal on the one hand, and the UNIDO, LM and ST approaches on the other, can be summarised in the following manner. Let us suppose that a project is set up to produce an export good and uses both domestic and foreign inputs. The most rudimentary approach would require that all tariffs and taxes be netted from the cost and benefits of the project; the Official Exchange Rate (OER) would then be applied to the 'border' price of the exported commodity (f.o.b. price) and to that of each of the imported inputs (c.i.f. price) to value them domestically and these values, together with the value of the domestically purchased inputs, would form the basis on which the net benefit stream could be calculated. Letting X stand for exports, M for imports, and D for domestic inputs, one may write:

$$NB = (OER)X - (OER)M - D \qquad \dots \qquad (4.1)$$

A decision rule would be to accept the project if $NB > O$ at the appropriate public sector discount rate.

---

[1] In this respect, Trotsky's views enunciated at the height of the Russian industrialisation debate are apposite: 'The more we become part of the system of international division of labour, the more directly will such elements of our home economics as prices and the quality of our goods become dependent on the corresponding elements of the world market.' L. Trotsky (1926), p. 63.

A first objection to the conventional approach turns upon whether the official exchange rate in most LDCs can be taken as accurately reflecting the true value of foreign exchange to the economy. There are really two arguments here. One is that protective policies (tariffs, quota restrictions, etc.) are such as to 'distort' the domestic price structure in a way which does not allow resources to be allocated efficiently between domestic production and trade; i.e. the 'gains from trade' argument set out in the preceding section. The second argument is that foreign exchange is necessary for investment and its scarcity limits the extent to which the desired rate of capital accumulation can be realised. Some early writers on this subject, such as Chenery (1953), recommended the use of a foreign exchange premium for project evaluation though not distinguishing clearly between the above concepts. Both the LMST and UNIDO approaches, however, distinguish between the problem of efficiency pricing under protective policies and that of sub-optimal savings (investment). Their treatment of the foreign exchange adjustment premium – the ratio of the Shadow Exchange Rate (SER) to the Official Exchange Rate (OER) – is essentially concerned with the former problem.

The UNIDO recommendation is that the conversion of foreign exchange into domestic consumption value be accomplished by using an SER. The SER is usually approximated by taking the domestic to border price ratio of traded commodities weighted by the share of each commodity in a country's marginal trade bill. In contrast to expression (4.1) above we may write:

$$NB = (SER)X - (SER)M - D, \text{ or more simply,}$$
$$NB = (SER)(X - M) - D \qquad \qquad .... \qquad (4.2)$$

The Little-Mirrlees recommendation, subsequently adopted by Squire and van der Tak (LMST), is in essence the converse of the above. Instead of expressing everything in terms of domestic consumption – or to use the more concise term, instead of taking domestic consumption as *numeraire* – everything is expressed in terms of foreign exchange. Foreign exchange is a more useful *numeraire* than domestic consumption, it is argued, because extra foreign exchange in Government hands is an addition to savings (investment).[1] Hence if we define NB' as the net benefits of the project expressed in terms of a foreign exchange *numeraire* and introduce the conversion factor a (alpha) defined as $a = OER/SER$, we may write:

$$NB' = (OER)(X - M) - aD \qquad \qquad .... \qquad (4.3)$$

1   Using foreign exchange as *numeraire* does not mean that project accounts are expressed in terms of dollars or some other foreign currency. The unit of account remains by convention the home currency, but the values recorded are 'foreign exchange equivalent pesos, rupees, etc.'.

It will be apparent that the two approaches are equivalent since multiplying expression (4.2) by OER/SER yields expression (4.3).

In practice, the domestic consumption component of net benefits is not usually translated into its foreign exchange equivalent value by means of a single 'summary' conversion factor (a). Instead, all non-traded goods are individually decomposed into traded goods and valued at border prices. One may visualise this as equivalent to calculating a conversion factor for each non-traded good which can be represented by a set of βs (beta). Hence if D_i is the ith domestic (non-traded) good, we may write:

$$NB' = OER(X - M) - \sum_i^n \beta_i D_i \qquad \dots \qquad (4.4)$$

Consequently, while the UNIDO and LMST methods may be thought of as formally equivalent in an abstract sense, the key difference arises from the level of aggregation used in deriving an index relating domestic consumption values to foreign exchange values. The UNIDO 'weights' are established from the composition of the marginal trade bill while the LMST 'weights' are established from the composition of the non-traded elements in the project itself. A more detailed discussion of these principles appears in later sections. It will suffice for the moment to note that while at one level of abstraction the methods may be considered equivalent, in practice they will not necessarily give equivalent results, UNIDO effectively being a 'second best' version of LMST, as will be argued subsequently.

A further problem of efficient pricing which is handled in both methodologies concerns the pricing of labour. Just as the operation of Government commercial policy may cause the marginal consumption value of foreign exchange to be understated, the operation of the (unskilled) labour market may cause the wage to overstate labour's foregone net output (m) resulting from its withdrawal from elsewhere in the economy for use in the project (see Chapter VI). Hence domestic inputs grouped together under the term D in (4.2) should be disaggregated into the value of labour (L) and non-labour (NL) inputs, and the cost of the former valued using an 'efficiency wage rate' (EWR) instead of the market wage. Let a wage adjustment factor (EWR*) initially be defined as the ratio of labour's marginal net product foregone (m) to the market wage (W), or EWR* = m/W. Then:

$$NB = (SER)(X - M) - \{(EWR^*)L + NL\} \qquad \dots \qquad (4.5)$$

As before, where a is defined in a manner analogous with the UNIDO use of the SER, the LMST treatment amounts to the same thing since:

$$NB' = (X - M) - a \{ (EWR^*)L + NL \} \qquad \dots \qquad (4.6)$$

4.08 Social Pricing

Expressions (4.2) to (4.6) summarise the essence of efficiency pricing adjustments in the two procedures. It has now become conventional to treat efficiency pricing as the subject of economic cost-benefit analysis (ECBA) in contrast to social cost-benefit analysis (SCBA) which requires extending the analytical framework to incorporate distributional judgements. Such judgements are essentially of two kinds: firstly, is consumption optimally distributed between contemporaries (intra-temporal) and, secondly, is it optimally distributed between generations (inter-temporal)? For the moment we shall be concerned with the latter question which is merely a way of asking whether the global savings (investment) ratio for the economy is adequate. Subsumed under this question is the notion of foreign exchange as a constraining factor on investment.

To demonstrate the essence of social pricing, assume that the net benefits of a project are paid out either to Government (in which case they are entirely re-invested) or to workers in the form of wages (in which case they are entirely consumed). Further assume that savings (investment) is sub-optimal. By sub-optimal in this sense is meant that the present value of the stream of consumption to which a marginal unit of investment would give rise is greater than unity when discounted at the 'ideal' discount rate for consumption, or CRI. For example, if an investment of 1 Peso yields a stream of consumption having an NPV of 1.50 Pesos, then an 'investment' Peso must be adjusted by a factor of 1.5 to make it commensurate with consumption in the hands of the average individual. In UNIDO terminology this factor is called the investment premium (P^{inv}) while under LMST conventions it is referred to as the 'value of public income' (v). Let NSB represent the net consumption value of project benefits at social prices in contrast to NB which measures these at efficiency prices. Then, for a given project, NSB will exceed NB to the extent that project benefits accruing as surplus to government are valued more highly than as wages to workers (P^{inv} or $v > 1$). Symbolically, let ΔL be the incremental wage bill and (NB - ΔL) be the surplus accruing to government, then:

$$NSB = v (NB - \Delta L) - \Delta L \qquad \dots \qquad (4.7)$$

Using LMST conventions, investible foreign exchange is taken as *numeraire*. Hence the procedure is reversed and it is workers' consumption which must be deflated to make it commensurate with investment, or:

$$NSB' = (NB' - \Delta L') - \Delta L'/v \qquad \dots \qquad (4.8)$$

This handles the inter-temporal distribution question; however, what of the problem of the distribution of consumption between contemporaries? The problem is clarified if one bears in mind that the value of investment has been measured in terms of the value of consumption in the hands of an *average* individual; more precisely, the man at average (per capita) consumption level. However, the term L in the above expression may be thought of as a composite term grouping payments to different individuals at different income (consumption) levels, and can be expanded as follows:

$$d_1 \Delta L_1 + \dots + d_i \Delta L_i + \dots d_n \Delta L_n \qquad \dots \qquad (4.9)$$

where there are 1...n recipients and the ds are 'distribution' weights reflecting the extra utility associated with the extra consumption of individuals in each group. If the ith recipient is designated the average man, d_i can be assigned a value of unity and $d_1 > d_i > d_n$ moving in ascending order of income. Hence an expression incorporating both dimensions of the distributional question may be formulated using LMST conventions:

$$NSB' = (NB' - \Delta L') - \sum_{i}^{n} \Delta L'_i . d_i / v \qquad \dots \qquad (4.10)$$

A modification to this procedure, discussed in later sections, involves assigning a unitary distributional weight not to the average income recipient but to the 'critical' income recipient; i.e. the man at that income (consumption) level, presumably well below average level, for whom an extra peso's worth of consumption is judged equally valuable as an extra investible peso in Government hands.[1]

4.09 *Summary*

The broad lines of the discussion presented in this Chapter suggest that the study of public sector investment methodology has gradually evolved away from a narrow concern for special types of non-commercial undertakings towards a more fully articulated set of concepts and tools applicable in principle to all investment decisions. In parallel manner, the assumed planning framework can no longer be perceived as one in which public sector intervention in direct investment is limited to dealing with a few special cases in an

1 Following along these lines, the revised version of Hansen (1975) redefines the UNIDO *numeraire* as 'critical consumption' rather than 'average consumption'.

otherwise smoothly functioning free-market economy but, instead, takes the existence of 'distortions' as the rule rather than the exception. That the latter view should have gained wide currency is closely associated with the growth of development economics in the post-war period and its emphasis on barriers to accumulation and structural imperfections in markets rather than on the analysis of static equilibrium positions emphasised by the neo-classical school. By implication, the corpus of theory and methodology which has developed under the SCBA rubric emphasises the need for improved resource allocation criteria, but raises further unresolved questions about the ideal scope of public control over investment decisions throughout the economy. As is suggested in subsequent chapters, it is only once the political setting is clearly defined that it becomes possible to judge the relevance of recent methodological innovations.

In looking at the new methodology, we have initially concentrated on the concept of trade efficiency which is at its core. While the discussion of comparative advantage theory has been couched at an elementary level, enough has been said to suggest the concept of trade efficiency is an ambiguous one and that capturing the short term gains from trade may involve serious costs to an economy. While such points are recognised in the formal theory, they are rarely discussed explicitly, and the main advocates of the new methodology have largely reserved their position to making the formally correct point that the methods are consistent with any policy (except pure autarky). By contrast, our own view is that the methods are useful precisely because, in focusing on the gains from trade, one is led to ask a series of questions about the nature of those economies which in the foreseeable future will need to trade a substantial proportion of total output. It seems not unreasonable to suggest that for such economies, capturing the potential gains from trade while minimising the deleterious side effects of 'openness' will require a substantial extension of direct public sector control. Finally, we have outlined the conceptual basis of the new methods distinguishing between 'efficiency' and 'social' parameters and showing the formal symmetry between the proposals originally advanced in the OECD *Manual* and the UNIDO *Guidelines*, and most recently by Squire and van der Tak. These are treated in greater detail in the chapters which follow.

4.10 *Further Reading*

Books on SCBA theory and methodology proliferate, although as we have suggested there is a clear dividing line between the old and the new which is historically situated at the end of the 1960s. Hence the student purchasing Mishan (1972), Pearce (1971), DasGupta and Pearce (1972) and Layard

(1972) will find these of interest as a guide to what was happening in the academic debate of the previous two decades but of little value in understanding the intricacies of what has happened since. Marglin (1967) is in this sense useful as it is a short and readable book which is specifically addressed to the development planning context. Harberger (1972), a collection of the author's own essays, is also instructive though written from a staunchly free-market oriented perspective. Standard review articles on the subject are Prest and Turvey (1965) and Henderson (1968). King (1967) sets out the traditional approach of the World Bank illustrated by case studies. For the more mechanical aspects of the older project evaluation methodology, UNO (1968) faithfully relates the state of the practical art as does Packard (1974). Self (1975) sets out an interesting and highly critical view of the role of 'traditional' SCBA in analysing public sector projects in developed countries.

Hansen (1975), ODM (1972) and OECD (1973) provide simple introductions to the principles of the UNIDO and LM methods, but the reader intent on gaining a proper understanding of the new methodology will eventually need to read OECD Vol. II (1968), UNIDO (1972) and Little and Mirrlees (1974). The latter is essentially a reworking of their OECD effort presented in more readable terms with some concessions made to their detractors. Their detractors' views initially appeared, together with those of some supporters, in a special issue of *BOUIES* (1972) in which particularly polemical pieces are provided by Stewart and Streeten as well as H. Joshi. Ancillary work referring to the application of the LM method is referred to in the next chapter; on the application of the UNIDO method there is much less work though Ruffing (1972) and Irvin (1975a) can be glanced at.

The most recent major contribution is the book by Squire and van der Tak (1975) which as explained above effectively synthesises the two approaches though adopting the LM *numeraire*. Background material immediately preceeding its publication is worth looking at, including the internal IBRD (1974) working paper on which it was based. A useful short summary of the basic thinking behind LMST is given by Linn (1976). A particularly useful book-cum-manual has recently appeared by FitzGerald (1976a) which explains much of the thinking behind the new methodology with the use of illustrative examples, and attempts to locate the role of micro-planning methods within a macro-planning context. This work also discusses some of the substantive political issues involved. Finally, readers interested in the state of the art in socialist countries will find Novozhilov (1970) instructive but somewhat unfamiliar semantically, and a practical illustration of project appraisal principles used in contemporary Cuba is given in the manual prepared by Castro Tato (1972).

V

EFFICIENCY PRICING AND TRADED GOODS

5.01 *The Application of SCBA*

One is now in a position to distinguish between three levels of analysis relevant to the evaluation of public sector projects:
(1) analysis at market prices — financial profitability;
(2) analysis at efficiency prices — economic profitability;
(3) analysis at social prices — social profitability.
The early chapters of this book have covered the essential concepts and tools required for the analysis of financial profitability. In particular, elementary notions of discounted cash flow and investment decision rules have been discussed, as have basic accounting conventions necessary for understanding what elements are properly included in cost and revenue flows. Elements of statistical theory have been included to clarify the principles involved in predicting costs and revenues. These constitute the essential foundation upon which, so to speak, it is now possible to erect a more elaborate superstructure. The present chapter and the two chapters which follow are concerned with the second of the above headings, the analysis of economic profitability.

In the light of what has been said above, it will be apparent that the analysis of economic profitability is now increasingly understood as predicated on the notion of trade efficiency as an 'ideal' benchmark against which actual investment performance can be measured. That one cannot consider trade efficiency — in the sense of pursuit of short-term comparative advantage — as an unambiguously desirable, or even well defined, objective is also clear. It has been argued, at a general level of abstraction, that external diseconomies in production and consumption may be associated with policies designed to open the economy more fully to trading possibilities, and that much may therefore depend on whether Government exercises sufficient control over the economy to minimise the possible costs of so doing. However, for expositional purposes, it will be useful to open the discussion by assuming that Government will want to plan investment decisions taking trade efficiency as a policy objective. At a later stage in the discussion it will

be seen that alternative assumptions regarding trade policies can be accommodated within the new methodology.

5.02 Correcting for Trade 'Distortions'

Imagine a two-good economy which exports food and imports machines
using a single factor of production, labour. Assume too that all markets are
perfect save for a single 'distortion' in the form of a tariff on the imported
good; e.g. a situation such as that shown in Figure 4.1 in the previous chapter.
We shall assume that a ton of food sells at $500 (f.o.b.), a ton of machines
costs $1000 (c.i.f.), and that a 50 percent tariff exists on machinery imports
such that the price of machines to domestic purchasers when converted to
Pesos at the official exchange rate (OER) of $1 = P.1 is P.1500. Further as-
sume that it take 50 man-days and 150 man-days respectively to produce
food and machines domestically at a wage (equal in both industries) of 10
pesos per man-day and that there is no unemployment. The information is
summarised in Figure 5.1.

Figure 5.1 *International and Domestic Costs of Food and Machine
              Production*

	Border Price ($)	Domestic Price (P.)	Domestic Cost (P.)	Wage (P./day)		Required Labour (man-days)
Machines (M)	1000*	1500	1500 =	10	x	150
Food (X)	500	500	500 =	10	x	50

*subject to 50% tariff

   Notice that in terms of domestic prices, marginal cost (MC) equals marginal value (MV) in both cases, there being no reason to switch labour between industries in order to produce more of either product. But the MC and
MV of foreign exchange are not equal. The MV of foreign exchange is the
domestic worth of what an extra unit of foreign exchange will buy while the
MC is the domestic cost of producing more foreign exchange. In the present
case, an extra $1000 will buy one extra unit of machines worth P.1500
domestically, but, the domestic cost of producing an extra $1000 of foreign
exchange is the production cost of 2 tons of food, or P.1000. Hence the MV
of $1000 of foreign exchange is P.1500 while its MC is P.1000. The source
of this discrepancy is the tariff on machines, and domestic prices are 'inefficient' in the sense that there is no incentive to increase foreign exchange
production through expanding the food industry until the MC and MV of
foreign exchange are brought into line.

The discrepancy can equally be visualised in terms of the foreign exchange productivity of the factor, labour. If foreign exchange is taken as *numeraire*, the marginal productivity of labour in food production is $10 (i.e. the border price of food, $500, divided by the number of man-days required in production, 50). In the case of machines though, the marginal productivity of labour is only $6.67 ($1000 ÷ 150). Hence labour should be shifted out of machines towards the food industry in which it has a higher marginal value product in terms of foreign exchange.

If domestic consumption is taken as *numeraire*, planners should use a shadow exchange rate (SER) to value foreign exchange if optimal use is to be made of resources. What is the SER? Broadly speaking, it is that rate of exchange which accurately reflects the consumption worth of an extra dollar (or other convertible foreign currency) in terms of one's own currency. In the above case, an 'extra' $1000 is worth P.1500, the domestic value of machines it is used to 'consume', and hence the SER[1] is $1 = P.1.5

Consider now what the profitability of *expanding the food industry* would be. As already noted, using traditional project appraisal methods (expression 4.1 in Chapter IV), the net benefit calculation would indicate zero profitability;[2] i.e.

$$NB = (OER)X - (OER)M - D$$
$$NB = (1.0)(\$500) - 0 - P.500$$
$$NB = P.500 - P.500 = 0$$

However, adopting UNIDO conventions, we get:

$$NB = (SER)X - (SER)M - D$$
$$NB = (1.5)(\$500) - 0 - P.500$$
$$NB = P.750 - P.500 = P.250$$

Similarly, if the LMST summary conversion factor, a, is defined as the reciprocal of the SER, the analysis can be made to yield equivalent results where foreign exchange rather than domestic consumption is taken as *numeraire*.

$$NB' = (OER)X - (OER)M - aD$$
$$NB' = (1.0)(\$500) - 0 - (.67)(P.500)$$
$$NB' = P.500 - 0 - P.334 = P.166$$

1   Because of the way in which the figures have been chosen, the ratio of the SER to the OER, or SER/OER, is also 1.5.
2   Note that using the traditional method involves netting for tax and tariff elements in output and input costs. In the case above there is no tax on food.

That the LMST and UNIDO methods are equivalent can easily be seen by noting that NB' (P.166) multiplied by the SER/OER (1.5) yields NB (P.250). Looking more closely at this logic though, several points might be noted. Firstly, the calculation of the SER is simplified by the assumption that the marginal trade bill consists of only one good, imported machines. Similarly, the LMST conversion of labour into its foreign exchange value using the summary conversion factor (a) is simplified by assuming that the product foregone (opportunity cost) is also machines since expanding one industry entails contraction of the other. In reality, though, the marginal trade bill would consist of a collection of different things, and thus the calculation of the SER and its reciprocal, a, would be more complex. More important, the composition of the marginal trade bill would not necessarily correspond to the bundle of goods constituting labour's foregone product or marginal consumption pattern. In applying the LMST method, it is therefore more appropriate to calculate a specific conversion factor for labour (β_1) as well as for any other major non-traded items such as transport (β_t) and power (β_p) which might appear in the project.

Consider the definition of the SER more carefully. Let us suppose foreign exchange to be 'consumed' by importing not merely machines but a variety of other products as well, such that one could write:

$$SER/OER = \sum_i^n f_i . P_i^d / P_i^w \qquad \dots \qquad (5.1)$$

This says that the ratio of the SER to the OER is equal to the fraction of foreign exchange earnings spent on the ith commodity (f_i) times the ratio of the domestic price of the commodity (P_i^d) to its world (c.i.f.) price (P_i^w). Such a formulation of the SER implies that the country uses foreign exchange at the margin wholly to increase imports. However, it is conceivable that a part of the country's foreign exchange might be used to relieve pressure on exports — for example, in the above case, consumers might wish to 'consume' extra foreign exchange not by purchasing an extra machine (increasing imports) but by eating more food (reducing exports). Hence, a more general expression for the foreign exchange adjustment factor would be:

$$SER/OER = \sum_i^n f_i . P_i^d / P_i^w + \sum_j^m x_j . P_j^d / P_j^w \qquad \dots \qquad (5.2)$$

where, as a result of a unit increase in foreign exchange availability, f_i is the fraction spent on the ith import summed over n imported commodities, and x_j is the fraction by which the jth export falls summed over m exports. Returning to the previous example one might imagine that, instead of foreign exchange being spent entirely on imported machines, half of it was spent on releasing food exports to domestic consumption. Substituting into (5.2), we get:

SER/OER = 0.5 (P.1500/$1000) + 0.5 (P.500/$500)
SER/OER = 1.25

In brief, the UNIDO approach to price distortions induced by the existence of non-optimal barriers to trade requires that, in evaluating a project, the
foreign exchange components be translated into domestic consumption value
using an SER. The value of the SER will depend on the domestic to world
price ratios of the set of goods entering into trade at the margin, weighted by
the proportion of each in rising imports (falling exports).[1]

5.03 *LMST or UNIDO?*

At the broadest level of abstraction there would appear to be little to choose
between in deciding whether to adopt one method or the other, the formal
difference being the choice of *numeraire* and the operational question being
whether the non-traded content of a project should be made commensurate
with the traded in terms of the former or the latter. But this way of viewing
the choice is somewhat misleading.

Suppose that one were dealing with a series of projects each of which had
both traded and non-traded inputs. To the extent that one was concerned
with the trade efficiency objective, the significant question would be that of
ascertaining the direct and indirect balance of payments effect of each
project. Hence, before attempting to value inputs, one would *decompose* the
non-traded elements into their traded constituents.[2] With all inputs expressed in terms of traded goods, these would then be *valued* at border
prices. If one were using LMST methods, that would be the end of the
story. Using the UNIDO approach, however, one would go on to calculate
an SER for the economy as a whole and translate foreign exchange

1 In practice, there are two problems associated with such a definition of the SER.
Firstly, 'at the margin' is a difficult concept to use when one is dealing with a country's
trade statistics since one is looking at aggregative commodity classifications over some
past period of time. Secondly, one is using such figures to derive a figure pertaining to
the value of foreign exchange in the future; if the pattern of foreign exchange use is expected to change, so too will the SER. More will be said of this latter problem below
under the heading of protectionism and general equilibrium (Chapter VI, section 6.06).
2 In the words of Scott, 'One does not have to be very sophisticated to realise that it is
insufficient to look at *direct* foreign exchange receipts or expenditures, but, once one
allows for *indirect* effects, where can one stop? In the author's view, the correct answer
is "nowhere"'; Scott (1974), p. 170.

values into domestic consumption. UNIDO therefore involves an extra (and redundant) step.[1]

The essential difference between the methods goes beyond the formal choice of *numeraire* and concerns the more critical question of how far indirect foreign exchange effects of a project are to be investigated. For projects whose inputs and outputs are entirely traded the application of UNIDO conventions is most obviously redundant while, at the other end of spectrum, for projects consisting entirely of non-traded items it is unclear what advocates of the UNIDO method would recommend. Either these should be valued at ruling domestic prices (in which case the trade efficiency objective is violated) or decomposed entirely into traded equivalents (in which case one is back to LMST). In short, it is difficult to see what advantage there can be from application of the UNIDO approach so long as the conventions regarding *decomposition* are symmetrically applied. In practice, since most projects consist of both traded and non-traded constituents, it is likely that the real difference between the two methods lies in the extent to which non-traded goods are decomposed, and hence that the UNIDO method can best be regarded as a 'rough and ready' variant of LMST rather than as a formally equivalent alternative.

The principle of decomposition and its relevance to the difference between the methods suggested by the above argument can best be illustrated by means of a further example. The initial country situation is now altered to allow for four traded goods, all of which (with the exception of food) are subject to tariff. Figure 5.2 shows the world price, tariff rate, and resulting domestic price of each.

Figure 5.2 *Protective Structure in a Hypothetical Four-Good Economy*

Good	Abbre-viation	World Price $ (cif, fob)	Tariff	Domestic Price (P.)	Accounting Ratio P^w/pd
Food (export)	F	500		500	1.00
Machines (import)	M	1000	50%	1500	0.67
Textiles (import)	T	200	25%	250	0.80
Appliances (import)	A	800	150%	2000	0.40

As before, the object is to assess the profitability of expanding the food industry. The official exchange rate remains $1 = P.1, the wage rate P.10 per man-day, but the production of food is now assumed to require 20 man-days of labour (L) and 0.2 units of machines, or:

$$1F = 20 L + 0.2M$$

1   The logic is explored at greater length in Balassa (1974).

Consumption out of wages is 50 percent food, 25 percent textiles and 25 percent appliances (radios, bicycles, etc.).

Figure 5.3 shows the basis on which the project is evaluated. Column 1 shows costs and returns of a unit expansion of the industry measured at domestic prices and is equivalent to performing conventional financial analysis. As before, it is unprofitable to expand the industry on purely financial criteria. Columns 2 and 3 show the direct and indirect foreign exchange impact of the project in dollars. Hence to produce $500 worth of food, $200 worth of machinery imports will be required. The payment of workers will constitute an indirect foreign exchange (FE) claim since the wage bill will be used to purchase textiles and appliances from abroad and workers' food consumption will reduce potential exports, adding a further $160 to costs. The project will therefore make a net foreign exchange profit of $140 as shown at the bottom of column 4, which is in fact the LMST solution.

Figure 5.3 *Decomposition of Costs and Returns into Foreign Exchange*

Column	(1) Domestic Costs and Returns (P.)	(2) Direct FE Contribu- tion or Use ($)	(3) Indirect FE Impact ($)	(4) Total FE Impact ($)	(5) SER	(6) Domestic Consumption Value (P.)
Returns						
Food	500	500	-	500	1.38	690
Costs						
Machines	300	200	-	200	1.38	276
Labour	(200)					
.Food	100	-	100	100	1.38	138
.Textiles	50	-	40	40	1.38	55
.Appliances	50	-	20	20	1.38	28
Net Benefit	0			140	1.38	193

If SER weights are now defined as those reflecting the marginal direct and indirect impact on trade of project costs, then, in accordance with expression (5.2) shown on p. 86, the incremental trade bill at peso border prices is P.360 (P.260 imports of machines, textiles and appliances and P.100 of food exports foregone), and the calculation is:

$$\text{SER/OER} \cong \text{proportion of good in trade} \times \text{domestic/world price ratio}$$

$$\text{SER/OER} = \{(200/360)\,(1500/1000) + (40/360)\,(250/200) +$$
$$\text{machines (M)} \qquad\qquad \text{textiles (M)}$$

$$(20/360)\,(2000/800)\} + \{(100/360)\,(500/500)\}$$
$$\text{appliances (M)} \qquad\qquad \text{food (X)}$$

$$= 1.38$$

where the first three terms in the expression are claims on imports (M) and the final term is exports foregone (X). The UNIDO solution using a *project specific* definition of the SER is thus P.193, but the SER calculation is in fact unnecessary since once project inputs and outputs are entirely decomposed into foreign exchange their reconversion into domestic values is an extra step which adds nothing to the exercise.

A slightly different way of visualising the difference between the two methods is shown in Figure 5.4. Table A illustrates in the conventional LMST format how an accounting ratio (AR) can be derived for aggregate project

Figure 5.4 *Contrasting LMST and UNIDO Conversion Procedures*
Table A *LMST Derivation of Cost Conversion Factor*

Inputs into Food production	Domestic % Cost Composition	AR (P^w/p^d)	FE Equivalent Econ. Value
Machines	0.60	0.67	0.40
Textiles	0.10	0.80	0.08
Appliances	0.10	0.40	0.04
Food	0.20	1.00	0.20
Total	1.00		0.72

Table B *UNIDO Derivation of Project Specific SER*

Inputs into Food Production	Trade % Cost Composition	1/AR (p^d/p^w)	Domestic Econ. Value
Machines	0.56	1.50	0.84
Textiles	0.11	1.25	0.14
Appliances	0.05	2.50	0.13
Food	0.28	1.00	0.28
Total	1.00		1.38

costs, each element being expressed as a percentage of total domestic cost per unit of food produced and multiplied by the relevant AR to obtain a foreign exchange equivalent value in pesos per unit total costs (AR of aggregate costs = 0.72). Table B shows the UNIDO treatment, the percentage weights used being those in trade (and hence at border prices), and the UNIDO ARs being reciprocals of the LMST ARs. The resulting SER/OER, as above, is 1.38. Note that the reciprocal of 1.38 is 0.72.

5.04 *LMST Terminology and Conventions in More Detail*

While the choice of *numeraire* was in earlier discussion treated as a formality, having now shown the advantages implicit in adopting LMST conventions these will be adhered to throughout. The LMST *numeraire*, referred to variously above as 'foreign exchange', 'savings' and 'investment' can now be defined more precisely. It is 'the present value of uncommitted Government income measured in terms of foreign exchange'. Since by extra 'uncommitted' foreign exchange in Government hands is meant foreign exchange available for investment, the equivalence of Government saving/investment and foreign exchange becomes apparent. The adoption of this *numeraire* has the obvious advantage of focusing attention more readily on the trade efficiency objective than its UNIDO counterpart 'the present value of domestic consumption in the hands of the average individual' which is, in a sense, the main point of the preceding sections.

Given the present volume of literature on public sector project appraisal, it is perhaps not surprising that there should be a good deal of confusion over terminology. On the whole, we try to avoid the term 'shadow price' which comes essentially from programming literature, 'accounting price' now being the preferred convention. Following the distinction sketched out at the end of the last chapter between efficiency (or economic) and social pricing, one may think of accounting prices as being either 'economic accounting' or 'social accounting' prices, both differing from ruling domestic market prices. The transformation of market prices into economic into social prices is accomplished using appropriate 'accounting ratios' (ARs), referred to as 'conversion factors' in the early LM literature. ARs may be either specific to a particular good or may be 'summary' in the sense of representing the average value for a bundle of commodities. While ST (Squire and van der Tak) represent these by the symbols β and a respectively, we shall normally use the AR notation in preference to a and β. Similarly (see Chapter VII) what is generally the 'discount rate' may be termed an 'accounting rate of interest' (ARI), this being the conventional term applied to the discount rate for investment as distinct from the rate appropriate where consumption is *numeraire* or 'consumption rate of interest' (CRI).[1] Finally, the term 'shadow wage rate' is replaced by 'economic wage rate' and 'social wage rate'.

Some further points merit attention with regard to the substantive problems of derivation and use of the various LMST parameters. The essence of LMST, we have seen, consists of valuing all traded commodities at border prices and breaking down all non-traded project components into traded equivalents. (The distinction between actually traded and potentially traded is taken up below.) While the valuation of traded goods (TG) appears straightforward enough, in practice there is usually a significant discrepancy between

1   A further distinction now adopted in the World Bank literature is between the economic accounting rate of interest (EARI) and the social accounting rate of interest (SARI).

the domestic retail price and border price of a traded good. This arises in part because of tariffs and taxes, and in part because the retail price of a traded good contains elements of port handling, transport, and distribution costs. Hence the foreign exchange valuation of a traded good includes, in addition to its border price, an estimate of these 'extra' costs. While the project evaluator may be expected to work these out for himself in the case of major project items, his task will be greatly facilitated to the extent that ARs for important single goods or groups of goods have already been estimated by the Central Planning Office. Examples of group specific ARs (βs) for traded goods which may be worked out in advance are for imports of consumer durables (luxury and non-luxury), intermediates (including fuel and raw materials), capital goods, and for major food items (both as imports and exports). Often there are a number of minor purchased tradable inputs entering a project which it would be hopelessly time consuming to attempt to estimate singly, and group specific ARs will prove useful for dealing with these. At the crudest level of aggregation, minor traded inputs can be dealt with using the summary trade conversion factor, a, which as we have seen is the weighted average of border to domestic price ratios for the collection of goods in the marginal trade bill. The factor a is sometimes also used to handle minor non-traded items since any non-traded item is essentially an aggregate of traded components and labour.

Non-traded goods (NTG) are broken down into traded goods and labour. Estimating labour's efficiency price (and its social price) involves information on the marginal product of the representative worker as well as marginal consumption data. Normally one attempts to estimate marginal product by category of worker (skilled, unskilled) and sometimes additionally by region. Direct estimates of the border/domestic price ratio of labour's consumption, sometimes called the 'consumption conversion factor', are conventionally designated by income group; viz. $\beta_l 1$, $\beta_l 2$, etc. Conversion factors for other major non-traded categories also need to be worked out (viz. construction, β_c; power β_p; transport β_t, etc.) and once again, such calculations are ideally performed by the planning office rather than left to the individual project evaluator. Because such parameters are likely to be relatively stable between different regions and points in time, there are obviously significant economies involved in working them out centrally and using them repeatedly, updating such estimates from time to time. But it will also be obvious that where a particular item is a significant proportion of project costs, the evaluator will need to refine centrally provided accounting ratios.

5.05 *Problems in the Valuation of Traded Goods (TG)*

Any project input or output which could enter into trade, regardless of whether it is actually purchased or sold abroad in the case of the project in question, can be treated as a traded good. On the other hand, any input or output which cannot by its very nature be traded, or which is subject to prohibitive restriction in force at the time of the good's purchase or sale, is to be treated as non-traded. The definition of traded goods derives from the principle that the opportunity cost of any commodity, as long as it could be traded under present (or predicted future) conditions, is its border price.

In practice, there are a number of practical problems associated with the valuation of a traded good. A special case is where there is a significant gap between the f.o.b. (export) and c.i.f. (import) prices of a commodity. Figure 5.5 illustrates such a situation.

Figure 5.5 *The 'Border Price Gap' Problem*

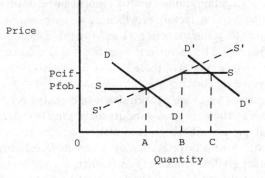

Suppose that the domestic demand curve is initially DD and the domestic supply curve S'S'. The domestic cost of quantity OA is shown by the domestic supply curve, but its *opportunity* cost (since it could be exported) is P_{fob}. Now suppose demand to increase in a manner represented by the demand curve D'D'. This will require producing an extra quantity AB domestically and importing BC at price P_{cif}. The problem is to value domestic production AB. Over this range, the commodity should formally be treated as 'non-traded' and its cost elements decomposed. A convenient shortcut, though, is to take an appropriate average of the f.o.b. and c.i.f. prices as representing the opportunity cost. The same logic will apply where the commodity is a project output.

A different problem arises where foreign import supply (or export demand) is less than perfectly elastic such that the project has an impact on the price of the commodity in question. It is, of course, relatively rare for the extra input requirement or output of a project to be of such a magnitude relative to quantities entering world trade as to give rise to such a situation. However, where this is the case, one must calculate the marginal import cost or export revenue rather than using the average figure, and price elasticities of import supply and export demand must be estimated. The relevant expressions are:

$$MC = P_{cif}(1 + 1/e_s); MR = P_{fob}(1 + 1/e_d) \qquad \dots \qquad (5.3)$$

where e_s and e_d are the elasticities of import supply and export demand respectively. Note that where these elasticities have a value of infinity as is conventionally assumed, marginal cost and revenue are equal to the respective border prices.

A more frequently encountered difficulty is that the home produced 'traded' commodity differs in kind or quality from the imported one. While it is analytically convenient to speak of a particular commodity as if it were of universally standard specification, country X's milling machines or cotton shirts may be quite different from those which can be purchased on the world market. Indeed, the problem may be compounded by the fact that in looking at trade data, the level of aggregation at which commodities are shown (number of digits in the Standard Industrial Commodity Classification) may be such that the unit values derived cover a range of differing products having different prices. One must therefore be sure that the world price data used relate to that commodity whose specification most closely resembles that of the project input or output. If the input or output is actually to be purchased from (or sold) abroad, price data can sometimes be obtained directly from the foreign supplier (purchaser). If the input or output is domestically purchased (or sold) and a perfectly analogous traded commodity cannot be found, a useful approximation will be to take the border price of the nearest equivalent traded good and multiply it by the ratio of the domestic price of the home variety to the domestic price of the imported variety. Generally speaking, while such difficulties are sometimes glossed over in the literature, their importance in practice is considerable, and much will depend on the experience and good judgement of the project analyst.

5.06 Traded Goods: Tariffs, Taxes and Domestic Cost Components

With these qualifications in mind, let us consider how accounting ratios (or βs if one prefers World Bank conventions) are derived for goods in practice, starting with the case of traded goods and gradually extending the analysis. A first and most obvious point concerns the treatment of tariffs and taxes. Although these are 'costs' to the domestic user, they are not costs from a national economic point of view but rather transfer payments to government. However, they do affect the border to domestic price ratio (accounting ratio) of the good, import duties resulting in an AR of less than unity and export taxes leading to an AR greater than unity. Returning to the earlier example of machine imports and food exports, Figure 5.6 shows ARs calculated for milling machines and coffee.

Figure 5.6 *The Treatment of Tariffs and Taxes*

Milling Machine Import		*Coffee Export*	
	pesos		*pesos*
Import price (c.i.f.)	1000	Export price (f.o.b.)	500
Duty	+500	Export tax	– 100
Domestic price	1500	Domestic price	400
AR = 0.67		AR = 1.25	

However, this is only the beginning of the story since, in addition to tax elements will enter into the determination of the final price to the consumer: viz. handling charges at port, transport to the point of consumption, and distribution charges (including the distributor's profit). Figure 5.7 shows how such costs are taken into account in a typical AR calculation, in this case, the imported milling machine.

Figure 5.7 *Calculating AR of Imported Milling Machine Delivered to User*

	1 Cost Components (pesos)	2 % Final Price	3 AR	4 Accounting Cost
Imports (c.i.f.)	1000	0.50	1.00	0.50
Duty	500	0.25	0.00	0.00
Port handling	100	0.05	0.90	0.05
Transport	100	0.05	0.70	0.04
Distrib. Margin	300	0.15	0.80	0.12
Total	2000	1.00		0.71

Column 1 shows the components of the domestic retail price (P.2000) while column 2 shows each component as a percentage of the retail price. Column 3 shows the AR of each of these components. Since the c.i.f. price is a pure foreign exchange cost, it has an AR of 1 by definition, just as the duty element, since it is a pure transfer, has an AR of zero. The other three cost elements have ARs of less than unity since it is assumed that there will be tax or duty elements in their own composition. Column 4 is derived by multiplying column 2 by column 3, and the sum of the elements of column 4 gives the

AR for the good in question (0.71). While the above figures are hypothetical, they are not unrepresentative of the sorts of magnitudes typically encountered, and a short-cut for deriving ARs of an imported commodity is to break down the commodity into its c.i.f. cost, its duty and 'the rest'. ARs of 1.0 and 0.0 being applied to the two former components while 0.8 is a typical order of magnitude for a 'summary AR' applied to minor non-traded items.

Figure 5.8 *Calculating AR of Coffee Export*

Example A

With tax and subsidy elements	Cost Components (pesos)	% Final Price	AR	Accounting cost
Export (f.o.b.)	+500	+1.00	1.00	+1.00
Tax	− 50	− .10	0.00	0.00
Port handling	− 20	− .04	0.90	− 0.04
Transport	− 20	− .04	0.70	− 0.03
Margin	− 60	− .12	0.80	− 0.10
Farmer subsidy	+150	+ .30	0.00	0.00
Total	500	1.00	-	+0.83

Example B
Without tax
or subsidy

Export (f.o.b.)	+500	+1.25	1.00	+1.25
Port handling	− 20	− 0.05	0.90	− .05
Transport	− 20	− 0.05	0.70	− .04
Margin	− 60	− 0.15	0.80	− .12
Total	400	1.00		+1.04

The same procedure is used in calculating the AR of an exportable good. Figure 5.8 shows hypothetical figures for a food export, in one case where no distortions are assumed, and in the other case where there is both a tax on the export of the good and a subsidy paid to farmers to maintain domestic price. The logic of the calculation will be clear if the following principle is borne in mind. In calculating the marginal foreign exchange cost of an extra import delivered to the point of purchase, the foreign exchange cost of handling, transport, etc. must be added to the c.i.f. cost. In the case of an export, however, the marginal foreign exchange earning is the f.o.b. price minus the real cost of resources required to get the export to port. Hence the plus and minus signs in the Accounting Cost column show foreign exchange revenue (+) and cost (−) items. (Adopting this convention in Figure 5.7, all entries would be negative.) Where a net subsidy element exists, as in example A shown in the upper part of Figure 5.8, an accounting ratio of less than unity (0.83) says that every peso's worth of the good (valued at the point of collection) has a net foreign exchange equivalent value of P.0.83. The subsidy has raised the domestic price. In the alternative case, example B, a peso's worth of production generates slightly more than a peso's worth of foreign exchange. In general, where Government relies on import tariffs rather than on export taxes or subsidies, ARs of imports will tend to be less than unity and ARs of exports slightly greater than unity.

5.07 *Solving for ARs Simultaneously*

In calculating the ARs for tradables, information is required both on tariffs (subsidies) and on 'other costs' consisting in this case of non-traded goods. But in calculating the ARs of non-traded goods, as shown below, one needs to know the ARs of the traded goods into which NTGs are decomposed. This suggests a chicken-and-egg situation; formally, one needs to solve a large number of simultaneous equations. In practice, one may start by making some assumption about the ARs for non-traded goods (using a 'standard' AR) in order to work out ARs for a large number of tradables. One then uses these in calculating the ARs of non-traded goods and the latter are then used to recalculate the traded good ARs.[1] It will be apparent that one is dealing with an iterative solution process though, in practice, two rounds of iteration will usually suffice to approximate an overall solution.

Figure 5.9 illustrates the principles of simultaneous solution where there are only two goods, imported fuel (TG) and transport (NTG) and two unknowns (the ARs of fuel and transport). The cost breakdown is known and standardised on a unit domestic price basis as before. The AR of the c.i.f. cost is 1.00 and of taxes 0.00 by definition. An AR of 0.80 is assumed for labour.

Figure 5.9 *Simultaneous Determination of ARs*

| | % Cost Breakdown of Each Good | | |
	Fuel (traded)	Transport (non-traded)	AR
Import (c.i.f.)	0.35	-	1.00
Taxes	0.05	0.10	0.00
Transport	0.40	-	AR_t
Fuel	-	0.50	AR_f
Labour	0.20	0.40	0.80
Total	1.00	1.00	

Since the AR of a good is defined as the sum of its percentage cost components times their respective ARs, we have the following expressions:

1 The procedure suggested is that advocated by Scott, MacArthur and Newbery (1976). Squire and van der Tak (1975), like more recent World Bank publications on the subject, suggest that a single round of decomposition and valuation of non-traded goods is sufficient.

$$AR_f = (0.35)(1.00) + (0.05)(0) + (0.40)(AR_t) + (0.20)(0.80)$$
$$AR_t = (0.10)(0) + (0.50)(AR_f) + (0.40)(0.80)$$

which can be simplified to:

$$AR_f = (0.40)(AR_t) + 0.51$$
$$AR_t = (0.50)(AR_f) + 0.32$$

and solved to obtain:

$AR_f = 0.79; AR_t = 0.70$

Checking back to Figures 5.7 and 5.8 it will be seen that 0.70 has in fact been used as the AR for transport in calculating the ARs for milling machines and coffee in our hypothetical example. To obtain consistency over a very large number of goods and services, however, computer facilities will be essential.

5.08 *How Representative are Average ARs?*

A word concerning the use of commodity specific ARs as opposed to summary ARs. Where a great many ARs are derived, it will be useful to measure their central tendency and dispersion. If the latter is small, one may then be justified in taking the central tendency value as summary AR to be applied to all goods and services in a particular category. For example, Scott's[1] work in Kenya resulted in median AR values of 1.00 for exports and 0.86 for imports, both having relatively large standard deviation (0.25). In the case of non-traded goods and services, however, the median AR value was 0.77 with a standard deviation of only 0.06. This result will not be surprising if one recalls that ARs of non-traded goods are weighted averages of ARs of traded goods. Similarly, observed ARs for those items constituting 'urban consumer goods and services' (used as seen below in deriving the AR for labour's consumption) were found to cluster around a median of 0.80 since the category comprised both traded and non-traded components. Hence if one were presently evaluating a project in Kenya, while it might be safer to estimate ARs individually for particularly important inputs and outputs, one would not go far wrong in using 0.77 as the AR for non-tradables while 0.80 might conveniently be used as a summary AR (or Standard Conversion Factor) to cover miscellaneous small items consisting of both tradables and non-tradables. Figure 5.10 shows how some typical frequency distributions of

1 See Scott, MacArthur & Newbery (1976) and Scott (1974).

ARs associated with different categories of goods and services might look.

Figure 5.10 *Hypothetical Frequency Distributions of ARs by Category*

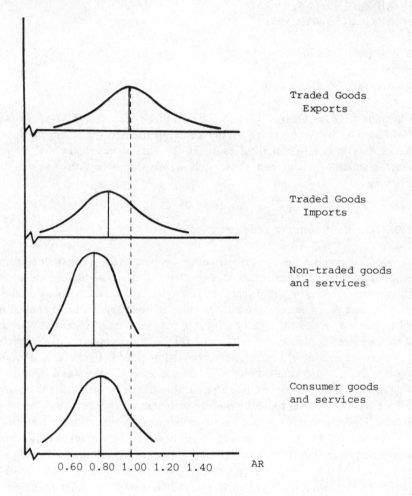

5.09 *Summary*

The present chapter has developed the essential methodological elements necessary to understanding the notion of economic pricing and its relation to the trade efficiency objective. We have seen, by means of simple examples, how protectionist measures necessitate adjusting the value of foreign exchange for planning purposes or, equivalently, how such measures drive a wedge between factor productivity measurement at domestic values and at foreign exchange values. The derivation of a shadow exchange rate has been illustrated adopting UNIDO conventions as has that of the summary trade conversion factor, the reciprocal of the SER adopting LMST conventions. However, the latter method has been seen to entail decomposing all project elements into direct and indirect trade effects. Since both methodologies ultimately take trade efficiency as the basis of economic pricing, it follows that where identical conventions are adopted with respect to the extent of decomposition, the UNIDO methodology becomes redundant. Hence our adoption of LMST terminology and conventions which we have developed at length.

We have then gone on to concentrate on the treatment of traded goods and, while non-traded goods and factor valuation have been touched on, these matters are examined in greater detail in the chapters which follow. Key problems in the treatment of traded goods have been examined both in principle and in practice. It has been seen that while for purposes of abstraction it is convenient to speak of valuing traded goods at border prices as though this were a simple operation, in practice a number of complications exist. Where goods are actually imported or exported, domestic distribution costs will need to be taken into account in deriving the foreign exchange equivalent value of the domestic retail price, and some of these costs will consist of non-traded items. Since the treatment of non-traded goods requires that they be broken down into traded components, there is in principle a problem of simultaneity to be dealt with. Crude estimates of parameter values will need to be used in the initial instance and then refined by successive iteration. Equally, where goods are both traded and produced at home, valuing the latter raises problems of product comparability. Hence, 'efficiency pricing' will require an element of good judgement on the part of the project evaluator, the degree of refinement sought depending on the importance of the particular input or output in total project costs. Finally, it has been suggested that there are significant advantages in working out a number of accounting ratios centrally. One is that so doing saves a good deal of work for the individual project evaluator since these can be used for a variety of projects and periodically updated. Secondly, variance estimates of ARs for different commodity groups are particularly useful in judging the degree to which it will be appropriate for the project evaluator to apply standard (central tendency) conversion factors to the valuation of minor items as well as indicating the extent of further work needed in refining his own estimates of major items.

5.10 *Further Reading*

A good theoretical discussion on the relationship between the UNIDO, LM and other methods (viz. Bruno) is provided by Lal (1974a). For the more theoretically minded, the symposium on shadow exchange rates which appears in *OEP* (1974) contains a number of interesting contributions, particularly those by Scott and by Balassa.

Early work on the derivation of shadow prices for commodities includes that contained in OECD Vol. II (1968) as well as a series of ancillary case studies published separately, of which Lal (1972a) and Little and Tipping (1972) are illustrative. More recently there is the work reported in Little and Scott (eds) (1976) as well as the long awaited book by Scott, MacArthur & Newbery (1976) which shows the application of the LM method to the 'million acre settlement scheme' in Kenya. Additionally, a series of pilot studies is being sponsored by the World Bank with the aim of ascertaining the applicability of LMST. Some of these are referred to in the following Chapter, but Bruce (1976) gives the best indication of the general approach. Finally there is a useful article by Guisinger and Papageorgious (1976) which is concerned with the empirical problems associated with pricing traded goods, particularly that of international comparability.

Of the many other strands making up the debate, one should also mention the seminal work done on effective protection which is reviewed in Balassa (1971), the 'domestic resource costs' approach first set out by Bruno (1967), and the contributions of Schydlowsky (1968) and Kruger (1966) particularly. These are essentially variants of the approach discussed above and we have therefore omitted them in the text.

VI

POTENTIALLY TRADED AND NON-TRADED GOODS

6.01 *Introduction*

The present chapter begins by drawing the distinction between non-traded and potentially traded goods, the treatment of the latter category depending essentially on how government policies are expected to change in future. The valuation of non-traded goods is then discussed in more detail, particular attention being paid to problems raised where such goods are project outputs. For non-traded goods as inputs, it is shown how valuation will differ according to whether their use has an impact on production or consumption if neoclassical marginal equality conditions do not hold. The argument is accompanied by a detailed example showing how an average conversion factor may be worked out. The discussion next moves to considering the effects of relaxing the assumption of 'unchanged' policies; notably the removal of protective barriers and accompanying devaluation. The general equilibrium of 'free trade' exchange rate concept (FTER) is introduced and illustrated, as is the notion of valuing labour's consumption according to whether protectionist policies are maintained or abandoned. Finally we consider the notion of the 'optimal' tariff or tax and examine the argument about 'freeing' trade in the light of some general political and institutional considerations.

6.02 *Non-Traded Goods and Services*

A point which is typically the source of some confusion is whether some goods and services are non-traded because *by their very nature* they do not enter into trade — a frequently cited example is electricity which is only rarely transmitted across frontiers — or rather because protection is presently such that they cannot enter into trade at the margin, as in the case of a good subject to a fully taken-up quota or prohibitive tariff. Properly speaking, it is only the former category which is non-traded, while the latter consists of potentially traded goods which *because of present policies* are non-traded.

Such goods are variously referred to by different authors as 'tradable', 'partially traded' and 'potentially traded' and we shall generally use the latter term.

6.03 *Valuing Potentially Traded Goods (PTG)*

How this category of goods is to be valued depends on the view taken about the likelihood of present restrictive policies continuing to hold in future. Figure 6.1 illustrates the principles involved. Assume that one of the key inputs of a project is presently subject to a fully taken-up quota restriction as shown by the vertical line QM. Present imports are thus OM and are obtained at a world price of P^w; however, all further demand must be met from the domestic supply curve (S_d), and the project requires quantity MD of the good. If the quota restriction were suitably relaxed, the total cost of the

Figure 6.1 *Valuation of Potentially Traded Good*

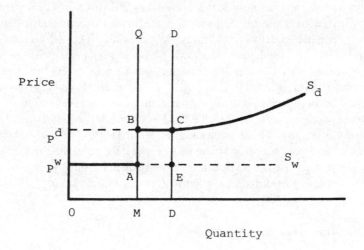

required amount would be MAED (or simply the extra quantity valued at its world price). However, if the quota restriction is to remain in force, the total cost of the input will be MBCD; i.e. it will need to be treated like a non-traded good and decomposed into its marginal domestic cost elements, the traded and non-traded components of which can be multiplied by their respective ARs.

In general, then, PTGs are to be treated like fully traded goods if it is thought that restrictions will be removed, or like non-traded goods (i.e. decomposed) if the opposite is the case. This point is important since the original OECD *Manual* was unclear about judgements concerning the nature of future commercial policies and seemed to suggest that 'movement towards optimal policies' – i.e. the dismantling of 'non-optimal' trade restrictions – should be assumed. However, as now understood, the adoption of LMST evaluation conventions in the public sector does not in any sense depend on a rationalisation of trade policies taking place. Trade rationalisation is only important insofar as the private or 'market price' sector is to be induced to allocate investment resources more efficiently.

6.04 *Non-Traded Goods (NTG) and Decomposition*

Where goods do not enter into trade by their very nature, decomposition is a pre-requisite to their valuation in terms of world prices. Implicit in the characterisation of decomposition outlined so far is that the domestic marginal cost (MC) and marginal value (MV) of a good can be assumed equal. While such an assumption is consistent with the usual textbook representation of equilibrium pricing, there are many reasons why it may not hold in practice. Most industries do not price their products on a marginal cost basis and, even if prices can be characterised as 'tending towards' marginal costs in the long term, the existence of short term disequilibria (particularly in the form of spare capacity) means that there will be a discrepancy between MC and MV. In this event it will be important to assess, where project *inputs* are non-traded, whether the requisite input supply is made available by increasing domestic production of the non-traded good, or by restricting its consumption in other uses, or both.

Figure 6.2 shows one such possible situation. Suppose that one of the inputs into a project is electricity. In the conventional representation of supply-demand equilibrium (Diagram A), a price of P_e prevails and MC equals MV. Since, however, the provision of extra electricity generation capacity typically requires large 'lumpy' investment, a more appropriate representation of the situation is given by the L-shaped supply curve shown in Diagram B labelled SUP. The equilibrium price, P_e, is determined by some view of future demand growth in relation to the long run supply curve (not shown). Under current demand conditions (the demand curve DD), OE electricity is therefore supplied at the going price P_e, which is higher than the marginal supply price P_m.

Suppose the project uses an increment in total electricity supply equivalent to EF. This can be met from spare capacity, and the power supply to the

Figure 6.2 *Valuation of Non-Traded Good*

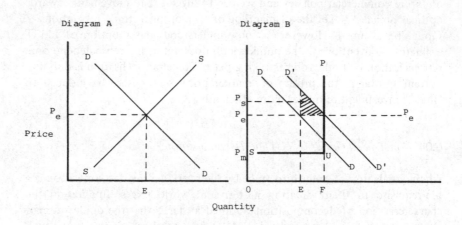

project should be valued at *marginal cost of supply* (P_m) valued at border prices. However, suppose that demand is D'D' and that no spare capacity exists. In such a situation, extra supplies for the project could be made available by cutting back supplies to other users by an amount EF; project electricity would in this case be costed on the basis of its equivalent *marginal value* in terms of foregone consumption, or P_s. The price P_s will be seen to correspond to average 'consumer willingness to pay' over that segment of the demand curve D'D' lying between E and F. This is the familiar problem of measuring 'consumer surplus'; i.e. the difference between what the consumer now pays for unit F and what he would be willing to pay for unit E shown by the shaded triangular area.

In short, in valuing NTGs as *inputs* to a project, a situation may exist such that P_e is not the relevant reference datum and some judgement needs to be made about whether extra supplies come from extra production, from a cut-back in consumption, or from a combination of both. If the former is the case (extra production) the components of P_m will need to be decomposed into traded and non-traded constituents and valued using appropriate ARs. If the latter situation holds (cutback in consumption) one will need to ascertain the marginal composition of the representative consumption bundle value using the relevant ARs (see section 6.08 of the present chapter). In some cases, representative ARs (βs) for short-term and long-term electricity supply may already have been worked out by the Planning Office; as illustrated in the section which follows.

But what of the valuation of NTGs where they are project *outputs*; i.e. how would one set about evaluating a project providing extra electricity generating capacity equivalent to EF? Obviously it would make no sense to cost the inputs and then value the output at that cost. One answer is to attempt to assess consumers 'willingness to pay' (WTP) valued at border prices from inspection of the long run demand curve. Besides raising the practical objection that in typical LDCs many more consumers are 'willing to pay' than those connected to the supply system, there is a principled objection to re-introducing WTP on grounds which are central to the LMST rationale; notably, that the inherent usefulness of LMST relies upon removing production decisions from the sphere of influence of domestic price signals. The seriousness of this latter argument is to be judged in relation to the fact that, in many LDCs, the bulk of public investment is directed to the provision of non-traded outputs.[1] One way of circumventing the WTP problem would be to evaluate all end-uses of the non-traded good in terms of their balance of payments impact in production rather than looking at consumption. Hence, in the case of an irrigation project, the value of water is assessed not by looking at what consumers would be willing to pay but by looking at its net economic contribution to increased crop production. Such a procedure would be difficult to adopt for electricity, however, because of the multiplicity of end-uses both as an intermediate and as a consumption good.

An alternative is provided by Fitzgerald (1977) who suggests that the core of the problem lies in attempting to separate project analysis from central planning. On this view, searching for an 'objective' economic price for certain types of non-traded goods and services is meaningless as is most apparent in the case of, say, health and education. The problem is, rather, to ensure that sectoral physical output targets are reasonably and consistently specified, the ultimate provision of such goods depending on political decisions. In such a context, the role of project appraisal is limited to ascertaining least-cost ways of meeting a given target.

6.05 *Valuation of Non-Traded Items: An Example*

From the above discussion it will be apparent that the valuation of an NTG such as electricity raises questions of theory as well as significant problems in practice. Let us assume that electricity is being valued as an input to a project in a country where electricity is generated thermally using coal imports.

1 See Toye (1976) who sees this as the central objection to the Little & Mirrlees approach.

Figure 6.3 *Valuation of Average Cost of Electricity as Project Input*

Row/column	Cost per Kwh Supplied 3 year average at Mkt Prices (Kobos)			Weighted Average Cost per Kwh at Mkt Prices	AR	Weighted Average Cost per Kwh at Econ. Prices
	Region 1	Region 2	Region 3			
	(1)	(2)	(3)	(4)	(5)	(6)
(1) Wages & Salaries	1.25	0.95	1.14	1.11	0.80	0.89
(2) Social Security	0.08	0.08	0.10	0.08	0.00	0.00
(3) Coal imports (C.i.f.)	3.32	3.24	3.90	3.40	1.00	3.40
(4) Transport to site	0.33	0.24	0.29	0.29	0.70	0.20
(5) Other Materials	0.42	0.40	0.48	0.42	0.85	0.36
(6) Capital Maintenance	0.83	0.79	0.95	0.83	0.90	0.75
(7) Extra Capital (Depreciation)	0.83	0.95	1.14	0.93	0.90	0.84
(8) Transmission Costs	0.83	0.87	1.05	0.88	0.85	0.75
(9) Office Overheads	0.42	0.40	0.48	0.42	0.70	0.29
(10) Total cost per Kwh	8.31	7.92	9.53	8.36		7.48
(11) Weights; n⁰ of Kwh x 10^7 (total 500 MW)	23.2 (46%)	18.6 (38%)	8.2 (16%)			

AR for electricity supply = $7.48/8.36 = 0.89$.

Valuation of marginal economic costs in the short term will require dealing carefully with problems of excess capacity and/or cutbacks in consumption to existing users. However, a useful point of departure will be to work out a long term average AR for electricity as an input, it then being up to the project analyst to determine how sensitive project NPV will be to using a range of different AR values.

Figure 6.3 illustrates the basis of the calculation. A hypothetical African country has generating capacity of 500 megawatts (MW) produced by three thermal stations in different regions of the country with different cost structures. Major cost elements are coal and its transport to site, wages and salaries, and transmission costs. Maintenance of existing plant and equipment is about 10 percent of cost while depreciation covers the anticipated cost of increased capacity. Costs per Kilowatt-hour (Kwh) are worked out for each regional generating station on the basis of the average of the past three years. These are then weighted by each region's average share in total production, the weighted average composition of costs (at market prices) being shown in column (4). ARs shown in column (5) are hypothetical but their orders of magnitude are broadly representative; (viz. capital items are unprotected relative to consumption goods, imports c.i.f. have an AR of unity and social security payments are a form of taxation). The average AR calculated for electricity supply is 0.89 in this case.

6.06 Protectionism and General Equilibrium

What view one takes about possible future changes in commercial policies determines whether potentially traded goods are to be treated as traded or non-traded. What view one takes of how extra project demand for non-traded inputs is met then determines how these are to be decomposed. If currently ruling commercial policies are thought likely to remain unchanged, then all potentially traded goods which because of prohibitive restrictions are not presently traded must obviously continue to be treated as non-traded and so decomposed. But what if policies are expected to change; i.e. what is the effect of removing restrictions and lowering tariffs on some goods (and possibly raising tariffs on others)? Clearly, the set of potentially traded commodities to be treated as non-traded will alter in composition — if the movement is towards generally less restrictive policies, the number of goods which are actually traded will increase. But more important, changed commercial policies will alter the structure of ruling domestic prices with consequent effects on the structure of consumption. What implications does this have for the analysis?

A lowering of barriers to trade, although it will affect the total volume of currently traded goods consumed, will not affect their valuation for project analysis purposes since the supply of imports (and demand for exports) can in most cases be assumed perfectly elastic at going world market prices.[1] However, in the absence of corresponding exchange rate adjustment, dismantling protection will mean that some import substituting industries go out of business and, if serious balance of payment difficulties are to be avoided, the resources released must be transferred to increasing the volume of exports by a corresponding amount. But this is more easily said than done. One solution is for the price of non-traded goods to fall relative to imports, thus shifting demand away from imports and increasing employment in the home goods sector (viz. services) until a new equilibrium is reached. On this view, unemployed workers bid down money wages in home industries until they are once again employed, and non-traded good prices fall relative to those of imports. If money wages cannot be bid down, then of course rising unemployment can reduce the real wage and home demand to some level compatible with balance of payments equilibrium. Devaluation is an alternative adjustment mechanism since exports become more profitable and imports more expensive relative to non-traded goods, although real wages are again affected since imports tend to figure significantly in workers' consumption. In brief, liberalisation entails either an exchange rate adjustment raising the price of traded relative to non-traded goods, or a more roundabout internal adjustment process which, by lowering the price of non-traded goods, achieves the same result.[2]

Whether in practice those countries which have attempted to remove trade restrictions and accompanied this by devaluation/wage cuts have always succeeded in attaining a new equilibrium is another matter. Often export supplies are inelastic in the short term and the rise in import prices occasioned by devaluation sets off an inflationary process which, even where real wages are falling, raises other costs in the home goods sector, which work their way through to the export sector. Hence the dismantling of trade restrictions may in reality have to be accompanied by successive rounds of devaluation and real wage cuts. In theory, of course, there is *some* level at which equilibrium can be reached.[3]

1 If ARs are being used to value traded goods, these would obviously need adjustment; i.e. domestic/world price *ratios* will change even though world prices remain constant.
2 I am grateful to Maurice Scott for pointing out that where import restrictions are combined with export subsidies, trade liberalisation need not necessarily entail devaluation.
3 The recent experience of Chile under the junta is a case in point. Successive devaluations and continuing real wage cuts would appear to have finally brought about balance of payments equilibrium, though one might legitimately enquire at what cost?

6.07 *The Free Trade Exchange Rate*

It will be useful to assume that a reduction in protection will always be accompanied by a corresponding devaluation. Consider the case in which protection is removed completely. At an earlier stage we discussed deriving that particular shadow rate of exchange (SER) which correctly values foreign exchange in terms of domestic consumption (see expression 5.2 on page 85 above) or, in analogous LMST terms, the summary conversion factor (a) which correctly values domestic consumption in terms of foreign exchange. With protection removed, determination of the SER using the ruling commodity composition of foreign exchange consumption as weights — the f_i's and x_j's as shown in expression (5.2) — is no longer appropriate. Rather, we are concerned with determining the set of weights reflecting foreign exchange consumption at the margin with restrictions removed; i.e. under conditions of changing domestic to world price relatives. The relevant weights are therefore elasticities of export supply and import demand with respect to price changes, and the resulting SER is called the 'free trade exchange rate' (FTER).[1] A simplified general expression for the FTER (expressed as a percentage of the actural rate is given by:

$$\frac{\text{FTER}}{\text{OER}} = \frac{\sum\limits_{i}^{n} \epsilon_i X_i (1+S_i) + \sum\limits_{j}^{m} \eta_j M_j (1+T_j)}{\sum\limits_{i}^{n} \epsilon_i X_i + \sum\limits_{j}^{m} \eta_j M_j} \qquad \dots \qquad (6.1)$$

where X_i and M_j are the total values entering trade (at border prices) of the ith export and j^{th} import summed respectively over n exports and m imports, S_i is the subsidy rate on the ith export and T_j the tariff (or tariff equivalent in the case of a quota) on the jth import, and ϵ_i (epsilon) and η_j (eta) the elasticity of foreign exchange earnings from the ith export and foreign exchange demand for purchase of the jth import.[2]

To illustrate the logic of the FTER, recall the two-good example given in the previous chapter (Figure 5.1). Suppose that five machines are imported and 10 units of food exported, the border prices of each being \$ 1000 and \$500 respectively. Since the OER is P.1 = \$1, the total import bill equals

---

1 This is sometimes referred to as the Bacha-Taylor SER.
2 If foreign demand for some of the country's exports is not infinitely elastic, the elasticity of supply of foreign exchange will be a function of both the elasticity of domestic supply (ϵ_x) and the elasticity of foreign demand (η_x), or:

$$\epsilon_i = \frac{\epsilon_x(\epsilon_x - 1)}{\epsilon_x + \eta_x}$$

total export receipts (P.5000). Imagine that it is planned to remove the present tariff on machines (50%), that the elasticity of import demand is 2.0 and that of export supply is 0.5; substituting into (6.1):

$$\frac{FTER}{OER} = \frac{(0.5)\,(P.5000)\,(1+0) + (2)\,(P.5000)\,(1+0.5)}{(0.5)\,(P.5000) \;+\; (2)\,(P.5000)}$$

$$\frac{FTER}{OER} \; (=\frac{1}{a'}) = 1.40; \; a^1 = \frac{1}{1.40} = 0.71$$

The free trade equilibrium exchange rate therefore values foreign exchange 40 percent more highly than the official exchange rate, of P.1 = \$1, or P. 1.40 = \$1.

Figure 6.4 below shows trade figures in the before/after situations. Although dollar border prices remain unchanged, peso border prices have risen .by 40 percent, and domestic price relatives have been brought into line with border prices. The peso value of total trade has increased from P.5000 to P.8400. The slight fall in the domestic price of machines is explained by the fact that the extent of devaluation is less than the tariff rate; hence the volume of machine imports has increased. However, the rise in the peso price of food is such as to bring forth an increase in export supply such that increased export receipts exactly offset the increased import bill.[1]

Figure 6.4 *Effect of Devaluation on Trade*

	Commodity	Domestic Price (pesos)	Border Price (pesos)	Quantity	Total (pesos)
Before	Machines (M)	1500	1000	5	5000
(P.1 = \$1)	Food (X)	500	500	10	5000
After	Machines (M)	1400	1400	6	8400
(P.1 = \$0.71)	Food (X)	700	700	12	8400

If the FTER revalues the domestic consumption value of foreign exchange (traded goods) under the assumption of full trade liberalisation, it follows that with foreign exchange as *numeraire* (LMST) it will be necessary to adjust the value of non-traded goods by the reciprocal of the FTER (a') in order to express their new foreign exchange value. Since domestic non-traded good

1 The reasoning can quickly be checked through by noting that the removal of the 50% tariff on machines has been offset by a 40% increase in the peso border price; hence there has been a net fall in machine prices of 10% which, given the import elasticity coefficient ($\eta = 2.0$), has occasioned a 20% increase in demand. With food, a 40% increase in the peso price has led to a 20% increase in output ($\epsilon = 0.5$).

prices have been assumed downwardly rigid, it follows that their accounting ratios (P^w/P^d) will tend to rise as P^w (the peso border price of their constituent traded elements) rises relative to P^d. Application of the LMST method in a post-devaluation context implicitly achieves this result by decomposing and valuing non-traded goods, including that proportion decomposed into labour's consumption, at the newly prevailing set of intermediate and factor combinations and prices. But the obvious problem is that where devaluation is expected but has not yet taken place, application of the LMST procedure requires one to predict how changes in domestic price relatives of traded goods, and of traded to non-traded goods, will affect *both the composition of non-traded goods* and the composition of labour's *consumption bundle*. Using the reciprocal of the FTER as a summary conversion factor is an extremely crude way of dealing with the problem; for the moment, however, it appears to remain the most practical, if not the most fully satisfactory, approach. In the words of Squire and van der Tak:

The information required to trace through these effects is formidable, and in practice, it may be necessary to ignore the substitution possibilities in both production and consumption and to concentrate solely on the immediate (relative) reduction in the cost of consumption when making new estimates of shadow wage rates and of marginal social costs for non-tradables.[1]

6.08 *Labour's Consumption Bundle*

In the previous chapter, a hypothetical example was used to show how a non-traded item (transport) could be decomposed into traded inputs and labour, the assumed AR for labour being shown as 0.80 (Figure 5.9). We now briefly examine the logic of how such an estimate is obtained.

In principle, the economic cost of employing labour in a given occupation is the foreign exchange equivalent of labour's consumption while the economic cost of moving labour from one occupation to another is the resulting net loss in output. It is the former concept which is relevant to 'costing' labour in the present context; the latter concept is relevant to costing labour as a direct project input. When one refers to labour's consumption, one is of course abstracting away from this or that individual and referring to a standard or

1   Squire and van der Tak (1975), p. 95; on the other hand, Lal (1974) has argued that composition of non-traded goods is relatively insensitive to tariff and exchange rate adjustments. It follows that the more non-traded goods appear in labour's marginal consumption bundle, the less sensitive will its composition be to such an adjustment. Balassa (1974) has suggested that consumption bundle elasticities be estimated directly.

'composite' worker. The consumption bundles of the skilled industrial worker, the artisan, the small farmer, and the casual day labourer will all differ, just as for any given category of labour the particular consumption pattern may vary according to region. How far it will be necessary to dis-aggregate labour into sub-categories depends on the importance of the labour item in total costs; in general, though, it will be useful to determine ARs for broad categories of labour such as skilled/unskilled and urban/rural, leaving it to the project analyst to undertake further refinements according to circum-stances. In the case of labour entering, let us say, transport it will probably be safe to assume that one can take the consumption bundle of the average ur-ban working class family as appropriate. Estimates of its composition will usually be available from household budget surveys (normally carried out by income group), though in cases where survey data is not available, the com-position of the retail cost of living index will provide some basis on which to work.

In an example given in Chapter V, section 5.4, we imagined a hypothetical worker spending his wage at the margin on one export (food) and two im-ported commodities (textile and appliances). Because one is concerned with the valuation of a marginal increase in the provision of a non-traded good, one must therefore consider labour's marginal consumption. Typically, how-ever, survey data relates to average consumption patterns and thus, if one is to be strictly accurate, average data must be supplemented by data on income elasticities of consumption for various product groups. Figure 6.5 shows how the AR for labour's marginal consumption in the hypothetical example is derived.

Figure 6.5 *Calculating the AR for Labour's Marginal Consumption*

Good	% of Average Consumption	Income Elasticity	% of Marginal Consumption	AR	Economic Value
Food (X)	0.60	0.83	0.50	1.00	0.50
Textiles (M)	0.25	1.00	0.25	0.80	0.20
Appliances (H)	0.15	1.67	0.25	0.40	0.10
Total	1.00		1.00		0.80

If present protectionist policies (determining the ARs of the various com-modities in consumption) are expected to be abolished and a corresponding exchange rate adjustment made then, as has been suggested above, the sum-mary 'general equilibrium' conversion factor (a') might be used as a crude measure of the foreign exchange value of labour's consumption; i.e. 0.71 in place of 0.80.[1] In terms of the example, one can see that removing the tariffs

1 Since the FTER calculated in the previous section had a value of 1.40, a' is equal to 0.71 (1/1.40).

of textiles and appliances would make these cheaper domestically relative to food, and that a resulting increase in their share in marginal consumption relative to food would tend to lower the AR. Strictly speaking, one must first work out, for a given percentage devaluation, the ratio of existing domestic prices of the commodities to their new peso border prices, and then use specific price elasticity information to determine a 'general equilibrium' conversion factor for labour's consumption.

6.09 *'Optimal' Protection*

In theory, equating the notion of removing protection with that of 'free trade' is incorrect since under certain conditions it is possible that a country may be able to order tariffs in such a way as to improve its terms of trade; hence the notion of an 'optimal' import tariff or export tax. Until recently, this notion has remained something of a theoretical *curiosum* since the conditions under which individual countries can improve their terms of trade hardly ever obtain. In any event, let us briefly examine the notion of the 'optimal' tariff to see what application it might have.

Figure 6.6 sets out the essentials of the analysis. Imagine initially that there are only two countries in the world (the UK and the USA) trading cloth and wheat respectively. The curve labelled OB in Diagram A is Britain's 'offer curve' for cloth in exchange for wheat and tends to slope upwards since, so to speak, the more cloth Britain exports, the less well-clothed everyone becomes and the more bread the inhabitants need to stay warm. The same logic applies in America where for every additional unit of wheat exported, a larger bundle of clothing is needed in compensation (curve OA). The intersection of OB and OA establishes the terms of trade (OT) between the two countries. Hence Britain can sell WC exports of cloth in return for OW imports of wheat. Now, however, Britain places a tariff on wheat imports such that its new 'tariff distorted' offer curve is OB'. This is equivalent to saying that Britain is willing to offer less cloth for a given amount of wheat, and since the Americans cannot sell their wheat elsewhere (there being only two countries), OW American wheat at the higher price commands only WC' cloth, C'C accruing as a net gain in 'cloth' foreign exchange to Britain. The new terms of trade, more favourable to Britain, are OT'. Exactly the same logic holds if Britain levies an export tax on cloth instead of a tariff on wheat.

Now consider Diagram B. Here one may abandon the assumption that there are only two countries and assume that America can buy its cloth (or Britain purchase its wheat requirements) from some third party at terms of trade OT. If Britain imposes a tax or tariff, the net effect is merely to reduce the volume of trade between the two countries, W'C' cloth being traded for

Figure 6.6 *Terms of Trade and the Optimal Tariff (Tax) Argument*

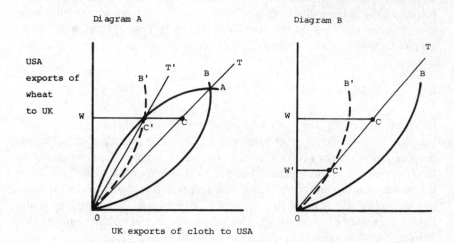

OW' wheat. In other words, Britain faces a perfectly elastic foreign demand curve for its exports of cloth, and a perfectly elastic foreign supply curve for its imports of wheat. In general this will be the case where there are many countries buying and selling the same product.

In the context of present day relations between developed and less developed countries, and particularly since the successful oil price rise negotiated by OPEC, the moral of the story is no longer that tariffs and taxes are always to be avoided. It is, rather, that where suppliers of a commodity can collude in driving up price, they can for a time at least secure a favourable movement in their terms of trade as long as the countries with which they trade do not retaliate – either directly by collectively taxing what they sell or buy from LDCs, or indirectly by passing on higher prices to primary producers through inflation.

6.10 *Some Political Remarks*

The present and the previous chapters have been concerned with the 'trade efficiency' basis of economic pricing. How potentially traded goods are to be priced has been shown to depend on how Government's commercial policies are expected to change in future. If the movement is towards free trade, PTGs become TGs, and NTGs (including labour's consumption) will need to be revalued. If no change is expected in current policies, PTGs are priced like NTGs. In either case, TGs are priced with reference to exogenously determined world market forces, while the foreign exchange equivalent value of NTGs is mediated by domestic market forces. Hence, adoption of LMST methods constitutes a movement away from market prices as reference datum, but does not entirely break the link between production and consumption. Finally we have seen that it may in certain circumstances be possible to favourably influence world market prices of some TGs.

In addition to questions of methodology, the discussion raises broad issues about the institutional framework within which policy decisions are made, particularly about the role of the public sector in pursuing the trade efficiency objective. The key question here is how far economic or 'efficiency' prices are to be used in evaluating *all* investment decisions. Broadly there are two positions which may loosely be characterised as 'first best' and 'second best'.[1] The early debate about the relative merits of LM and UNIDO approaches saw this distinction in terms of the power, or lack of it, assumed to be vested in the 'Central Office of Project Evaluation'. The UNIDO position was to accept a 'second best' position arguing that the project planning office could not be assumed sufficiently powerful to effect the removal of all restrictions. The LM position was to opt for 'first best' policies, arguing that COPE should have the power to effect the implementation of a rational tariff structure such that market price relatives could be brought into line with economic price relatives. The current LMST approach is basically to ignore the problem.

However, the implicit assumption of the LM first best solution is that the public and private shares of control over investment will not be decisively altered, for if the public sector planned *all* investment activity, why should trade restrictions be removed? Accounting prices could be universally adopted for production decisions and market prices used merely to ration consumption. Under socialism, the role of the public sector would be to use domestic tariffs, taxes and quotas to control final consumption, the broad lines of production strategy being determined by the planning process and 'economic' project evaluation being used as a second line of defence to ensure consistency between centrally determined trade efficiency objectives and administratively decentralised operating decisions. Ultimately this line of reasoning leads to a set of arguments about appropriate degrees of decentralised decision making under socialism, the extreme positions characterised by fully centralised physical balance planning (or what may be termed 'Stalinist'

1   For economic purists, 'n^{th} best' and '$(n-1)^{th}$ best' where $n > 1$.

planning) on the one hand, and decentralised planning of the sort first hypothesised by Lange (1938) and Lerner (1944) and more recently advocated in practice by Liberman (1964), Kantarovich (1965), and Kornai (1967).

There are a number of reasons in practice why LM 'first best' policies may prove difficult to adopt. For one thing, the private sector (including multinationals) may have a vested interest in maintaining present levels of protection such that tariffs can neither be dismantled nor even made uniform. Again, the public sector may be heavily dependent on tariff revenue, particularly if there are constraints on raising total savings through taxation (which is, as will be seen, the essential argument for LMST 'social' pricing). Finally, since protection is often seen as a method of alleviating Balance of Payments difficulties, abolishing protection may necessitate successive rounds of devaluation and be accompanied by domestic inflation, hence entailing political consequences similar to those suggested above. In short, the movement to a first best position under a mixed economy ultimately raises questions which are no less political in nature than the question of whether first bestness can better be achieved under capitalism or socialism.

6.11 *Data Sources*

It will be useful, in concluding the section on efficiency pricing to say something about sources from which relevant data can be obtained. *Trade accounts* will clearly be essential in determining what categories of goods are in fact traded as well as indicating c.i.f. and f.o.b. unit values. Equally, some goods which one might expect to be traded may not appear in trade accounts (or else appear in very small quantities) suggesting that either trade restrictions exist or that the explanation is to be sought in terms of quality differences. Furthermore, a good appearing as an import in some years may be an export in others (or both simultaneously) and such situations will need to be carefully investigated. An element of judgement will be required both in assessing what constitutes a sufficient volume of trade for the good to count as traded, and if traded both as an import and an export, how it is to be handled in the case of the project in question.

Customs and Excise schedules will be important for determining tariff rates and usually provide very detailed information although where, as in some cases, specific rates of tariff are shown (viz. per kilo), it will be necessary to translate these into *ad valorem* terms. *Commodity publications* will be important for determining border prices of important traded goods as well as for forecasting possible future changes in such prices. Wholesale and retail prices for domestic goods and services will normally be available from central statistical offices as part of the data necessary for compiling national income and expenditure but the breakdown of goods and services into their various cost components will typically be more difficult to obtain. *Production census* figures used for national income purposes usually show value-added by product broken down into wages and profits. In decomposing non-traded goods, *input-output tables* may be of some use, but typically these are too aggregative to provide anything more than a rough indication of the lines along which further research needs to take place. Finally, *household expenditure surveys* will be particularly useful in providing data on consumption patterns (by region and income group) necessary for valuing labour.

6.12 *Further Reading*

The original characterisation of the difference between the OECD and UNIDO approaches to the treatment of potentially traded goods is P. Dasgupta (1972). Much of the practical work on non-traded commodity valuation has already been mentioned, including the most recent work of Little and Scott (1976) and Scott, MacArthur and Newbery (1976). This is supplemented by a series of current World Bank studies, references to which appear in the text.

Our treatment of the FTER essentially follows Squire and van der Tak (1975), though earlier work may be consulted including Balassa and Schydlowsky (1968), Balassa (1971), Bacha and Taylor (1971), Batra and Guisinger (1974), Balassa (1974). The approaches are well summarised in Lal (1974a), and more compactly in Lal (1974b).

On the more general problem of effective protection and its measurement which lies behind much of the present thinking on efficiency pricing, there is a large body of literature stemming from the 1960s. Extensive coverage of these problems, both theoretical and empirical, is to be found variously in Corden (1971), Balassa (1971) and Little, Scitovsky and Scott (1970).

Optimal tariff theory is discussed in any of the standard texts on international trade theory of which a better known example is Kindleberger (1969). A particularly useful early paper on the pure theory is by Mrs Robinson (1951), while the recent debate on 'unequal exchange' stems from Emmanuel (1972).

Current debates on centralised and decentralised planning under Soviet socialism are well summarised in Ellman (1972).

VII

ECONOMIC PRICING OF FACTORS OF PRODUCTION

7.01 *Introduction*

In the present chapter we examine the economic pricing of factors of production: labour, land and capital. Here the discussion centres initially on the concept of foregone output, the treatment of labour requiring a brief excursion into aspects of labour market theory. The problem of valuing land (including both renewable and non-renewable resources) is examined briefly in the context of the 'with/without project' situation. In looking at capital, attention is first drawn to definitional problems, and some simple theory is introduced to relate notions of time preference, marginal productivity, and the interest rate. The STP vs. SOC debate is introduced and seen to relate to the distinction between efficiency and social pricing. It is argued that because the concept of a social discount rate is ultimately related to the effective power (or lack of power) of the public sector, the notion of 'efficiency' price must implicitly assume either that global savings and its distribution between private and public sectors is optimal, or else ignore the question altogether. Finally some reasons are given for treating the economic discount rate as a pure rationing device. The chapter concludes with a brief section on measuring the effective cost of adding to public financial resources through borrowing.

7.02 *Valuing Factors of Production*

Classical and neo-classical theory distinguish three main factors of production — labour, land and capital — commanding remuneration in the form of wages, rent and interest (profits) respectively. Price formation takes place in factor markets where, in the absence of imperfections, prices of each factor reflect their marginal contribution to final output. But orthodox neo-classical theory goes one step further in asserting that since factor prices reflect marginal productivities, factors must therefore be receiving their 'just' reward. Since the remuneration of factors determines the distribution of income, it follows that the prevailing distribution of income must be 'just'.

At one level, the argument is merely circular since it is possible to reverse the direction of causality and argue that the prevailing distribution of income determines marginal factor productivities. More importantly, the notion of *rewards* is fundamentally misleading; i.e. labour is rewarded for working, capitalists are rewarded for 'waiting', etc. Basically, the worker's wage reflects his cost of maintenance just as in the case of a machine or a piece of land. Machines and land (or other natural resources) become productive when combined with labour, and it is the ownership of machines and land (or the finance to acquire these) and the bargaining position of their owners relative to workers which determines how the surplus is apportioned. Capitalist profit and landlord rent can therefore be decomposed into maintenance cost (keeping capital intact), payment for managerial services (which is basically a wage), and surplus. In speaking of factor payments, one must be careful to keep these concepts distinct.

The marginal concepts of neo-classical economics, purged of these normative elements, do retain an important value particularly at the project level with which we are concerned. For here one is concerned with pricing quantities of physical goods or services (including labour) which are small relative to total volume available. More precisely, one is concerned with estimating the cost of shifting factors at the margin between one occupation and another, hence the importance of 'output foregone' or opportunity cost.[1]

7.03 *The Economic Cost of Unskilled Labour as a Project Input*

For the purposes of financial analysis, the cost of employing an extra worker is his wage. For the purposes of economic analysis, though, two questions must be asked. First, does the going wage accurately reflect opportunity cost (i.e. output foregone as a result of shifting him out of his previous employment) and, next, is the foregone economic value of output correctly measured at domestic prices. Having adopted the LMST convention of pricing output at its foreign exchange equivalent value and explaining how this is done in practice, one may concentrate on the first question.[2]

The discussion until now has been concerned primarily with trade distortions. The question of whether the wage accurately reflects opportunity cost (at domestic consumption value) introduces a second magnitude of market

1 The notion of opportunity cost is not wholly clear in the literature, as it can variously be interpreted to mean that output foregone in the activity from which a factor is drawn, or output foregone in the optimal alternative employment. A useful distinction to make is between 'predictive opportunity cost' and 'ideal opportunity cost'. This will be seen as a problem of the 'second best', and operationally one can only use the term in the 'predictive' sense.

2 See Chapter 5, section 5.02 on the 'trade efficiency' value of labour.

imperfection into the analysis. Imperfections in the labour market have, indeed, been a subject of debate for some years in economic theory, and more particularly in the development literature where the problem of wage market inefficiency constitutes a field of specialisation in itself. Very generally, the problem is stated as follows. Unskilled wages in urban industrial occupations in LDCs are typically very much higher than casual agricultural wages. On the premises of neo-classical theory, this should not be so since rural workers should migrate to the modern sector and bid down industrial wages to a level such that real wages in both sectors are equivalent and migration ceases. However, while migration is observed, the real wage differential between the modern sector and the traditional sector persists, and migrants swell the ranks of the partially employed urban slum dwellers belonging to the 'urban informal sector'. Moreover, wages in agriculture, while lower than those in modern industry, and even those in the urban informal sector, are not low enough to absorb the whole of the rural work force into permanent employment. Hence, when one creates extra unskilled employment in the modern sector (since any large project may by definition be thought of as coming under the modern sector) then, to the extent that workers are drawn directly or indirectly from agriculture, the wage actually paid on the project (W) will overstate the worker's net contribution to production (m) in his previous occupation, assuming that he was employed at all.

Various theories have been put forward to deal with this apparent perversity in the operation of the labour market. One variety of theory, now generally discredited, concentrates on 'backward bending supply curves' and the 'disutility of effort' which, loosely interpreted, means that if the rural (or urban) unemployed fail to bid down modern sector wages it is merely that they place a high value on leisure. Another variety of theory, originally put forward by Mazumdar (1965) but more recently elaborated with ingenuity by Todaro (1969) and Harris and Todaro (1970), sees the migrant weighing the certainty of earning a given rural wage against the probability of earning a higher urban wage, hence maintaining an 'equilibrium' differential between traditional and modern sector wage rates.[1] Still others, for example Harberger (1971), argue that modern sector wages are maintained artificially high by trade unions, while the apparent difference between real wages in agriculture and the urban informal sector can be explained largely by maintenance costs

---

1 This has the interesting corollary that the creation of an extra job by marginally changing the subjective probability assessment of all potential migrants, may bring more than one migrant into the urban sector, thus increasing urban unemployment and discouraging further migrants.

(rent, transport, food, etc.) differentials between town and country.[1]

Another set of arguments relates to the extent and nature of rural unemployment and underemployment *per se*. Early writers such as Nurkse (1957) saw the existence of rural 'disguised' unemployment as evidence for arguing that the opportunity cost of withdrawing labour from agriculture was close to zero, a view broadly consistent with the 'unlimited supply of labour' notion advanced by Lewis (1954). The view was later challenged from several quarters, most polemically perhaps by Schultz (1964). Much work has been done in defining the concept of agricultural underemployment in more precise terms, the importance of seasonal variations in employment demand and slack season occupations now being generally accepted and, hence, the 'zero marginal product' view largely abandoned. A useful interpretation, advanced by Sen (1966), is that underemployment exists in the sense that rural workers can withdraw with little loss in output where others can work longer hours; i.e. marginal labour time is 'underemployed' rather than men.

These issues are worth reviewing briefly in the present context because one's approach to the interpretation and measurement of opportunity cost is influenced by the weight given to different authors' arguments. Formally, the 'efficiency shadow wage rate' (SWR), or what is more appropriately termed the *economic wage rate* (EWR), is defined as:

$$EWR = m.AR_m \qquad \qquad .... \qquad (7.1)$$

where m is the product foregone, and AR_m is the conversion factor translating m (measured in market prices) into foreign exchange equivalent.[2] The definition is simple enough. In practice, everything depends on how one estimates m.

For those whose view of the labour market is essentially in line with neoclassical theory, the best estimator of m is the wage. However, for a modern sector project, there are broadly four categories of average unskilled wage rates to choose between: W_m (the modern sector wage), W_i (the informal sec-

1 There is also what might loosely be called the 'classical' interpretation which sees the modern/traditional wage rate differential in the first instance as institutionally determined. Low traditional wages provide the surplus for industrialisation through ensuring cheap wage goods (food) to the modern sector, migrant labour, and rentier transfers of savings, the relative importance of these different modes of surplus extraction and transfer varying according to the particular institutional setting. As the modern sector grows in size, agriculture is gradually capitalised and real output per worker increases; ultimately the whole of agriculture is brought into the modern sector and the real wage differential disappears.

2 Squire and van der Tak (1975) use slightly different notational conventions. A conversion factor, β_1, is defined such that $\beta_1 = EWR/W$; EWR is then defined as $EWR = m.\beta_c$ where β_c is the conversion factor for labour's consumption used as a proxy for what we have called AR_m, the conversion factor for labour's foregone output.

tor wage), W_a (the average agricultural wage for the sector as a whole), and W_{ca} (the wage for casual agricultural labour) where $W_m > W_i > W_a > W_{ca}$.

Setting m equal to W_m, the procedure adopted in financial analysis, is equivalent to assuming that the new job is filled by drawing labour from a similar occupation elsewhere in the modern sector and that there are no further migration effects. Alternatively, it may be argued along Harris and Todaro (1970) lines that $m = W_a$ and that the creation of an extra modern sector job induces more than one worker out of agriculture such that total opportunity cost is W_m — see Lal (1973). $W_i = m$ is the view adopted by Harberger (1971), the essence of his argument being that the apparent differential between W_i and W_{ca} is illusory. This view really amounts to saying that although the extra worker is ultimately drawn from the rural sector, his economic cost consists of both foregone output *and* net additional resource claims on urban services from which he derives no net welfare gain. An alternative is to set $m = W_a$, where W_a is defined as total agricultural value added divided by the agricultural work force. This has the advantage that W_a can be estimated from national income data, but it amounts to asserting either that there is equal income and work sharing (as might be the case where agriculture consisted entirely of family farms) *and* that remaining family members do not increase their output after migration, or that such an increase in output is exactly offset by the disutility of extra effort which accompanies it to which society should give weight. Finally, one may let $m = W_{ca}$. Unfortunately, W_{ca} varies considerably between regions and between seasons, and since subsistence sets a lower bound on its value, there may be many more workers seeking employment at some times of year at this wage than can be accommodated. Thus, m may be lower than W_{ca}.

Current orthodoxy is to take the latter view and to attempt to derive m (ideally by region) by weighting W_{ca} by some estimate of the degree of underemployment. Hence Bruce (1976) suggests the following definition:

$$m = \frac{\sum\limits_{i}^{n} (D_i/S_i).W_i}{n} \qquad \ldots \qquad (7.2)$$

where:

  W_i is the monthly casual wage rate;
  S_i is the monthly supply of casual labour;
  D_i is monthly demand for casual employment;
  n   is the number of months (or time periods if above figures are expressed on some other time basis).

Other suggestions have also been made along similar lines. Little and Mirrlees (1974) have suggested observing variations in the daily casual wage rate over the year and taking a seasonally weighted average, multiplying this seasonally weighted daily wage by the estimated average number of man-days worked per annum in the region. Finally, a very crude estimate of m may be derived by calculating average value added per man in agriculture (W_a) and simply halving it.

As to estimating AR_m, in principle one will need to estimate the composition of the representative bundle of agricultural output foregone. Regional agricultural production data will normally provide a reasonable basis on which to do this, but in the absence of such information Squire and van der Tak have recommended applying the conversion factor for *rural* workers' consumption, AR_{rc} (β_{rc}), on the grounds that, in rural subsistence areas at least, production and consumption patterns are reasonably similar.

7.04 *Skilled Labour*

The economic cost of skilled labour is in principle estimated in exactly the same way as for unskilled labour. The significant difference, though, is that there is more general agreement in the literature that skilled labour's wage reflects its marginal product reasonably accurately. There are two reasons for so arguing. One is that skilled labour is more specific, often being highly mobile in nature and circulating in a well organised modern sector market where wages tend to be competitive and full employment is the rule. Hence there is no problem, as with unskilled workers, of determining what the net migration effect is of withdrawing a unit of skilled labour from its present occupation. Secondly, the supply of skilled labour is increasingly equated to its present and future demand by the use of 'manpower planning' techniques which has the virtue of minimising discrepancies between supply and demand, and hence relieving the price mechanism of part of the burden of adjustment.[1]

Against this line of argument it can be claimed that certain types of skilled labour (particularly professional salary earners) are in a position to exert considerable influence on their level of remuneration, in part through trade union and professional organisations, and in part through the more general political and cultural conventions which relate earnings to 'status' rather than productivity. Undoubtedly this argument contains a strong element of truth as will be apparent to any undergraduate who has ever had to write an essay on why university lecturers earn more than dustmen. Moreover, the suggestion that the price mechanism efficiently equates supply and demand when manpower plans go wrong seems to be refuted by the experience of certain countries (viz. Sri Lanka) where an oversupply of university graduates in certain professions has not been mopped up by a fall in levels of remuner-

1   See FitzGerald (1976a).

ation. On balance, valuing skilled labour at its wage (translated into foreign exchange at the appropriate AR) involves something of an element of judgement, particularly when dealing with professional categories.

Two further points are worth noting which apply to most types of projects. Firstly, while there may be some doubt about whether the going wage (or salary) of skilled labour drawn from other sectors of the economy accurately reflects its opportunity cost, in the case of imported labour, wage (or salary) *is* the relevant concept. The cost of an imported man is here treated exactly like the cost of an imported good. Secondly, to the extent that a project provides on-the-job training which transforms an unskilled man into a skilled one, one might be tempted to treat this as part of the economic wage determination exercise. The more appropriate procedure, however, is to treat the 'cost of training' and the 'benefits of training' as separate elements. In some cases these can be assumed to offset each other, and therefore the further calculation becomes unnecessary.

7.05 *Labour: Special Cases*

There are a number of other areas in which the value of labour figures in applied cost-benefit analysis but is not treated as an input. Here, rather, the problem is to value labour as a productive asset. One approach to educational investment suggests treating the return to investment as the present value of the extra stream of earnings he may expect to receive as a result of extra education — see, for example, Blaug (1968). Such an approach has been criticised on various grounds, one being that part of the benefit of education is an intangible 'consumption' benefit not amenable to measurement, and another that it is wealth which gives access to education and not the other way round.

Another difficult area is that of assessing the value of human life. Recent litigation arising out of the Turkish Airlines DC-10 disaster has involved voluminous reports citing different principles. Still another area is that of assessing the value of 'time saved' as where, for example, a motorway decreases a journey time thus benefitting users in the form of extra leisure or extra time to work. The application of cost-benefit methods has undoubtedly been of use in improving the conceptualisation of such problems, and in some cases has produced quantitative results of sufficient validity to decisively affect the accept/reject decision, as for example in the case of London's Victoria Line. Often, however, the urge to quantify merely taxes the credibility of the subject. One may cite the apocryphal story of the £150 per week construction worker who fell from the top storey of London's Post Office Tower. One side argued that his widow should receive lump sum compensation equivalent to his discounted expected lifetime earnings stream plus a bonus for 'psychic' loss; the other side argued that since the wage implicitly included an 'acceptable' risk premium to the worker, his widow should receive nothing.

7.06 The Valuation of Land

The valuation of land is usually omitted from books on project appraisal, presumably because much recent work has been concerned with industrial projects.[1] For some types of projects though – typically in agriculture and transport – land costs may form a significant amount of the total. Moreover, the generic meaning of the term covers not merely land *per se*, but other natural resources such as forests, fishing reserves and mineral deposits. Consequently, it is worth briefly examining the principles which govern economic as opposed to financial evaluation.

In principle, the capital value of land is the discounted value of the stream of future earnings which it can command, net of the cost of purchased inputs and labour; i.e. it is the capitalised rental element. This means that the value of land varies as a function of expectations about its future use. Where there is a free market in land, the market price will reflect purchasers' assessment of these future net earnings; viz. in the case of urban building land, if it is thought that zoning regulations will in future permit the construction of luxury office blocks, shopping centres, etc., the value of land will rise. Similarly in the case of 'land' in the natural resource sense, the expectation that future mineral prices will be high will raise the present financial value. This is why presently idle land can be held as a profitable speculative asset. In other situations, the use and disposition of land may be determined exclusively by social structure and tradition – as in the case of communally-owned tribal grazing land – and hence there may be no market place at all. In still other cases, where the private market for land is relatively narrow, a degree of collusion may exist in keeping land values artificially low so as to reduce tax liability, a situation not uncommon in certain regions of Latin America. In short, while the valuation of land is based upon best expectations about the future net returns to which it gives rise, the market price of land is not always useful as a guide to economic valuation.

For land, just as for labour, one wants to determine the foreign exchange value of the stream of net output foregone as a result of taking land out of one use and transferring it into another. This is normally implicitly achieved in the case of land by defining net project benefit as the difference between

1   A good discussion of land valuation in practice can be found in Scott, MacArthur and Newbery (1976), Chapter 15.

the 'with' and 'without' project situation. Suppose that it is planned to invest 500 kobos of foreign exchange per acre in creating an irrigated settlement scheme growing rice which presently has to be imported. At present, farming is based on a mixture of cash and subsistence crops and land ownership rights are vested in the kinship group. Present net returns per acre are valued at K.100 foreign exchange equivalent and productivity has traditionally been stagnant. The new scheme is expected to result in first year net benefits of K.150 in net foreign exchange, productivity rising thereafter at a rate of 5% (compound) per annum. Figure 7.1 illustrates the basis of the calculation showing the expected future net benefit streams in the 'with' and 'without' situations. Subtracting the latter from the former, an incremental net benefit stream is obtained for the assumed 40-year life of the project which, discounted at, say, 20% results in a negative NPV (minus 121 Kobos per acre); hence the project should not be undertaken, or at best will require further work to ascertain whether an improved version would be worthwhile.

Figure 7.1 *'With' and 'Without' Project Benefits*

Figures in Kobos per acre	0	1	2	3	4	....	40
(1) Net benefits in present use	100	100	100	100	100		100
(2) Net benefits in project use	–500	150	155	161	167		2057
(3) Incremental net benefits	–400	50	55	61	67		1357
NPV at 20%	–121						

An alternative way of handling the problem would be to treat the economic cost of land as the present value of net benefits in present use (row 1) and add this figure to the capital cost (K.500 per acre) appearing in year zero, which would give the same result. The central point, however, is that there are two different types of predictions to be made. The prediction of the 'with project' situation may be reasonably straightforward where agronomic evidence of productivity improvements under scheme conditions is 'hard'. The prediction for the 'without project' situation will be more problematic, particularly if there is reason to believe that traditional practices and institutions are under pressure and are undergoing rapid change. In short, the valuation of land will require forecasting not merely technical and economic variables but a variety of other factors which, by their very nature, may be difficult to quantify and predict.

While land *per se* is a renewable resource, in the sense that its productivity can be maintained by avoiding overcropping and/or replenishing the supply of soil nutrients,[1] some resources (such as mineral deposits, oil and natural gas) are non-renewable. This raises special problems of valuing use of the resource, since using more now means that less will be available in future. Hence the foreign exchange equivalent value of, say, an extra barrel of domestically produced and consumed oil is not simply its opportunity cost as an import or export; rather its value depends on how future oil prices are expected to move. In essence, if the discounted real present value of a barrel of future oil is greater than the present border price, one should be storing one's oil in the ground.[2]

7.07 *The Valuation of Capital and the Accounting Rate of Interest*

As noted earlier, the term 'capital' is often used in an ambiguous manner. The essential distinction is between capital as a stock of existing machines in production, and as 'finance' (or savings) which can be used to purchase machines in future. The valuation of existing capital stock is a complex subject which, besides raising problems of definition and measurement, opens a set of theoretical issues the major positions on which now constitute a dividing line between neo-classical and 'radical' economists.[3] For present purposes, the valuation of *existing* capital stock can be ignored and one may concentrate on the valuation of capital at the margin. In one sense, this is a simple problem since the valuation of an extra machine is simply its foreign exchange cost. The central problem, though, is that of assessing the 'opportunity cost' of tying up finance (foreign exchange viewed as savings) in the machine, and what alternative yield could be realised on funds used for other purposes in the public or private sectors. This in turn raises the question of whether the private sector is generating sufficient savings (investment) and, if not, what constraints exist on raising the rate of accumulation to a level compatible with the 'optimal' trade-off between present and future consumption.

A simplified way of characterising the problem (taken from Ricardo) is as follows. Suppose the economy to consist of a single farmer growing corn for consumption and saving part of his corn for planting next year's crop. Initially he divides his harvest into two parts: one which is just large enough to meet his subsistence consumption needs in the coming year (which we shall

1 The same logic applies to fisheries and forests.
2 Hence the meaning of Sheik Yamani's remark that 'Oil in the ground is more valuable than money in the bank'.
3 This is the subject of the so-called 'Cambridge controversy' (Cambridge, England vs. Cambridge, USA) which is summarised in Harcourt and Laing (1971).

now ignore) and another which is a residual. If he wanted to maximise next year's output, he would plant the whole of the residual corn. However, being a good marginalist, he performs the following calculation.

One unit of 'residual' corn will produce $(1 + q)$ units of corn next year where q is the marginal product of 'corn capital' and tends to decline as more corn is planted.[1] Alternatively, he would be 'subjectively indifferent' between consuming one unit of corn this year and $(1 + i)$ units next year, i tending to be larger the greater his present hunger. His decision about how to divide the residual pile is thus determined by two kinds of information; one his 'subjective rate of time preference' schedule, and the other his 'objective' productivity of capital schedule. He will ultimately divide the corn such that, at the margin, $i = q$.

In generalising this story to apply to a realistic economic setting in which there are many investors and consumers and many different goods, earlier neo-classical theory saw the rate of interest as performing this equilibrating function.[2] However, since Keynes, this view has been largely abandoned and the role of the State in ensuring that sufficient investment takes place has tended to be stressed increasingly, particularly in the development literature. Just how the State (or more precisely Treasury officials and their Minister) is presumed to determine society's 'rate of social time preference' is something of a vexed question, but more will be said about this in the chapter on 'social' pricing. Suffice it to say that for the purposes of economic pricing, one possible assumption is that the global savings/investment rate is implicitly deemed adequate. If this is so, two things seem to follow. The first is that a unit of potential investment (foreign exchange) and a unit of consumption can be considered equally valuable. This does not mean incidently that the foreign exchange *numeraire* is to be abandoned but rather that a marginal 'border peso' can be indifferently allocated between raising investment and raising consumption. The second is that if, *ex hypothesi*, $i = q$, q can be taken as a reasonable measure of the rate at which future consumption can be discounted into present value terms. But how does one define q (marginal public or private yield) and how does one measure it?

Before continuing these remarks, though, a brief word on terminological conventions will be in order. The terms 'accounting rate of interest' (ARI) and 'consumption rate of interest' (CRI or often simply i) have been mentioned in several earlier sections. The CRI measures the rate at which the value of one unit of average consumption in successive future years falls relative to a present unit. The ARI measures the rate at which the unit value of future investment falls. Since, for the moment, we are assuming investment

1 One may imagine that the more corn he plants, the more he has to move onto stonier ground where yields are low.
2 The classical exposition is to be found in Irving Fisher (1930).

and average consumption equally valuable at the margin, the CRI and ARI are equal. Finally, one may distinguish between 'investment in general' and 'investment in Government hands' as *numeraire*. Although it is possible that global investment may be adequate, its division between public and private sector may not be considered optimal. Once again, this is a matter which will be further discussed and for the moment one may start by assuming that marginal value of:

Consumption $\cong$ Investment $\cong$ Public Investment

For convenience (and following ST conventions) let the discount rate for economic evaluation be called the Economic Accounting Rate of Interest (EARI) where, as a first approximation,

$$EARI = q.AR_q \qquad \qquad .... \qquad (7.3)$$

and q is the marginal product of capital measured at domestic prices and AR_q the accounting ratio transforming domestic into foreign exchange equivalent value. Unfortunately, defining and measuring the marginal product of capital raises serious difficulties. In principle, it is the rate of return on the marginal project in the economy estimated using the conventions described so far in this book. In practice, a variety of different approaches have been suggested.

One approach is to treat q as the 'economy wide' marginal product of capital using national income data (UNIDO); here one looks at the projected output capital ratio for the next planning period subtracting the wage bill from output. A variant of this approach is to estimate the elasticity of output with respect to changes in capital using an aggregate production function approach.[1] The conventional approach in the early SCBA literature is to treat q as the opportunity cost of public borrowing at the margin or what is called the social opportunity cost (SOC). Alternative methods for estimating SOC have variously included direct estimates of rates of return in private industry, tax incidence weighted averages of real rates of return on private investment and saving, or weighted average interest rates. A common questionable feature of all these approaches is that they assume that the 'revealed preferences' of many different individuals and firms acting in the market can be taken as evidence for what individuals as citizens would regard collective interests to be – see Sen (1967) – hence the alternative notion of some social time preference rate (STP) which would in general be lower than the SOC. These arguments are resumed in detail by Feldstein (1973). The STP approach is indeed part of the conceptual basis adopted by OECD (1968) and

1   See, for example, Yang (1975).

UNIDO (1972) in which the distinction is fully drawn between treating investment at a premium in relation to consumption and choosing of discount rate. (This is dealt with in the chapter which follows.)

A different approach is to ignore q altogether, treating the discount rate instead as a rationing device. According to this line of reasoning, the function of the discount rate is not to measure the rate at which 'society' values future in relation to present consumption (investment); indeed, some would argue that the whole notion is 'metaphysical' to use Mrs. Robinson's term.[1] Rather, it is to ensure that the total number of public projects undertaken does not exceed available investment funds.

Figure 7.2 will help to illustrate the principles involved. Let us suppose the total supply of funds to the public sector to be shown by PS. Public sector investment demand (a series of candidate projects ranked in declining order of profitability) is shown by the schedule DD. If PS is total available public sector savings, only projects along segment DA of the demand curve can be carried out, EARI being set such that the marginal project (point A) will have an NPV of zero. Suppose, though, that a further net increase in public savings equivalent to SS' were made available. At discount rate EARI all projects along segment AB of the demand curve would have a negative NPV; the discount rate must therefore be lowered to EARI' if these further projects are to be passed to make use of extra available funds. Here, the EARI is equal to the marginal rate of return (q) on *public* investment.

Figure 7.2 *The Accounting Rate of Interest as a Rationing Device*

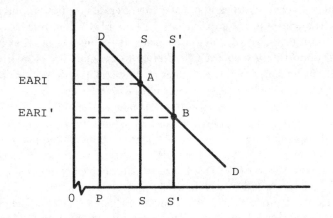

It follows that if the supply of public sector investment funds is extremely limited, the equilibrium discount rate used to ration investment may possibly exceed the opportunity cost of funds (q) in the private sector More likely, though, public sector marginal rates of return will be lower than those in the private sector because public authorities are charged with undertaking 'non-commercial' types of projects. It is sometimes argued that the 'balance' of public and private shares in total investment must be changed on the grounds of increasing 'efficiency' through the equation of marginal rates of return in both sectors.[1] But more will be said on this in speaking of 'social' pricing.

In summary, one might argue that economic analysis is the special case of 'social' analysis in which global savings is deemed 'optimal'. There is then a further question about whether 'optimal' global savings is correctly apportioned between the private and public sectors. But although some economists might interpret efficiency as requiring public and private rates of return to be equated at the margin, there are both theoretical and practical reasons for rejecting such a view. Alternatively, one may assume that for the purposes of economic analysis 'optimal savings' considerations are ignored and hence the appropriate discount rate is simply whatever 'equilibrium' rate prevails.

A related aspect is the choice of investment decision rules. In the first chapter, the question of ranking projects was discussed and related to the choice of an equilibrium discount rate, the general argument being that as long as an equilibrium rate was selected, NPV was an adequate criterion. (This was also seen to hold true for mutually exclusive projects.) It may in some

---

1 Returning to the Ricardian example, we may now imagine the economy as consisting of two farmers both growing corn, one 'capitalist' (the private sector) and the other 'socialist' (the public sector). On neo-classical grounds one would argue that total investment is optimal where q_p (private sector corn interest rate) equals q_s (socialist sector). Where the socialist farm is small in relation to the private one, the former must rely on the latter to lend it corn, and hence the socialist sector discount rate can never fall below the capitalist sector's q, or revealed market rate of time preference. This is the essence of the neo-classical (SOC) position. The socialist farmer may respond by saying that this richer colleague discounts the future too highly, and that he (the State) must assume responsibility for long term corn provision hence leading to $q_s < q_p$ (STP argument) which is financed by 'optimal' taxation. Alternatively, if he is a good Marxist, the socialist farmer may wish to abolish private property altogether. If the economy as a whole is relatively poor and the capitalist farmer exploitative and inefficient, the latter position may make good sense. In this event, one forgets about determining some ultimate measure of the rate of time indifference and concentrates on raising the rate of investment subject to all farmers and their families having enough corn for their basic requirements. At the rate of saving set by the new revolutionary Government, the discount rate will only be useful insofar as it is necessary to supplement central planning with some way of checking that branch level investment decisions are consistent with available finance.

cases be difficult, for a variety of practical reasons, to ensure that the current public sector rate is effectively an equilibrium rate. For example, the planned supply of public sector investment funds may be critically influenced by incorrect expectations about aid availability, or the growth of fiscal revenue, or else may change abruptly for political reasons. Where the discount rate cannot be taken as an equilibrium rate, second best 'ranking' criteria such as PV/K (or NPV/K) may need to be applied measuring the efficiency of resource use with respect to available current finance.

Ultimately one may argue that at the core of the choice of discount rate discussion is a mistaken emphasis on attempting to arrive at 'first best' solutions which render macro- and micro-level planning decisions (as well as the public-private balance of investment) perfectly consistent. Indeed the way to ensure such consistency does not lie in continuing to refine parameters such that the burden of achieving growth, efficiency and equity can safely be left in the hands of the project planner. Rather it is only to the extent that the State is both able to set the broad priorities of public policy through the planning process and secure the necessary finance to implement its aims that public investment decisions need tight co-ordination. Such co-ordination will take place predominantly through the administration of the planning effort and the careful elaboration of sectoral targets. This in itself will help ensure that inefficient projects are avoided. Where, on the other hand, the State has only a marginal role to play in investment planning, many of the indicated refinements, while undoubtedly providing well-paid jobs for the initiated, will have little influence on the overall direction of the economy.

7.08 *The Effective Cost of Foreign Borrowing*

Since the 'equilibrium' EARI is determined by total available public finance in a given year relative to the number of projects competing for funds, a related question is that of the conditions under which it pays to supplement domestically mobilised public savings by recourse to foreign borrowing. In principle it would seem that, where the mobilisation of domestic finance for public investment is constrained by tax or other reasons, it should be possible to supplement domestic funds with 'aid' in order to raise the volume of savings to the desired level.[1] In practice there are two complications. The first is that official development assistance is subject to a complex system of country quotas, often specifying types of project acceptable, such that suf-

1   This is the essence of the 'savings gap' argument which has been challenged on various grounds by Bauer (1966) and by Griffin (1970), the latter arguing that increased borrowing may lead to an offsetting fall in domestic savings.

ficient extra funds may not be available to significantly lower the EARI.[1] Second, and more simply, 'aid' may be too expensive.

One advantage of LMST is that, since project values are expressed in terms of foreign exchange equivalent, the benefits and costs of aid are directly commensurate. It should therefore be possible to compare the economic rate of return of projects directly with the cost of borrowing. But the effective cost of borrowing may differ significantly from its nominal cost. For one thing, bi-lateral aid is often tied to purchases in the donor country and prices quoted for aid-financed purchases may be significantly above world market prices.[2] For another, obtaining development assistance for projects may involve significant delay, a not untypical figure being one or two years in contrast to commercial credit which is normally available within weeks. The relative merits of different forms of credit is a subject well beyond the scope of the present discussion and in the present section we confine ourselves to examining a few simple principles relevant to calculating the effective costs of aid.

Suppose that a country wishes to finance a project which, at the equilibrium rate of discount (assumed to be 10 percent) has an NPV of $0.60 million and a capital cost of $1.20 million. Its options are to borrow the money commercially or seek bilateral assistance. Assume that commercial credit is available at 10 percent, repayment to be made over five years with no grace period, and the money is available immediately. The alternative option involves a government loan at seven percent with a 10 year repayment period and five year grace period (during which only interest is paid). Superficially it would seem that the latter terms are preferable and that the bilateral option should be taken.

On closer investigation, however, it turns out that the average delay period for government assistance in question is two years, and that aid is 'tied' to donor suppliers quoting prices 25 percent above those of alternative manufacturers. Two calculations must be performed. The first is to calculate that 'cost of delay' if bilateral aid is sought for the project which is simply the difference between the project's NPV if it were done immediately and its NPV if it were set back two years in the future, or:

$0.60 m - $0.60 m (0.826) = $0.10 m

where (0.826) is the discount factor for 10 percent two years hence. The second is to compute the rate of return which equates the effective cost of

---

1   It can also be argued that recipients make an assumption of the likely availability of aid in calculating the EARI. They may then find, in calculating the real cost of such aid, that some projects passed at the EARI turn out to be uneconomic when aid financed.
2   The seminal work in this field is Mahbub ul Haq (1967).

loan repayment (including delay cost) with the capital cost of the project (£1.20 m).[1]

Figure 7.3 shows the basis of calculation of the second step. Assume that the capital cost consists entirely of equipment purchased abroad. If tying involves paying prices for equipment 25 percent above world price, then to finance $1.2 m. worth of capital investment, $1.5 m. will have to be borrowed ($1.2 m x 1.25). Row (1) shows the money borrowed while rows (2) and (4) show the loan amortisation and interest repayment schedules respectively which, added together, give the total repayment schedule (row 5). To this stream must be added the cost of delay (row 6) which gives the total cost stream for the loan (row 7).[2] The discount rate which equates the stream of loan costs of the project when financed bilaterally with the capital cost is 12.5 percent. In short, the effective internal rate of return on the loan is

Figure 7.3 *Calculating the Effective Rate of Interest on Foreign Borrowing*

Years	All figures in $ x 10^3										
	0	1	2	3	4	5	6	7	8	9	10
(1) Capital borrowed	1500										
(2) Capital repayment							300	300	300	300	300
(3) Balance outstanding		1500	1500	1500	1500	1500	1200	900	600	300	
(4) Interest paid (7%)		105	105	105	105	105	105	84	63	42	21
(5) Capital + interest		105	105	105	105	105	405	384	363	342	321
(6) Cost of delay	100										
(7) Total cost of loan	100	105	105	105	105	105	405	384	363	342	321

(8) PV of row (7) at 12.5% $\cong$ 1200

nearly twice the nominal interest rate and, in this case, Government would do better to finance the loan internally or take commercial credit (alternatives between which Government is assumed to be indifferent in this case) than to seek 'aid'.

1   This is, so to speak, the IRR of the loan and may be compared with the country's EARI. Alternatively, the NPV of the loan could be calculated.
2   All flows are assumed to be at constant foreign exchange prices.

7.09 *Data Sources*

The valuation of unskilled labour's foregone output, as has been said, will depend on what view one takes of the operation of the labour market and on the particular circumstances of the country. Figures on average casual wage rates can normally be got from survey data. Official estimates of regional unemployment are usually risky unless one has some knowledge of the way in which sample surveys have been carried out. *Per contra*, skilled wage rates are usually well reported. Land valuation figures can normally be obtained from local tax offices though, for the purposes of economic analysis, *farm budget surveys* supplemented by direct observation will be necessary. Finally, on the choice of discount rate, we have argued that the appropriate figure is what the Planning Office takes this to be. Although this may be supplemented by calculations on the effective cost of foreign borrowing, few governments carry out such calculations in practice. Inspection of domestic interest rate structures, normally reviewed regularly in Central Bank publications, are useful only insofar as one feels the need to delve further into the question of how Government sets the discount rate.

7.10 *Further Reading*

The term 'disguised unemployment' was first coined by Joan Robinson (1936), and applied to the development context by various writers including Lewis and Nurske cited above, and also Eckaus (1955), Georgescu-Roegen (1963) and Leibenstein (1957). Early empirical studies are associated with Mellor and Stevens (1956) and Rosenstein-Rodan (1957). The early debate is best summarised in Kao et al (1964). Rural-urban migration theory springs from the early notion of social dualism advanced, amongst others, by Boeke (1954). A recent contribution illustrating the complexities of the current debate initiated by Todaro is to be found in Stiglitz (1974), while Marglin (1976) contains a more general theoretical discussion of valuation in a labour surplus economy as well as an interesting incursion into questions of political economy.

The classical exposition on interest rates is that already mentioned by Fisher (1930), but the debate on the public sector discount rate emerges in part from the early literature in water resource development of which well known examples are Eckstein (1958) and Krutilla and Eckstein (1958), and in part from the theoretical development literature on optimum saving such as Tinbergen (1956) and Dobb (1960). Feldstein (1964) reviews the SOC vs. STP debate at an early stage while Feldstein (1973) reviews the issues which later emerged. Other important pieces on the opportunity cost notion of the use of public funds include Galenson and Leibenstein (1955), Marglin (1963b), Baumol (1968) and Harberger (1969). Arrow and Kurz (1970) relates at length the interrelationship between optimal savings, optimal fiscal policies, and the public sector discount rate. A lucid discussion of these issues appears in Pearce (1971). In the contemporary context, Scott (1977) discusses setting the test discount rate while the chapter by Newbery in Little & Scott (1976) considers the valuation of private relative to public investment in Kenya.

On the theory of bridging the savings 'gap' by foreign borrowing see Chenery and Strout (1966), while a provocative alternative view is provided by Griffin (1970). These issues are discussed more fully in Mikesell (1968), Byres (1972) and White (1974). A recent paper on evaluating aid flows using current conventions is Lal (1976).

VIII

SOCIAL PRICING, DISTRIBUTION, AND THE PUBLIC SECTOR

8.01 *Introduction*

The present chapter deals with the third and final category of cost-benefit analysis, the 'social' dimension. Just as financial analysis may be thought of as a second-best substitute for economic analysis where market prices incorrectly reflect factor productivity in trade, so economic CBA may be considered as a second-best alternative to social CBA where Government wishes to compensate for inadequate global savings and income inequalities by incorporating explicit distributional objectives into micro-level planning.

The chapter begins by distinguishing the several dimensions of the distributional problem, focusing initially on distribution between contemporaries. The orthodox position on interpersonal utility comparisons is discussed briefly, and the conventional 'efficiency' approach to the measurement of consumption benefits is seen as a special case in which Government values marginal additions to savings at par with marginal additions to the consumption of any income group or region irrespective of whether it is rich or poor. LM and ST approaches to the derivation of income weights are discussed introducing the notion of 'investment standardised' weights and illustrating their conceptualisation and derivation by means of simple examples. Next, the derivation of the 'social wage rate' (SWR) is introduced and possible refinements to the treatment noted, the discussion then relating the SWR to choice of techniques and, ultimately, to the choice of sectoral investment strategy.

A feature of the ST treatment of distribution weights is that these are derived with reference to 'extra consumption in the hands of the average man' (the original UNIDO *numeraire*) and hence average consumption must be translated into the LMST *numeraire* by means of a 'social' accounting ratio, v, or 'value of public income'. The parameter v is the LMST equivalent of the UNIDO 'premium on investment' (P^{inv}) which assumes the normative function of increasing global savings (investment) via choice of technique in accordance with some 'ideal' social discount rate for consumption, the CRI. The analytical distinction between the ideal consumption discount rate, the economic discount rate for investment (EARI), and the social discount rate (SARI) is discussed and the conditions under which these coincide are examined. Attention is then focused briefly on the UNIDO-ST approach to direct estimation of the parameter v, but it is ultimately argued that v and the SARI may be seen as alternative mechanisms for achieving capital budgeting equilibrium. A brief discussion follows on the relationship between the use of distribution weights at micro-level and welfare assumptions implicit in orthodox National Income accounting conventions and, in this context, the essential features of the Chenery et al (1974) approach to poverty weighting is examined and illustrated.

The chapter closes with a critical examination of the role of social cost-benefit analysis in planning, and it is argued essentially that such a role can only be understood within a broader context requiring some notion of the power of the public sector in relation to private interests. More particularly, a distinction is drawn between the use of SCBA as means of achieving consistency between central planning guidelines and enterprise level investment decisions in a decentralised socialist economy, and the use of SCBA in a predominantly capitalist economy where, if constraints on changing commercial and fiscal policies are assumed, the adoption of more sophisticated investment appraisal techniques in the public sector alone is unlikely to have much impact. For most readers, it is argued, understanding SCBA is more likely to be useful because of the nature of the underlying policy questions raised than because of its value as a planning technique.

8.02 Distribution of Benefits between Nationals and Non-Nationals

Traditional cost-benefit theory contains implicit assumptions about the weighting of project benefits, the convention being that all benefits are to count equally 'regardless of to whom they accrue'.[1] The implication is that whether benefits accrue to Government, firms, or private individuals rich or poor, all are given a weight of unity. Historically, the principle marked an important transition from the application of private sector accounting conventions which recognised only receipts accruing directly to the entity in question as 'benefits' since it now became possible, as in the case of, say, an irrigation scheme, to count amongst the benefits both receipts to the scheme

---

1 This was the principle first laid down in the United States Flood Control Act of 1936, and later codified in the Report of the Federal Inter-Agency River Basin Committee (1950).

authority in the form of water charges and extra income (net of charges) to farmers.

The exceptional case is where part of the benefits accrue to foreigners; in principle, such benefits should be given zero weight since it is conventional to confine oneself to national welfare gains as opposed to world welfare gains. A simple illustration of this principle is given in Figure 8.1 which shows hypothetical costs and benefits (expressed in present value terms) for a harbour improvement scheme. Total investment is Dinars 750 m., the bulk of the money coming from the public sector (D.650 m.). Direct returns accrue to three categories of recipient, the public sector (D.100 m.), these benefits being primarily existing user savings 'and the savings to extra shipping traffic

Figure 8.1 *Distribution of Benefits of Harbour Improvement Scheme*

	Domestic Public	Domestic Private	Domestic Total	Foreign Private	Total
Investment	−650	−100	−750	-	−750
Returns	+100	+400	+500	+300	+800
Pre-tax Surplus	−550	+300	−250	+300	+ 50
Tax	+200	−150	+ 50	− 50	-
Post-tax Surplus	−350	+150	−200	+250	+ 50

which the port is expected to draw, a significant part of this traffic being foreign. Toll charges and taxes are expected to siphon-off a part of the returns, D.150 m. and D.50 m. being remitted to Government by the domestic private and foreign private sectors respectively. Whether or not the project is accepted depends critically on the view taken as to whether post-tax net benefits to foreigners are to count; if they are, the net project surplus is D.50 m., while if they are ignored the net domestic loss is D.200 million. In effect the question is whether the 'cost' to the country of a net transfer to foreigners of D.250 million should be offset by the 'benefit' which they enjoy as a result. Governments and international aid agencies sometimes disagree about such questions.

8.03 *Distribution of Benefits between Nationals and SCBA*

If the question of how to treat benefits to foreigners is occasionally important in practice, it is nevertheless of little consequence theoretically since according these benefits zero weight merely follows from the definition of the scope of benefits to be counted. The distribution of benefits amongst nationals, on the other hand, raises theoretical issues, the history of which goes back to the early days of neo-classical theory. At the heart of the theory is an apparent paradox. Since the marginalist approach requires one to assume that the more one has of a good, the less utility one derives from an additional unit, it would seem to follow that total welfare can be increased by redistributing marginal units of a good (or of income in general) from those who have a great deal of it to those with very little; i.e. by moving towards a fully egalitarian distribution of income. Formally, though, such a conclusion only follows if the utility of different individuals is commensurate and all individuals have identical and declining marginal utility functions. By denying the possibility of 'interpersonal utility comparisons', orthodox theory conveniently avoided drawing egalitarian conclusions.[1]

On the other hand, there is one important area in which orthodox theory accepts the legitimacy of interpersonal utility comparisons of a special sort, notably in the operation of the capital market where individuals are presumed to weigh up the relative merits of present consumption as against future consumption which is assumed to include that of future unborn generations. Only on the assumption that the individual is a good judge of other people's welfare in this sense can orthodox theory be made to work.[2] Oddly, it is the connection between the criticisms levelled against this aspect of orthodox capital market theory on the one hand, and on the other the growing body of post-war development literature stressing inadequate savings as a constraint on growth, which served as the nexus for reviving interpersonal comparisons in the form of a value judgement about 'planners time preference' (or STP approach to choice of the public sector discount rate as discussed in the previous chapter).[3]

1   While Marshall appears to have accepted the principle of making interpersonal comparisons, Jevons, Edgeworth, Pareto and later Robbins denied the possibility of so doing. Robbins (1938) quotes Jevons as saying: 'I see no means whereby such comparisons can be accomplished. Every mind is inscrutable to every other mind and no common denomination of feeling is possible.' See Dobb (1969), pp. 80-81.

2   The best known early statement of the problem is that of Professor Pigou (1920) who suggests that 'defective telescopic faculty' may limit the rate of saving.

3   Strictly speaking, there are a number of problems here. The first is that it is difficult to ascribe a clear meaning to 'rational' individual preference for present over future consumption. Arguments about this centre on such factors as imperfect future knowledge, particularly about other individuals' savings intentions, the fact that individuals 'vote' in the capital market according to their wealth, etc. Once the notion of capital market imperfection is established, the problem is conventionally treated as one of finding alternative means of aggregating individual preferences. Since referenda on the ideal interest rate are ruled out, planners must take some decision, justifying it either by reference to the democratic nature of political institutions, or else justifying it by virtue of their accorded role (planners' time preference). Hence, one is using the term 'interpersonal comparison' in a slightly misleading way in this context and should instead refer to difficulties in the *aggregation* of somewhat suspect 'individual' preferences.

In its modern form, the essential idea is that the public sector is charged with the responsibility for making up any shortfall in total savings either by fiscal means or, where there are constraints on the use of these, by 'choice of technique' in project selection. Setting the public sector (consumption) discount rate low relative to the opportunity cost (marginal productivity) of investment funds at the margin — or, equivalently, setting marginal investment at a premium relative to marginal consumption — will encourage the selection of those projects which employ relatively little labour, or in Sen's (1960) terms are 'surplus maximising'.[1] Hence planners are imagined to work with some implicit notion of a socially 'optimal' trade-off between current and future consumption, and it is only a short step to the further question of determining the 'optimal' distribution of consumption between contemporaries. If judgements about the appropriate premium on investment relative to consumption are acceptable, then so too must be judgements about the appropriate premium to attach to extra consumption to the poor relative to extra consumption to the rich. The weighting of consumption benefits, then, has two dimensions; between present and future generation (inter-temporal), and between members of the present generation (intra-temporal).[2] It is the quantification of these further dimensions which constitutes the transition from 'economic' to 'social' cost-benefit analysis.

8.04 *Weighting Incremental Consumption Benefits*

At the level of cost-benefit methodology, the suggestion that current benefits be accorded different weights according to the region or income group to which they accrue is not entirely a new one. Krutilla and Eckstein (1958) suggested that the reciprocals of marginal tax rates might be used as weights while Foster (1966) suggested what is essentially a modern 'elasticity' approach setting n equal to unity (see below). Other suggestions for deriving weights 'implicitly' from planners' choice of project mix have been put forward by Marglin (1967), Weisbrod (1968), and McGuire and Garn (1969). The UNIDO *Guidelines* treatment of the choice of discount rate from observed 'switching values' is essentially an extension of the same principle to the inter-temporal dimension.

The OECD *Manual*, while treating the sub-optimal savings problem rather more elaborately than did the authors of the subsequent *Guidelines*, nevertheless had little to say about inter-temporal weights other than to suggest

---

1 The introduction of the notion of maximising 're-investible surplus' as an appropriate investment criterion for LDCs is normally attributed to Galenson and Leibenstein (1955) though its origins are broadly in the tradition of much earlier socialist writing.

2 Under this second category may be included the distribution of benefits between the rich and poor regions.

that capitalist consumption might under some circumstances be accorded a weight of zero. The basis of the now conventionally accepted approach to weighting is to be found in Little and Mirrlees (1974) and subsequently reappeared with slight modifications in IBRD (1974) and Squire and van der Tak (1975).

The essential principles can best be visualised by making the simplifying assumption that all project benefits are paid out either in the form of wages to workers or surplus to the State and that workers at all income levels have a zero marginal propensity to save.[1] At the margin, then, the State chooses between holding on to investible surplus and spending it on increasing private consumption, both valued in terms of the *numeraire*. Let d_i be the weight associated with an extra peso's worth of consumption going to the ith group presently enjoying level C_i of consumption, let $\check{C}$ be the average (per capita) consumption level, and let n be the rate at which utility increases relative to a unit rate of increase in consumption (or 'elasticity of marginal utility'), then:

$$d_i = (\check{C}/C_i)^n \qquad\qquad (8.1)$$

This says that as long as $n>0$, an extra unit of consumption accruing to an income group whose present consumption, C_i, is greater than average per capita consumption, $\check{C}$, will receive a weight of less than unity. The computed value of d_i will then depend on two things: firstly, how rich group i is relative to reference level consumption, and secondly, what value is chosen for n.

Figure 8.2 will help to clarify the principle. Here we have assumed for convenience that n=1 and, that average per capita consumption is P.1000 per annum. If the ith group has an income equal to the per capita level, the value of d_i is unity; where the current consumption level is lower (P.800), d_i is greater than unity (1.25). Clearly, the poorer the ith recipient group relative to the reference (or base level) income group and/or the larger the value of n, the greater will be the computed value of d_i.[2]

There is, however, one more important problem. Although this procedure gives us a series of weights for valuing consumption increments of different income groups relative to *per capita* consumption, it does not tell us how

1   In reality, savings propensities need to be calculated for different income groups of course, and there is the further question of whether savings or consumption in private sector hands are equally valuable as public sector savings or consumption.

2   A change in the value of n will cause the curve to rotate through the fixed point A defined with reference to base level consumption ($\check{C}$). A shift in the entire curve (say, to the right) will occur where there is a change in the availability of public investment funds (an   increase) and hence the valuation of public funds (v) relative to base level consumption changes.

Government values increments in its own investible surplus relative to increments in consumption at base (average consumption) level. The ratio of
these values is conventionally denoted by the symbol v (for 'value of public
income'). If global savings is at a level such that Government does not place a
premium on raising savings relative to raising consumption of the average man
(the 'optimal' savings situation), the answer is simply that v = 1; i.e. $\hat{C}$ is equal
to C_{cr} as explained below. If, however, savings is 'sub-optimal' the value of
public income must be greater than unity, but how much greater?

Figure 8.2 *The Diminishing Marginal Utility of Extra Consumption*

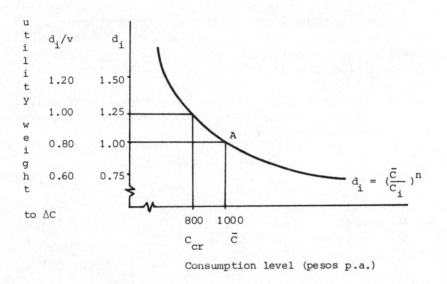

LM (1974) and ST (1975), although adopting equivalent definitions, differ
with respect to how v is to be estimated. LM suggest approaching the question directly by determining that level of income (consumption), or 'critical
level' (C_{cr}), at which Government is indifferent between spending more on
consumption and investment. ST suggest an indirect approach which involves
calculating a number of other parameters (see section 8.08) and using C_{cr} as
a crosscheck on the validity of the estimate. Hence, following LM procedures
one would examine such things as minimum wage legislation, threshold levels
of taxation, welfare benefit entitlement and possibly regional subsidy policy
to determine C_{cr}. Using the above example, let us suppose that this 'critical

level' was found to be P.800 per annum. One would then use P.800 rather than average per capita income (P.1000) as the reference level, the resulting distribution weight (d) for the P.800 per annum group being unity. Inspection of the graph (Figure 8.2) will show that this is equivalent to dividing through the original d_i's by v (or using 'Government savings standardised' weights). Summarising briefly, the ST approach defines the distribution weight (d) with reference to average per capita income level as shown in expression (8.1) while the latest LM approach is to determine a 'savings standardised' d (which for clarity might be written d^S) such that:

$$d_i^S = (C_{cr}/C_i)^n = d_i/v \qquad \qquad \dots \qquad (8.2)$$

Figure 8.3 shows a range of values derived for the distribution weight (d) under differing assumptions about the value of the elasticity coefficient (n) following the definition given in expression (8.1). For n = 0, an extra unit of consumption receives equal weight regardless of the present income (consumption) level of the group to which it accrues.[1] Setting n equal to unity

Figure 8.3 *Values of Distribution Weight (d) for Marginal Changes in Consumption Accruing to Different Consumption Groups Using Alternative Values for n*

Present Consumption		Value of elasticity coefficient (n)				
Level (C)	Č/C	0	0.5	1	2	3
(pesos per annum)						
500	2.00	1.00	1.41	2.00	4.00	8.00
Č = 1000	1.00	1.00	1.00	1.00	1.00	1.00
1500	0.66	1.00	0.81	0.66	0.44	0.29
3000	0.33	1 00	0.57	0.33	0.11	0.04
5000	0.20	1.00	0.45	0.20	0.04	0.04

corresponds to our earlier example while if n is increased to 2, note that the corresponding weights (d-values) are the squares of the weights for the n=1 case. Because the value of the weights is an exponential function of n, it follows that the spread between the weights associated with the lowest and highest consumption groups grows very large as n is increased above 3.[2] Note

1   This is the implicit assumption used in 'economic' CBA; similarly ECBA assumes that no premium is placed on Government savings relative to extra consumption at average per capita level (or $\check{C} = C_{cr}$). Hence ECBA can be viewed as a special case of the more general SCBA approach.
2   For n=4, the d-value for the lowest income group would be 64 while that for the highest would be 0.0016.

too that these results are meant to apply to weighting *marginal* additions to the consumption of the respective groups. Where such changes are non-marginal, it will be necessary to work out the d's on a different basis allowing for *both* the magnitude of change in the recipient group's income *and* the change in the (average) reference group's income.[1]

All this raises the somewhat vexed question of how the value of n is to be chosen in practice. The LM (1974) view was that 'most people would put n in the range 1 - 3'[2] while ST appear to have opted for a more cautious approach, suggesting that n should initially be set equal to unity and sensitivity analysis performed according to particular circumstances using values in the range $0.5 \leqslant n \leqslant 1.5$, values lower than 1 being recommended for those countries 'expressing a mild interest in redistribution'.[3] Such a recommendation might be thought somewhat paradoxical if one goes on to speculate that countries whose governments show little interest in redistribution are likely to be most in need of it. This is in a sense the objection put by Musgrave (1969) and others to basing estimates of distributional parameters on existing Government policies. An alternative is to attempt direct estimation of the marginal utility of consumption increments to different groups along the lines attempted in Fellner (1967). Lal (1972b) reports that in applying such an approach to India, a value of n = 2.3 was derived, though given the difficulties associated with the scope and interpretation of consumer expenditure data on which such an approach is usually based, such results must be treated with caution. Finally, DasGupta and Pearce (1972) have suggested explicity distinguishing between the empirical derivation of the shape of the utility function and the determination of 'equity' weights, or 'double tier' weighting.

More important, though, is the question of the role of public sector project appraisal in redistribution strategy, for whatever degree of sophistication is used in estimating the required parameters, such an exercise will only be of value to the extent that a significant proportion of total investment is evaluated along the lines proposed. Such questions are examined in more detail in a later section.

8.05 *The Social Wage Rate*

In the previous chapter the economic wage rate (EWR) was defined as the net output foregone (valued at border prices) resulting from committing labour to the project as opposed to leaving it in its previous occupation. The social wage rate (SWR) differs from the EWR in that a further element of 'cost'

1   See Squire and van der Tak (1975), pp. 65-66.
2   Little and Mirrlees (1974), p. 240.
3   Squire and van der Tak (1975), p. 103.

must be included (which may be positive or negative). To understand the nature of this extra cost, one must imagine broadly that the employment of an extra worker commits Government to finding extra consumption now, assumed for simplicity as equivalent to the difference between the wage and net foregone output. Extra consumption 'now' is clearly a benefit from the point of view of the worker though we are essentially concerned with how Government values this benefit. Extra consumption 'now' is also a cost in the sense that it constitutes a claim on limited investment resources and hence means sacrificing future consumption. It is the difference between value of such *future* consumption foregone and the value of additional workers' present consumption that constitutes the further social cost element. Use of the term 'social' in this context underlines the fact that two 'subjective' policy parameters are needed for the valuation; i.e. inter-temporal and intra-temporal distributional parameters.

$$SWR = m_i .AR_m + \{(W_i - m_i) - (W_i - m_i)d_i/v\} AR_c \quad .... \qquad (8.3)$$

where the first term in the expression is simply the 'economic' opportunity cost of the ith worker as defined in expression (7.1) in the previous chapter. One is basically interested in the social cost element which is that part contained in parentheses and which contains two elements, $(W_i - m_i)$ and $(W_i - m_i)d_i/v$. The former is simply the extra consumption cost which is borne as a result of hiring the worker. Since it is measured in terms of investible foreign exchange – everything within the parentheses is multiplied by the appropriate AR for consumption (AR_c) – it is investment foregone. The latter expression represents the social assessment of the benefit to the worker which results from his receiving $(W_i - m_i)$ extra consumption; i.e. $(W_i - m_i)$ must be multiplied by the standardised distribution weight appropriate to the ith worker consumption group (d_i/v). Referring back to Figure 8.2 it will be seen that if the worker belongs to that income group for which extra consumption is valued at par with extra investment $(d_i/v = 1)$ the whole part of expression (8.3) enclosed in parentheses drops out; i.e. there is no extra social 'cost' element in creating an extra job and SWR = EWR. Alternatively, if the worker belongs to a richer (poorer) consumption group, $d_i/v<1$ (>1), and the extra cost element will be positive (negative).

An arithmetic example will serve to illustrate the 'social cost' element in the SWR. Assume that the worker's wage (W_i) is 15, that output foregone (m_i) is 5, and that $AR_m = 0.80$. Further assume that the worker is drawn from the ranks of the very poorest and hence the associated standardised distributional weight is high $(d_i/v = 1.40)$. Calculation of the EWR is simple since it is merely:

$$EWR = m_i .AR_m = (5) (0.80) = 4$$

The extra social cost element is:

$$\{(W_i\text{-}m_i) \text{ - } (W_i\text{-}m_i)d_i/v\} = \{(15\text{-}5) \text{ - } (15\text{-}5)(1.40)\} = \text{-} 4$$

which must be valued at economic prices (multiplied by $AR_c = 0.8$) to arrive at a compatible value of -3.20. Hence:

$$SWR = (EWR + \text{'social cost'}) = 4 + (\text{-}3.2) = 0.8$$

It might be noted that had the value of the standardised distributional weight been greater than 1.5, a negative SWR would have resulted while for $d_i/v < 1$ (the case of a 'rich worker'), SWR $>$ EWR.

Although the logic of the SWR appears straightforward, a number of points must be borne in mind. Besides the problem of estimating standardised distributional weights (social parameters) discussed briefly above, the estimation of labour's economic cost (m) has been seen to relate to a set of issues still under debate in labour market and migration theory, some of which were raised in the previous chapter. A detailed example of empirical application of the original OECD (1968) SWR formulation to a particular country (Chile) is to be found in Seton (1972). An important paper on the inter-relationship between the valuation of labour and the internal terms of trade is by Dixit (1971) who argues that under certain conditions the extra consumption cost of labour may be understated, while Fitzgerald (1976b) points out that the consumption cost may be overstated either where the supply of urban wage goods is constrained by foreign exchange shortage (hence tending to reduce the urban real wage and migration) or where expanded employment created at the cost of public sector savings widens consumer goods markets and induces a compensating increase in private sector savings (investment). In a different vein, Irvin (1975b) has examined the implications for consumption costs of introducing wage remittance effects, particularly where monetary and real rural savings propensities differ significantly. Finally, for a discussion of the case where increased employment bids up wages, see section 4.6 of Scott, MacArthur and Newbery (1976).

However one views such difficulties, the salient feature of the SWR is to capture in single term (d_i/v) the relative weight Government accords to savings in its own hands relative to consumption in the hands of every category of income earner (including rentiers and capitalists), the terms 'worker' and 'wage' being used in the generic rather than the literal sense. Income redistribution between contemporaries, employment generation, trade efficiency, and extra savings (foreign exchange) generation objectives are all merged within a relatively simple conceptual framework applicable to project choice. The logic of the methodology then leads to placing the burden or regulation on 'choice of techniques' since, *ex hypothesis*, fiscal and other measures are not available. This is the next problem examined.

8.06 *Choice of Techniques and Macro-Policy Objectives*

Figure 8.4 illustrates the essence of the choice of techniques logic using the conventional neo-classical representation. Assume that a collection of projects in different sectors and of different capital intensities producing the same present value of output are arrayed along isoquant i. The price of (homogeneous) machines is a fixed datum in terms of savings since these are assumed to be imported at a constant price, while the social wage rate varies according to how increments in consumption to (homogeneously) poor

Figure 8.4 *Choice of Techniques*

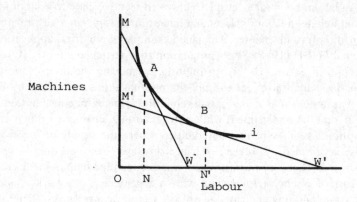

workers at a fixed real wage are valued relative to savings. Where increased savings (investment) is at a premium (i.e. workers' extra consumption now deemed expensive relative to extra savings) the machine-labour price relative is MW and projects of type A (viz. modern industries) tend to be chosen such that total employment is ON. Where extra consumption 'now' is at a premium, the price relative is M'W' and projects of type B (viz. artisan manufacture) tend to be chosen and employment moves towards ON'. Increased employment means (by assumption) a more adequate equitable income distribution. Similarly (by assumption), all projects arrayed along the isoquant are equally 'efficient' foreign exchange earners since all costs and benefits are expressed in terms of foreign exchange.

The broader strategic implications of choice of techniques will be more clearly understood by looking at Figure 8.5 which is a simplified version of the Raj-Sen (1961) model. Here one is imagined to be choosing between alternative sectoral uses of scarce foreign exchange (investment), the alternatives being as follows. If a constant annual stream of foreign exchange is spent entirely on consumption, the consumption path through time does not grow (strategy I). If foreign exchange is invested in importing the machines to make consumption goods (manufacturing sector) growth path II will be achieved, while if it is spent on machine tools (capital goods sector) which make the machines to make the consumption goods, the resulting growth path is III. Strategy II 'overtakes' strategy I at time t' while strategy III overtakes strategy II at time t''. Broadly, the relative weight given to consumption and investment at the margin (or value of public income, v) can be viewed as determining the appropriate sectoral allocation strategy and the 'degree of roundaboutness' with which foreign exchange is turned into consumption.[1]

Figure 8.5 *Simple Illustration of Alternative Growth Strategies*

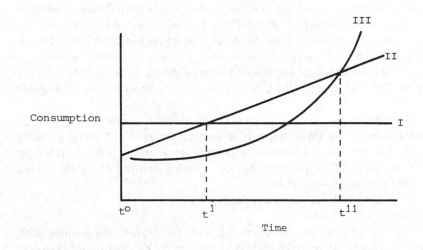

8.07 *The Social Accounting Rate of Interest (SARI)*

With the relative valuation of increased consumption and savings (investment) now located in the SWR, one way of treating the social accounting rate of interest is as a rationing device along similar lines to those suggested in the previous chapter (see Figure 7.2); i.e. it is that discount rate which passes just

1   A useful book to consult on growth models which combines lucid exposition and illustration is Qayum (1966).

sufficient projects to exhaust current available public investment funds.[1] Its numerical value will be determined on a trial and error basis. Indeed, some governments regularly review the discount rate used for public sector projects, raising it when a budgetary constraint is anticipated and lowering it when the supply of investible funds is expected to increase.

For a given available total of investment funds, however, the equilibrium SARI will not necessarily coincide with the equilibrium EARI. To understand why this is so, part of the argument of the previous chapter needs to be briefly reviewed. The EARI was defined as the marginal rate of return on public investment valued in terms of the foreign exchange (investment) *numeraire*. We saw that it might be higher or lower than the marginal rate of return on private sector investment measured on an equivalent basis. Similarly, it was argued that while the traditional (SOC) view was that these two rates should be equated, there were various grounds for believing that the private sector did not invest sufficiently. This led to some notion of an 'optimum' discount rate for the public sector (STP) which measured 'society's' indifferent transformation rate between present and future consumption (now conventionally called the CRI). This is equivalent to saying that the State places its own investment funds at a premium over current private sector consumption (at average level), or that the value of public income (v) is greater than 1. Hence the State would tend to choose those projects maximising 'surplus', adopting social CBA conventions. In short we may distinguish between:

(1) the opportunity cost of capital (SOC) borrowed from the private sector;
(2) the equilibrium EARI which is an implicit measure of the rate at which the future value of investment (consumption) falls as determined not by some ideal STP rate (CRI) but by existing constraints on the State's ability to mobilise finance;
(3) the CRI[2] which is an ideal rate; and,
(4) the equilibrium SARI.

Now we may ask how all these discount rates relate and, in particular, what is the relation between the EARI and the SARI? Firstly, let us accept typically that SOC > CRI. Then let us assume that Government will only use *economic cost-benefit analysis* (ECBA) when no premium is placed on Government investible surplus relative to average level consumption. If this is the case, then EARI = CRI, since ECBA is only relevant (and SCBA irrelevant) in an ideal world where savings is optimal. If ECBA is applied 'perversely' (which seems the more plausible assumption), then the equilibrium EARI

1   This is the essential principle of the OECD (1968) treatment of the ARI.
2   We are using the terms CRI and STP interchangeably; strictly, the STP is the 'pure' time preference rate and equals the CRI only where average consumption is not growing through time.

may exceed the CRI or even the opportunity cost of private capital, but we shall ignore this possibility.

Next consider the case where investment is sub-optimal. Here there are two possibilities. The first is that it will continue to remain sub-optimal indefinitely and that public savings will be at a constant premium (v) relative to average consumption. The second possibility is that through judicious application of SCBA, or else a relaxation of fiscal constraints, public savings will be at a declining premium relative to average consumption.[1] It is only in the latter case that the SARI will exceed the 'ideal' EARI (CRI). This is because with savings growing towards optimality, the rate of fall in the social value of future *extra* savings will be greater than the rate of fall in the value of extra consumption. Formally this may be written:

$$ \text{SARI} = \text{CRI} + \left(\frac{v_t - v_{t+1}}{v_{t+1}} \right) \qquad \dots \qquad (8.4) $$

where v_t is the value of public income[2] relative to average consumption at time t. Since by assumption $v_{t+1} < v_t$, the expression in brackets will always be positive and therefore SARI > CRI. Alternatively, if savings is expected to continue to be sub-optimal indefinitely and $v_t = v_{t+1}$, then SARI = CRI.

One conclusion is that if there were some reliable way of independently estimating the CRI, determination of the equilibrium SARI by trial and error could act as a cross-check on the estimated value of v; i.e. if the SARI derived from (8.4) and the equilibrium SARI were found to differ, the annual estimate of v could be revised. Hence the 'equilibrating function' would be thrown on to v rather than on to the discount rate. Formally, the effect on choice of techniques should be the same. We shall nevertheless explore some suggested methods of cross-checking v in more detail.

8.08 *Cross-checking the Value of Public Income (v)*

As already noted, there is a broad division of opinion as to how v should best be estimated, LM (1974) recommending a direct estimate of the consumption level at which additional units of consumption are treated at par with

---

1 This requires predicting the evolution of both public and private savings since we are interested in the global savings rate.
2 Note the relationship of expression (8.4) to the original OECD (1968) formulation in which the value of public income was expressed as the compound average difference between the SARI and the CRI, or (with slight modification to the original formula):
$v = \{1 + \frac{1}{2} (\text{SARI} - \text{CRI})\}^T$

increased public sector savings, and ST (1975) suggesting an indirect procedure the results of which are then compared to the direct (LM type) estimate.

In essence, the ST procedure follows the lines originally suggested in the UNIDO *Guidelines*, v (or what the *Guidelines* termed P^{inv}) being defined as:

$$v = \{ (q-sq)/(CRI-sq) \} . AR_c^{-1} \qquad \qquad \dots \qquad (8.5)$$

and

$$v = (q/CRI) . AR_c^{-1} \qquad \qquad \dots \qquad (8.6)$$

where expressions (8.5) and (8.6) serve to define upper and lower bounds respectively for the value of v.[1] The terms are defined as follows:

q: marginal product (yield) of net aggregate investment,
s :   marginal propensity to save (re-invest) out of yield, and,
CRI: consumption rate of interest.

Since these are presumed to be estimated at border prices, they must be re-translated into domestic consumption values by deflating by the accounting ratio for consumption (AR_c), where v is the premium on investment valued in terms of domestic consumption. The effective distinction between (8.5) and (8.6) is that the former makes allowance for further saving out of yield (hence making investment even more valuable relative to consumption). We can now deal briefly with the estimation of the CRI, s and q in that order.

The CRI measures the rate at which the social value of consumption falls over time and is notionally composed of a 'pure time preference' element and a growth element; or,

$$CRI = ng + p \qquad \qquad \dots \qquad (8.7)$$

where p is the pure time preference rate, g is the average expected rate of growth per capita income over some future period, and n (see section 8.04) is the elasticity of marginal utility of extra consumption with respect to present consumption level. The expected rate of growth of per capita income can be established from Plan projections, but measurement of n and p raises difficult (some would argue insurmountable) problems. A discussion of these appears in Scott, MacArthur and Newbery (1976), Scott using a modified version of expression (8.7) to derive an estimate of 6 percent for the ARI in Kenya

1 Expression (8.5) will be recognised as the expression for the premium on investment (P^{inv}) given in UNIDO (1972).

which was subsequently thought too low and abandoned.[1] A more practical procedure may be simple to guess initially plausible upper and lower values for the CRI, testing the sensitivity of the derived estimate of v to changes in the assumptions.

Estimation of the parameters s and q, the economy-wide marginal savings propensity and marginal product of capital respectively, raises a further set of difficulties. The approach originally advocated in the *Guidelines* was to base estimates on plan projections. Hence, s would be total incremental savings as a percentage of incremental national income growth and q would be the incremental output (value added) capital ratio net of the incremental wage bill. In the case of the latter estimate, Irvin (1975a) encountered problems in applying such an approach, while alternative attempts based on aggregate production function estimation techniques — see, for example, Yang (1975) — raise a series of further issues which have been much debated in other areas of the literature.[2]

In light of these difficulties, the view taken here is that while it may in some circumstances be possible to estimate a range of values for v using the UNIDO-ST approach and use these as a way of cross-checking results obtained using a more direct LM approach, it would be unwise to rely on UNIDO-ST type methods as the primary way of dealing with the question.

8.09 *Income Distribution Weights and National Income*

One of the more important implications of adopting consumption weighting procedures has to do with the way in which growth indices of national welfare are conceived. The difficulties associated with the use of GNP as an index of welfare are well known and are most recently discussed in Chenery et al (1974) who propose offsetting the distributional bias in existing GNP measurement conventions by the use of 'poverty' weights. Briefly, the argument is that where, typically, the top 40 percent of income earners receive some 75 percent of national income, to infer from the fact that per capita income grows at 'x' percent per annum that society is 'x' percent better off is to implicitly weight welfare in proportion to different groups' share in total product. The alternatives they suggest are 'one man one vote' equality weights, or weights inversely proportional to initial group income level (poverty weights). On this basis, past growth rates for a large number of

1   Scott's procedure was essentially to define the parameter g in expression (8.7) as the average growth rate of critical income level (Y_{cr}) rather than per capita income ($\bar{Y}$); Scott, MacArthur and Newbery (1976), pp. 45-48. A more recent attempt to apply these principles to deriving a public sector discount rate for the U.K. appears in Scott (1977).
2   See Sen (1971).

countries have been examined and adjusted with interesting results. While
detailed discussion of these matters is outside the scope of the present work,
the general point to be noted is that the use of income distribution weights
at project level is only one aspect of recent concern with problems of equity
and ways of incorporating distributional objectives into planning methodology at several levels.

Figure 8.6 illustrates the essential principles involved, though using somewhat different conventions from those proposed by Chenery at al (1974).
Imagine a hypothetical country consisting of 100 people, the highest and
lowest annual income levels being piastres 1600 and piastres 100 respectively.
Column 2 shows annual levels of remuneration while column 1 shows the
percentage of the population in each category. Columns 3 and 4 show total
income by group and each group's percentage share in the total. The top 40
percent of income recipients account for 74% of a total national income of
30,000 piastres while the bottom 40 percent receive only 13% of the total.
Average per capita income is piastres 300 per annum and we shall assume that
'critical' income level (Y_{cr}) – or that level at which Government is indifferent
between additions to current consumption and savings – is piastres 200.

Figure 8.6 *Weighting National Income Increments*

1	2	3	4	5	6	7	8	9
% Y earners	Y level (piastres p.a.)	Total Y	% share in total	10% Δ in Y	$d_{i/v}$ for $n = 1$	social value	ΔY equal- ly dis- tributed	social value
5	1600	8000	28%	800	0.13	100	150	20
5	800	4000	13%	400	0.25	100	150	40
10	400	4000	13%	400	0.50	200	300	150
20	300	6000	20%	600	0.67	400	600	400
20	200*	4000	13%	400	1.00	400	600	600
40	100	4000	13%	400	2.00	800	1200	2400
100		30000	100%	3000		2000	3000	3610

* 'critical' income level.

Suppose that national income grows by 10% in such a way as to leave the
current distribution of personal income unchanged as shown in column 5. An
implicit assumption in treating national income as an index of national welfare is that a unit of income to a rich man has the same marginal utility as to
a poor man; thus one may think of column 5 as incorporating unitary distributional weights ($n = 0$). An alternative approach is to derive a set of weights
using Y_{cr} as the 'reference' level and assuming that $n = 1$; i.e. that an extra 10
piastres to a man at the 100 piastres income level has the same social value as
an extra 80 piastres to a man at the 800 piastres income level. The corre-

sponding distribution weights are shown in column 6 while column 7 shows the social value of the income increment. On this basis national income has grown by 10 percent, but national welfare by 6.7 percent. Now consider a situation in which the 10 percent increment in income is distributed in a perfectively egalitarian manner; e.g. each man receives 30 piastres. Using the weights in column 6, the aggregate social value of the increment is piastres 3610, or a growth in national welfare of 12 percent.[1] In summary, the use of distributional weights at project level has important implications for the way in which one thinks of macro-level indices of welfare, and raises the problem of methodological consistency between different levels of planning.

8.10 *Politics, Planning and the New Methodology*

While the main focus of the present work has been didactic, it will be appropriate in concluding to comment briefly on the political context of planning which is implicitly assumed in much of the current literature on project appraisal. It will be useful, more particularly, to say something about different views of the role of the State in the planning process and how these influence both what importance is attributed to trade efficiency and distributional objectives and what instruments of policy are available for pursuing these.

Broadly speaking, one may distinguish between the State seen as playing a supportive role in the process of accumulation and growth, and the State seen as directly controlling this process. On the former view the State, in addition to its traditional 'law and order' function, is charged with the direct provision of collective goods and services (defence, education, health, some types of infrastructure) and with indirect regulation of private sector activity through fiscal and commercial policies. Although such a characterisation abstracts away from significant variations between countries in the scope of public sector provision and the nature of the instruments available for discharging the 'regulative' function, the crucial point is that control over capital accumulation in this case ultimately resides with the private sector through its ownership of productive assets, and investment decisions are influenced by the State largely to the extent that it is able to alter market price signals through fiscal and commercial policy.

In contrast, the notion of the State as controller implies, minimally, a significant extension of power over the use and disposition of productive

---

1 Note that if the average per capita income level (P.300) were used as reference level in place of Y_{cr} (P.200), the social value of the 'distribution neutral' increment would be identical to its nominal value (P.3000) but the social value of the 'equitably distributed' increment would be greater than the P.3610 shown.

assets, traditionally taking the form of nationalisation of key areas of mining, manufacturing, banking and in some cases land, while maximally the economy may be fully collectivised. Here, successful capital accumulation is no longer contingent upon the provision by public authorities of the right 'mix' of incentives, sanctions and complementary investment to the private sector but on the performance of public enterprise itself. The key problem is, having gained control over the surplus, how best to distribute it between alternative investment possibilities. While the suggested schema is somewhat simplified, it is only against a backdrop of political discourse that it becomes possible to enquire meaningfully about the relevance of adopting sophisticated methods for public sector project appraisal and, in particular, about the pursuit of trade efficiency and distributional objectives via project choice rather than other means.

Consider, firstly, the concept of trade efficiency. The early debate concerning the 'power' of the Central Office of Project Evaluation in influencing Government to adopt 'rational' trade policies (e.g. remove or restructure protection) presupposes a decentralised system of autonomous enterprises making investment decisions in response to market signals; i.e. either a decentralised socialist system or, what seems more likely, a predominantly private enterprise system as exists in much of the developing world. The removal of protection is not an end in itself; rather, it is a necessary condition for achieving trade efficiency where selection of investment alternatives is predominantly market determined. The alternative to bringing domestic and world prices into line via a rationalisation of commercial policy is to subject all investment decisions to central control either by applying accounting prices universally through the introduction of comprehensive investment licensing in the private sector, or simply by absorbing all important industries into the public sector. Moreover, to the extent that further distortions not due to trade policies exist, either further corrections are needed in a decentralised system to achieve efficiency objectives (viz. wage subsidies where the opportunity cost of labour is below its market price), or decisions themselves must be centralised.

The salient feature of the modern project appraisal literature is that it rigorously conceptualises distortions on a magnitude which undermines faith in market virtues while accepting as 'given' a system of economic organisation which perpetuates such distortions. The point is usually formalised in arguments about 'second-bestness'. In practice, though, it is the public sector through its adoption of advanced appraisal methods that is expected to bear the burden of adjustment. How this is to work in practice is unclear, particularly where the public sector is relatively small, or else predominantly responsible for the provision of non-trade goods and services in a manner consistent with the above characterisation of the supporting role of state activity. The authors of the OECD *Manual* were in this sense more consistent than those of the UNIDO *Guidelines* in stressing the importance of removing trade restrictions where the locus of effective economic power lies in the private sector.

Precisely the same objections apply when considering distributional objectives, though there is one important distinction. While Little and Mirrlees grant that use of the methods in the public sector *plus* trade liberalisation will enhance efficiency in their reference economy (there being some degree of leverage in counteracting private interests which benefit from protection), the inclusion of equality as a further dimension of project selection in the public sector is apparently necessary only because there is *no* available fiscal leverage. Here the burden of redressal falls (understandably) entirely on the public sector, and since a limit to effective redistribution through taxing the rich is (again understandably) assumed, the alternative is to distribute investible public funds to the poor in the form of labour intensive projects. But here is another apparent dilemma, for simultaneously, the public sector is assumed to make up for a global savings deficiency by adopting surplus maximising techniques. Now either Government does one or the other – but it cannot do both unless total saving can be increased at the expense of socially undesirable current consumption which, *ex hypothesis*, is ruled out. The argument does begin to sound very strange. The confusion can only be clarified by recognising that the nature of the dilemma is located in the adoption of implicit assumptions about the role of the State which are contradictory. Either the public sector is subordinate to powerful private interests which make it impossible to *both* increase global savings and achieve redistribution, which would be consistent with the 'supportive' view, or the political climate is such that the balance of private and public power can be decisively altered.[1] If, as suggested above, public investment activity is a relatively small part of the total and/or is limited to the provision of basic infrastructure (which with some exceptions such as construction is likely to offer little scope for the adoption of labour intensive techniques), it is difficult to see what significant redistribution can take place where the burden is thrown entirely onto choice of techniques at the margin. In this light, the attitude of those economists who dismiss the 'cost benefit parlour game'[2] as a diversionary technocratic exercise obscuring rather than illuminating fundamental problems begins to make sense.

What role, then, do techniques of investment appraisal have to play? At

1 Little and Mirrlees (1974) provides a most revealing, if somewhat unintentional, statement of this dilemma: 'Our belief is that most Governments would be happy if some quantified allowance for inequality were made. But many might prefer that it was done in a concealed manner, so that the weighting system did not become a subject of parliamentary or public debate. It may sometimes be politically expedient to do good by stealth.' (p. 75)
2 See Bienefeld (1975), p. 40.

one level the answer to this question, as we have suggested, turns on what role is accorded to the public sector. Unless one is a devout believer in marginalism, reasoning that any efficiency gain no matter how small is worth the effort, one must conclude that where the role of the public sector is small, so too will be the role of social cost-benefit analysis. Again, in those few cases where a major change in the balance of power takes place (often only after a protracted process of political struggle), the newly installed revolutionary Government is unlikely to accord high priority to polishing techniques of project appraisal to a high degree of methodological brilliance. In the words of Oskar Lange:

In both the socialist and the national revolutionary types of economic development we find that in the first period the main problem is not that of the details of accounting... The question of rapidity of growth overshadows the more subtle questions of high grade efficiency.[1]

The underlying significance of these techniques, one may speculatively venture, is twofold. Firstly, and least importantly, they serve as an aid to planning in the sense of providing a set of prices to be used at enterprise level where planned development has attained a degree of complexity such that it is no longer possible to rely exclusively on centralised decision making and physical production targets. In such a situation, by implication that of a developed socialist economy, production priorities are identified within the framework of the national plan while detailed investment decisions (including choice of specific techniques) are subject to cross-checking by the adoption of a set of accounting prices reflecting both efficiency and distributional objectives. Indeed, as previously noted, one strand in the development of the theory of shadow pricing comes from contemporary economic debate in Eastern Europe, though here too, theory is far ahead of practice. If the importance of such applications is deemed to be of marginal significance in the present context, it is because the prospect of future political changes in the Third World tending towards the adoption of a decentralised system of socialist planning appears remote.

A more important argument in defence of the relevance of social cost-benefit analysis stresses its heuristic value. To understand advances in the theory is to understand the changing perceptions of economists, many of whom are firmly in the mainstream of neo-classical orthodoxy, towards the question of how well market economies function in practice. At one level, contemporary cost-benefit theory is a crucial junction of neo-classical technique and development theory which has produced an impressive volume of traffic in new thinking, or at least in new constructs which have adapted old ideas to new settings. At another level, cost-benefit theory can be interpreted

1   O. Lange (1973), pp. 214-15.

as a foundation stone in the construction of a new economic paradigm which would finally purge normative notions of consumer sovereignty and just factor rewards from allocation and price theory (though such a claim is for the moment a bit ambitious). Again, one may argue that the justification of cost-benefit theory lies more in the questions which it raises than those it answers; the meaning of trade efficiency and the conditions under which gains from trade can best be secured; the relationship between trade, the evolution of consumer demand patterns in the Third World and technology selection; the relationship between employment and the distribution of income; and the precise meaning (if any) of redistribution and growth as conflicting objectives. Whether the present book is useful in understanding some of the conceptual baggage which must be acquired in order to come to terms more effectively with such issues is a question which is best left to the reader.

8.11 *Further Reading*

With reference to the early section on interpersonal welfare comparisons, elements of the problem are to be found in any book on welfare economics, of which Little (1950) and Graaff (1971) are prominent examples while Dobb (1969) and Sen (1970) provide important political critiques of contemporary theory. The philosophically-minded reader will also find Rawls (1972) particularly interesting on the concept of social justice. An illuminating short exposition of the measurement of inequality as well as the implications of assuming non-identical individual utility functions is provided in Sen (1973). References to the debate on intertemporal preferences and the discount rate are covered in Chapter VII above.

With regard to the derivation of consumption weights, a more rigorous treatment of the social valuation function appears in Seton (1972) and further useful discussions are to be found in Lal (1972b), Nash, Pearce and Stanley (1975) as well as most recently in Little and Scott (1976). Different approaches to social wage rate determination are summarised in Lal (1973). There is an enormous volume of literature on the relationship between growth, employment, choice of techniques and equity, but a useful short paper resuming the main issues is Stewart and Streeten (1971).

Although equally relevant in the above context, Chenery et al (1974) has been cited with reference to national income weighting procedures. A summary of the debate to which this book gave rise appears in IDS *Bulletin* (August 1975) which, incidently, contains a polemical exchange on different assumptions about the role of the State between Leys and Jolly which is relevant to the brief political comments contained in the concluding section of the chapter. The connection between the current SCBA debate and the role of the State is raised in Sen (1972) which also criticises an important orthodox contribution to the theory of optimal fiscal regulation advanced by Diamond and Mirrlees (1971). One of the few attempts to examine the role of the public sector in LDCs is that of Sachs (1964), while more recently, FitzGerald (1976c) has looked at changing public sector influence in the case of Peru. Further critical discussion of the political assumptions underlying the use of SCBA appears in Stewart (1975) and FitzGerald (1977).

APPENDICES

APPENDIX A

The appendix which follows contains a set of numerical exercises designed to supplement material presented in the main body of the text. Each *question set* consists of a number of problems requiring numerical solution; the answers to those questions marked with an asterisk are shown in the corresponding *answer set*.

Question Set I: Use of Discount Tables and Selection of Simple
Alternatives   (Based on Chapter 1)

*1. Find the present and future values (at end of year 4) for the fol-
lowing cash flows assuming an interest rate of 10% per annum:

Investment		Y E A R			
£	0	1	2	3	4
A	+20	+40	+60	+80	+100
B	+60	+60	+60	+60	+ 60
C	-50	-50	-50	-50	-100
D	-100	0	0	+100	+100

2. Solve the following assuming an interest rate of 4% per annum:

(a) $100 at the end of each year for 13 years will repay a present
debt of how much?

(b) An annual end-of-year investment of how much is required to provide $22000 at the end of 30 years?

(c) The present value of $5000 37 years hence is how much?

(d) A payment of how much now is acceptable in place of a payment
$1500 18 years hence?

(e) A present investment of $10000 will secure a perpetual income
of how much a year?

(f) A perpetual annual income of $100 has a present value of how
much?

*3. Using the net present value decision rule, evaluate the following
independent investment projects assuming an annual discount rate
of: (a) 5%; (b) 10%.

Investment		Y E A R			
$	0	1	2	3	4
A	-175	+100	+100	-	-
B	-200	+ 60	+ 60	+60	+60
C	+ 50	-100	-100	-100	+275

*4. Using the internal rate of return (IRR) decision rule, evaluate the following independent investment proposals, assuming an opportunity cost of capital of: (a) 4%, and (b) 6%.

Investment $	0	1	2	3
A	-1000	+1100	0	0
B	-1361.6	+ 500	+500	+500
C	-1000	+ 200	+854.5	0
D	+1000	-1100	0	0

*5. Choose between the following mutually exclusive investment projects assuming a cost of capital of: (a) 4%, and, (b) 10% per annum.

Investment $	0	1	2	3	IRR
A	-1000	+500	+500	+500	≃ 23%
B	-2361.6	+1000	+1000	+1000	≃ 13%

6. As part of an irrigation pumping scheme in a Latin American country, it is proposed to use either a 20 cm. or a 25 cm. pipe. The former has an initial cost of P. 9000 and annual pumping costs estimated at P. 1800. The latter has an initial cost of P. 12000 and annual pumping costs estimated at P. 1100. The scheme has an estimated life of 15 years and neither pipe is expected to have any salvage value at the end of this period. Users are to be charged an annual tax expected to be 5% of initial cost. Compare the present values of the net cost over the project's life using a discount rate of 6% per annum.

7. Two alternative projects are being considered in the U.K. Compare the present values of the net cost of providing the service for a

24-year period, assuming a discount rate of 6% per annum.

	PROJECT	
Cost/Revenue Breakdown	A	B
Initial cost	£18000	£40000
Estimated life	12 years	24 years
Estimated salvage value	none	£8000
Annual costs	£6000	£4000
Annual revenues	£1600	£1200

(Make any further assumptions explicit.)

8. A manufacturing company in the Middle East is required to install a plant to comply with air pollution standards specified by the local authority. The plant engineer has made the following estimates of costs in dinars for 4 alternative plants, each having an estimated life of 10 years.

Cost estimates	A	B	C	D
Installation cost	D. 12000	D. 15000	D. 18000	D. 20000
Annual costs:				
Power and water	2560	2560	2000	1900
Cleaning and maintenance	3600	3400	2920	2600
Labour	800	740	520	480
Property taxes and insurance	240	300	360	420
Expected salvage value	0	0	1000	1500

Which one would you recommend, given an after tax annual discount rate of 8%?

9. In the design of a road that is required to have an infinite economic life, two alternative plans have been proposed.

- Road A involves an initial cost of $300,000, has an estimated life
  of 20 years and is expected to have annual maintenance costs of
  $500.

- Road B involves an initial cost of $400,000, is expected to have
  an infinite life, but would involve maintenance costs of $1000 per
  year.

All salvage values are assumed to be negligible and road A can be
reconstructed at the end of its life at the same cost. The stipu-
lated discount rate is 5% per annum. Which of the two alternatives
would you recommend?

10. What are the problems with using the 'payback period' as a measure
    of investment performance?

11. What meaning, if any, would you attach to a negative internal rate
    of return; is there a lower limit to the value which the IRR may
    take?

Answer Set I

1. Present value $(P_o) = \sum\limits_{t=0}^{T} P_t/(1+r)^t$

    (i) $P_o(A)$ = 20(1.00) + 40(0.909) + 60(0.826) + 80(0.751) + 100(0.683)

                 = 20.00 + 36.36 + 49.56 + 60.08 + 68.30

                  = £234.30

    (ii) $P_o(B)$ = 60(4.170)

                  = £250.20

    (iii) $P_o(C)$ = -50(3.487) - 100(0.683)

                  = -174.35 - 68.30

                  = -£242.65

    (iv) $P_o(D)$ = 100(-1.00 + 0.751 + 0.683)

                  = 100(0.434)

                  = £43.40

Future value $(P_4) = \sum\limits_{t=0}^{T} P_t(1-r)^t$

    (i) $P_4(A)$ = 20(1.464) + 40(1.331) + 60(1.210) + 80(1.100) + 100(1.000)

                  = 29.28 + 53.24 + 72.60 + 88.00 + 100.00

                  = £343.12

    (ii) $P_4(B)$ = 60(6.105)

                  = £366.30

    (iii) $P_4(C)$ = -50(1.464 + 1.331 + 1.210 + 1.100) - 100(1.000)

                  = -50(5.105) - 100(1.000)

                  = -255.25 - 100

                  = -£355.25

    (iv) $P_4(D)$ = 100(-1.464 + 1.100 + 1.000)

                  = 100(0.636)

                  = £63.60

3. Investment A: $NPV_{(0.05)}$ $= -175 + 100(1.859)$
$$= -175 + 185.9$$
$$= \$10.9 \text{ therefore accept}$$

$NPV_{(0.10)}$ $= -175 + 100(1.736)$
$$= -175 + 173.6$$
$$= -\$1.4 \text{ therefore reject}$$

Investment B: $NPV_{(0.05)}$ $= -200 + 60(3.546)$
$$= -200 + 212.76$$
$$= \$12.76 \text{ therefore accept}$$

$NPV_{(0.10)}$ $= -200 + 60(3.170)$
$$= -200 + 190.20$$
$$= -\$9.80 \text{ therefore reject}$$

Investment C: $NPV_{(0.05)}$ $= 50 - 100(2.723) + 275(0.823)$
$$= 50 - 272.3 + 226.3$$
$$= \$4.02 \text{ therefore accept}$$

$NPV_{(0.10)}$ $= 50 - 100(2.487) + 275(0.683)$
$$= 50 - 248.7 + 187.82$$
$$= -\$10.88 \text{ therefore reject}$$

4. Let IRR = r

Investment A: $\$1000 = \$1100/(1+r)^1$
$$1 + r = 1100/1000$$
$$= 1.10$$
$$r = 0.10 \text{ or } 10\%$$

As $0.10 > 0.06 > 0.04$, investment A should be accepted at both rates for the opportunity cost of capital.

Investment B: $\$1361.6 = \$500/(1+r) + \$500/(1+r)^2 + \$500/(1+r)^3$

$\qquad\qquad\qquad = \$500 \cdot \{1 - (1+r)^{-3}/r\}$

$1-(1+r)^{-3}/r = 1361.6/500$

$\qquad\qquad\qquad\qquad = 2.723$

$\qquad\qquad\qquad r = 0.05$ or 5% (from Table 2, Appendix B)

As $0.06 > 0.05 > 0.04$, investment B should be accepted at an opportunity cost of capital of 4%, but rejected at 6%.

Investment C: $\$1000 = \$200/(1+r) + \$854.5/(1+r)^2$

By trial and error, $r = 0.03$

$\qquad\qquad\quad \$1000 = \$200(0.971) + \$854.5(0.943)$

$\qquad\qquad\qquad\quad = \$194.2 + \$805.8$

$\qquad\qquad\qquad\quad = \$1000$

As $0.03 < 0.04 < 0.06$, investment C should be rejected at both rates
for the opportunity cost of capital.

Investment D:

(It should be noted that the cash flow for this investment is the
same as the cash flow for investment A except for a reversal of the
signs. This implies that the NPV will be positively instead of inversely related to the discount rate, as for example, with a loan
seen from the point of view of the borrower. Such an investment is
only worthwhile if the IRR (10%) is *less* than the opportunity cost
of capital.)

As $0.10 > 0.06 > 0.04$, investment D should be rejected at both rates
for the opportunity cost of capital.

5. (a) Cost of capital = 4% per annum

    Method 1:   Calculate the IRR for the incremental cash flow (pro-
                ject B - project A) and choose B if IRR(B-A) is great-
                er than the cost of capital.

$$(B-A) = -\$1361.6 + \$500 + \$500 + \$500$$

$$1 - (1+r)^{-3}/r = 1316.6/500$$

$$= 2.723$$

$$r = 0.05 \text{ or } 5 \text{ percent (from Table 2, Appendix B)}$$

As IRR(B-A) > cost of capital, project B should be chosen.

Method 2: Calculate the NPV's for the two projects at a discount rate equal to the cost of capital and choose the project with the larger NPV.

$$NPV(A_{0.04}) = -\$1000(1.00) + \$500(2.775)$$
$$= -\$1000 + \$1387.5$$
$$= \$387.5$$

$$NPV(B_{0.04}) = -\$2361.6(1.00) + P. \ 1000(2.775)$$
$$= -\$2361.6 + \$2775$$
$$= \$413.4$$

As NPV(B) > NPV(A), project B should be chosen.

(b) Cost of capital = 10% per annum

Method 1: As IRR(B-A) < cost of capital, project A should be chosen. (Same IRR calculation as in part (a).)

Method 2: $NPV(A_{0.10}) = -\$1000 + \$500(2.487)$
$$= -\$1000 + \$1243.5$$
$$= \$243.5$$

$$NPV(B_{0.10}) = -\$2361.6 + \$1000(2.487)$$
$$= -\$2361.6 + \$2487$$
$$= \$125.4$$

As NPV(A) > NPV(B), project A should be chosen.

Question Set II: Financial Accounting (Based on Chapter 2)

* 1. From the following figures prepare full profit and loss and appro-
     priation accounts.

	£		£
Carriage	500	Administrative expenses	13,000
Factory depreciation	1,000	Other items, office expenses	10,000
Work in progress at start	10,000	Raw materials at start	10,000
Raw materials at close	8,000	Balance in profit and loss a/c	30,000
Work in progress at close	2,000	Finished goods at start	20,000
Salaries (factory)	10,000	Power, light and heat (factory)	1,000
Insurance (factory)	1,000	Finished goods at close	18,000
Wages (factory)	20,000	Sales	260,000
Rent, rates (factory)	2,000	Non-operating expenses	2,000
Maintenance (factory)	3,000	Non-operating income	4,000
Sales returns	2,000	Raw material purchases	105,000
Purchases returns	5,000	Dividend proposed 20% of year's net	
Office salaries	20,000	profit.	
Sales commissions	2,000	Tax, 40% of year's net profit.	
		Transfer to reserve, 10% of year's	
		net profit.	

(All the above figures correspond to the period January 1st - December
31st, 1974.)

* 2. *Part I*

   Here are some items from a balance sheet. Arrange them in the correct
   balance sheet layout (December 1, 1972).

	US$
Investments, market value	20,000
Depreciation of plant	10,000

	US$
Goodwill	20,000
Dividends due	10,000
Stocks (finished products)	20,000
Building at cost	80,000
Profit and loss balance	20,000
Short term loans (not repayable in 1 year)	30,000
Investments at cost	10,000
Shares	100,000
Long term loan	40,000
Debtors	70,000
Land at cost	80,000
Reserves	30,000
Creditors	50,000
Cash	10,000
Overdraft	20,000
Reserves for future taxation	10,000
Plant at cost	60,000
Tax due	10,000
Depreciation of buildings	20,000

Part II

Answer the following questions

a. What is the total value of current assets?

b. What is the total value of current liabilities?

c. What is the total value of external liabilities?

d. What are the quick assets? What is their total value?

e. What is the total value of owner's equity?

f. What is the working capital? What is its total value?

g. What is the acid-test ratio? Is it satisfactory?

h. What is the current liquidity ratio? Is it satisfactory?

i. What is the degree of solvency?

3. Below is a balance sheet (conventional accounting layout). Answer the questions that follow.

THE P. BENITEZ MANUFACTURING CO. LTD.
BALANCE SHEET AS AT DECEMBER 10, 1968

	Pesos		Pesos
Authorized capital		*Fixed assets*	
20,000 ordinary shares (at P. 1 each)	20,000	Freehold land at cost 1968	10,000
Issued capital		Buildings at cost 1968	20,000
15,000 ordinary shares (at P. 1 each		Plant (at cost P. 20,000 less	
fully paid)	15,000	P. 2,000 depreciation)	18,000
Reserves		Motor vehicles (at cost P. 10,000	
Capital	5,000	less P. 5,000 depreciation)	5,000
Revenue	5,000	*Investments*	
Profit and loss balance	5,000	Trade, quoted (market value P. 20,000)	10,000
Future taxation	4,000	*Current assets*	
Debentures		Stock	3,000
300 5% at P. 100 each	30,000	Debtors (less reserve for doubtful debts)	12,000
Current liabilities		Cash	1,000
Creditors	8,000		
Taxation	2,000		
Net dividend proposed	5,000		
	79,000		79,000
	=====		=====

a. Try to develop the more general layout used in project formulation.
b. Is the company solvent?
c. What is the capital employed?
d. What is the meaning of authorised and issued capital?
e. What is the net worth?
f. What is the acid-test ratio and the current-liquidity ratio?
g. How many further shares is this company permitted to offer for sale?
h. How much of the reserves is available for dividend distribution?

*4. From the following figures prepare a Sources and Application of Funds
    Statement.

Items	Increase during 1972 (Kobos)
Shares (ordinary)	80,000
Plant buildings	40,000
Office equipment	15,000
Current liabilities	3,000
Depreciation	1,000
Long term loan (A)	30,000
Inventories[+]	1,000
Plant equipment	25,000
Debtors (receivables)	4,000
Interest on loan (A)	3,000
Office buildings	20,000
Amortization of loan (A) (yearly basis)	5,000
Retained earnings	2,000

[+]Inventories increases are sub-divided in the following way:

    Work in progress   500
    Finished products   500

5. In what way can the method of depreciation adopted affect the net
   operating flow of a project?

6. Why might a project analyst not include tax as a cost in calculating
   a project's financial profitability?

7. Debt service charges should not be treated as a cost in deriving a
   net operating flow for financial evaluation purposes and yet a change
   in the amount or timing of these payments can affect the post-tax operating flow of a project. Explain.

8. Why might the post-tax operating flow of a private sector project differ from the post-tax flow on the equity component of the project's funds? Under what circumstances will the IRR of the latter be greater than, less than, or equal to the former?

9. The time stream of net consumption benefits of an investment project expressed in current prices, and the consumer price index (CPI) for each year of the project's life, are given below.

	1970	1971	1972	1973	1974	1975
Net benefits (£)	−2000	+330	+500	+700	+960	+1295
CPI	100	110	125	140	160	185

You are required to calculate the net present value of the project's consumption benefits expressed in constant (1970) prices, assuming a discount rate of 8% per annum.

10. If the project analyst is concerned primarily with a project's economic and social profitability, calculating its financial profitability is unnecessary. Discuss.

Answer Set II

1. *Manufacturing Account – January 1st–December 31st, 1974*

Opening stock:		Stock at close:	
– Work in progress	£ 10,000	– Work in progress	£ 2,000
– Raw materials	10,000	– Raw materials	8,000
Purchases	105,000	Purchases returns	5,000
Carriage	500	Balance (cost of	
Factory overheads:		manufactured goods)	148,500
– Light, heat, power	1,000		
– Salaries	10,000		
– Wages	20,000		
– Insurance	1,000		
– Rent, rates	2,000		
– Maintenance	3,000		
– Depreciation	1,000		
	£163,500		£163,500
	========		========

Trading Account – January 1st–December 31st, 1974

Stock of finished goods at start	£ 20,000	Stock of finished goods at close	£ 18,000
Cost of manufactured goods	148,500	Sales (less returns) (260,000 - 2,000)	258,000
Gross profit	107,500		
	£276,000		£276,000
	========		========

Profit and Loss Account - January 1st-December 31st, 1974

Office salaries	£ 20,000	Gross profit	£107,500
Administrative expenses	13,000	Non-operating income	4,000
Sales commissions	2,000		
Other items, office expenses	£ 10,000		
Non-operating expenses	2,000		
Net profit before tax	64,500		
	£111,500		£111,500
	========		========

Appropriation Account

Dividend proposed 20% of year's net profit	£ 12,900	Net profit	£ 64,500
Transfer to reserve account (10% of year's net profit)	6,450	Balance from previous year	30,000
Tax (40% of year's net profit)	25,800		
Balance	49,350		
	£ 94,500		£ 94,500
	========		========

2. *Part I*

BALANCE SHEET AS AT DECEMBER 1ST, 1974

I T E M	1972	1973	1974	- - -
1. LIABILITIES	$ 320,000			
1.1 *Equity and loans*	230,000			
1.1.1 Shares	100,000			
1.1.2 Reserves	30,000			
1.1.3 Retained earnings (Profit/loss account)	20,000			
1.1.4 Reserve for future taxation	10,000			
1.1.5 Long term loans (debentures)	40,000			
1.1.6 Short term loans	30,000			
1.1.7 Others	-			
1.2 *Current liabilities*	90,000			
1.2.1 Creditors	50,000			
1.2.2 Overdrafts	20,000			
1.2.3 Dividends due	10,000			
1.2.4 Tax due	10,000			
1.2.5 Others	-			
2. ASSETS	$ 320,000			
2.1 *Intangibles*	20,000			
2.1.1 Goodwill	20,000			
2.2 *Fixed assets (net)*	200,000			
2.2.1 Land	80,000			
2.2.2 Buildings (net)	60,000			
2.2.2.1 Buildings at cost	80,000			
2.2.2.2 Accumulated depreciation	20,000			
2.2.3 Plant and/or equipment (net)	50,000			
2.2.3.1 Plant and/or equipment at cost	60,000			
2.2.3.2 Accumulated depreciation	10,000			
2.2.4 Others (net)	-			
2.2.4.1 Others at cost	-			
2.2.4.2 Accumulated depreciation	-			
2.2.5 Investments (purchase price)	10,000			

I T E M	1972	1973	1974	- - -
2.3 Current investments	100,000			
2.3.1 Cash	10,000			
2.3.2 Debtors (receivable)	70,000			
2.3.3 Inventories (stocks)	20,000			
2.3.3.1 Work in progress (inputs)	-			
2.3.3.2 Finished products (outputs)	20,000			

Part II

a. Total current assets can be deduced either from the conventional layout or from the table above commonly used in project formulation.

Total current assets	US$ 100,000
b. Total current liabilities	US$ 90,000
c. Total external liabilities	

Debentures (long term loans)	US$	40,000
Loans (short term)	US$	30,000
Current liabilities	US$	90,000
T o t a l	US$	160,000

Note: Reserve for future taxation is not exactly a liability. It is at present a reserve earmarked for a future liability.

d. Quick assets are the most easily convertible into cash assets.

Total quick assets			
	Debtors	US$	70,000
	Cash	US$	10,000
	T o t a l	US$	80,000

e. Total owner's equity

Shares	US$	100,000
Reserves	US$	20,000
Profit and loss balance	US$	20,000
Tax reserve	US$	10,000
T o t a l	US$	160,000
		============

Note: Some companies would omit tax reserve from their total.

f. Working capital is the difference between current assets and current liabilities. It is also called net current assets.

Working capital			
or net current assets	Current assets	US$	100,000
	Current liabilities	US$	90,000
	T o t a l	US$	10,000
			============

g. Acid test ratio: US$ 80,000 : US$ 90,000 less than 1:1 so possibly not satisfactory. The business may have difficulty in meeting current commitments, unless it can obtain additional credit (a 1:1 ratio is *always advisable*).

h. Current liquidity ratio: US$ 100,000 : US$ 90,000 less than 2:1 so possibly not satisfactory.

i. Degree of solvency: External liabilities are US$ 160,000 which is 50% of total liabilities (US$ 320,000). Therefore the *solvency ratio* is: 100% - 50% = 50%

4.   SOURCES AND APPLICATION OF FUNDS STATEMENT 1972

	(Kobos)
1. SOURCES	113,000
1.1 Cash Income	3,000
1.1.1 Retained earnings [net profit (loss)]	2,000
1.1.2 Add: depreciation	1,000
1.2 Equity	80,000
1.2.1 Ordinary shares	80,000
1.2.2 Preference shares	–
1.2.3 Deferred shares	–
1.3 Loans	30,000
1.3.1 Long term loan from: (A)	30,000
1.3.2 Long term loan from: (B)	–
.	
.	
.	
1.3.n Others	–
2. APPLICATIONS	110,000
2.1 Buildings and Equipment	100,000
2.1.1 Plant buildings	40,000
2.1.2 Office buildings	20,000
2.1.3 Plant equipment	25,000
2.1.4 Office equipment	15,000
.	
.	
.	
2.1.n Others	–
2.2 Other Capital Expenditures	–
2.3 Replacements	–
2.4 Debt Service	8,000
2.4.1 Interest	3,000
2.4.1.1 Interest long term loan from:(A)	3,000
2.4.1.2 Interest long term loan from:(B)	–
.	
.	
.	
2.4.1.n Others	–
2.4.2 Amortization	5,000
2.4.2.1 Amortization long term loan from:(A)	5,000
2.4.2.2 Amortization long term loan from:(B)	–
.	
.	
.	
2.4.2.n Others	–

2.5 Increase in Accounts Receivable –
   Increase in Payables (debtor – current liabilities)   1,000

2.6 Increase in Inventories   1,000
   2.6.1 Work in progress   500
   2.6.2 Finished products   500

3. CASH SURPLUS (DEFICIT) [SOURCES – APPLICATIONS]   3,000

   3.1 Annual   3,000

   3.2 Cumulative   –

Question Set III: Discounting Exercises Involving Risk and Uncertainty
(Based on Chapter 3)

1. Distinguish between the concepts of "risk" and "uncertainty" and
   briefly illustrate and discuss decision-making criteria appropriate to each.

2. A project having an initial outlay of $1500 has a stream of annual
   net revenues for 10 years described by the following probability
   distribution:

Annual Net Revenues ($)	Probability
Years 1-4	
100	10%
120	20%
150	30%
200	25%
250	15%
Years 5-10	
150	5%
175	10%
200	40%
250	35%
300	10%

   Assuming a discount rate of 5% p.a., calculate the expected NPV for
   this project using as a measure of central tendency: (a) the mode;
   (b) the arithmetic mean; and (c) the expected value.

3. Under what circumstances will the mode, the arithmetic mean and the
   expected value of a given distribution coincide?

4. You are asked to evaluate a five-year agricultural project where the
   yield is sensitive to rainfall and operating costs depend on the performance of a new agricultural harvesting machine. You are supplied
   with the following information:

   (a) the project involves an outlay of $2000;

(b) the price of the output is fixed for the next 5 years at $10/ ton;

(c) the expected annual rainfall is described by the following probability distribution:

Rainfall (cm.)	Probability
5	0%
15	15%
30	20%
50	35%
70	15%
85	10%
100	5%

(d) expected annual yields from different levels of rainfall are:

Rainfall (cm.)	Yield (tons)
5	25
15	75
30	90
50	100
70	80
85	50
100	10

(e) annual operating costs are expected to be $300 p.a., but the machine supplier has indicated that depending on the machine's performance these might be as low as $200 p.a. (an optimistic estimate) or as high as $350 p.a. (a pessimistic estimate).

Assuming no salvage values after 5 years, and a discount rate of 4% p.a., show how you would evaluate this project and reach a decision. (If any further assumptions are necessary, make these explicit.)

5. (a) If the 'high' and 'low' estimated values for a certain variate are equidistant from the 'best' estimate, what is one assuming about the shape of the probability distribution when one uses some form of three-point distribution?

(b) What implicit judgement is one making about the expected occurence of the 'high' and 'low' estimates when one chooses the Beta in preference to the Triangular three-point distribution?

*6. For a certain irrigation project the present value of the return is
    a function of the cost of establishing a facility and n annual equal
    net returns thereafter. The annual net returns consist of revenues
    obtained from the increased production of three crops. Both the num-
    ber of acres and the yield per acre of crop 1 largely depend on wages
    farmers can earn in an alternative employment. The price of commodity
    2 is assumed to be negatively correlated with the output of crop 2
    by the project. Prices of commodities 1 and 3 are not affected by the
    project's output.

The model for calculating the present value of benefits is given in
Table 1, and the probability distributions of the 10 inputs needed
for estimating the model are given in Table 2.

You are required to calculate the expected NPV of this project assuming a discount rate of 8% per annum.

TABLE 1

(1) Acres in production of crop 1 (A) are a
    function of wage in an alternative $(A) = 10 - (W)$
    employment (W).

(2) Yield per acre of crop 1 (Y) is a
    function of wage in alternative $(Y) = 10 - 2(W)$
    employment (W).

(3) Production of crop 1 (X_1) is acres (A) $(X_1) = (A)(Y) + (e_1)$
    times yield (Y) and a random effect (e_1).

(4) Gross revenue from crop 1 (S_1) is price $(S_1) = (Z_1)(X_1)$
    (Z_1) times production (X_1).

(5) Price of crop 2 (Z_2) is a function of
    slope coefficient (b), production of $(Z_2) = 10 - (b)(X_2)$
    crop 2 (X_2) and a random effect (e_2). $+ (e_2)$

(6) Gross revenue from crop 2 (S_2) is price $(S_2) = (Z_2)(X_2)$
    (Z_2) times production (X_2).

(7) Gross revenue from crop 3 (S_3) is price $(S_3) = (Z_3)(X_3)$
    (Z_3) times production (X_3).

(8) Annual net benefit (B) is gross revenues (S_1, S_2, and S_3) less annual cost.

$$(B) = (S_1) + (S_2) + (S_3) - 70$$

(9) The sum of the discounting factors (Σa^t) is a function of the life of the investment (n).

$$(\Sigma a^t) = (1+.08)^{-t}$$
$$t = 1, \ldots n$$

(10) Present value (R) is a function of the discount factors (Σa^t) and the annual benefits (B), less the initial investment (B_1).

$$(R) = (\Sigma a^t)(B) - (B_1)$$

TABLE 2

Inputs	Outcome	Probability	Inputs	Outcome	Probability
	1	.30		1,600	.25
W ($)	2	.40	B_1 ($)	2,000	.50
	3	.30		2,400	.25
	2.4	.33		5	.33
Z_1 ($)	3.0	.33	n (years)	10	.33
	3.6	.33		15	.33
	3.5	.20		.06	.30
Z_3 ($)	5.0	.60	b	.10	.40
	6.5	.20		.14	.30
	30	.33		-10	.30
X_2 (tons)	50	.33	e_1 (tons)	0	.40
	70	.33		+10	.30
	14	.33		- 0.4	.30
X_3 (tons)	20	.33	e_2 ($)	0	.40
	26	.33		0.4	.30

Source of Tables: Reutlinger (1970), p.83.

7. If most of the variates entering the definition of the NPV can be
   assumed independent of one another, what can (in most cases) be
   assumed about the resulting distribution of NPV? Explain why the
   same is not true of distibutions generated by correlated variates.

*8. You are faced with making a decision between two projects, A and B,
   the outcomes of which depend upon the value of a certain variable
   which is known to vary from x_1 to x_3. The outcomes in terms of NPVs
   are given in the table below.

	x_1	x_2	x_3
A	12	10	7
B	15	8	3

   Use the various Games Theory criteria to show which of the two projects might be chosen by a decision-maker who is:

   (a) a compulsive gambler;
   (b) highly risk averse;
   (c) thoughtfully cautious.

9. An engineering consultant has claimed that by using a new piece of
   equipment, a textile project's production costs could be reduced
   substantially. As the project's economic advisor you have calculated that unless unit production time is reduced by 12%, the new machine will not be financially more profitable than the older alternative, as it involves higher maintenance costs. A sample survey of
   40 users of the new machine indicates that the mean reduction in production time is 10%. (The standard deviation of the distribution is
   1%.) Assuming that the sample has been randomly drawn from the population from which the new machine will be selected, you are required
   to answer the following questions:

   (a) What is the probability of the new machine being more profitable
       than the older one?

(b) What is the probability that a new machine will reduce production time by the following amounts: (i) 9%, (ii) 10%, (iii) 13%?

10. The Republic of Uhuria has called upon economists in the Ministry of Agriculture to evaluate an irrigation project which will produce cotton as its main crop. As part of the evaluation team, you have been called upon to forecast the world price of cotton from 1980 (when the crop is expected) until the year 2020.

All inputs and outputs of the project are to be expressed in terms of 1976 prices (the year when the first investment will be undertaken).

You have the following data on cotton prices, in US cents per pound (f.o.b. US East Coast). The data refer to Mexican SM 1 1/16" which is the likely staple length of the variety your scheme will be producing. All prices are expressed as annual seasonally weighted averages. (Table 1)

You also have an index of International Prices produced by IBRD based on all goods entering into international trade. Note that the major share of goods entering into international trade is that of manufacturers. (Table 2)

I. You are asked to:
   (a) convert Table 2 showing 1976 as the base year;
   (b) convert Table 1 into 1976 constant prices;
   (c) comment on the appropriateness of using the IBRD international price index.

TABLE 1

Average Annual Price Cotton in US Cents/Lb.

	Mexican SM 1 – 1/16"		Mexican SM 1 – 1/16"
1961	30.36	1968	31.92
1962	30.08	1969	28.89
1963	29.11	1970	29.34
1964	29.52	1971	33.12
1965	29.19	1972	38.22
1966	18.27	1973	43.67
1967	29.34		

(Source: 'Cotton World Statistics', ICAC, Washington)

TABLE 2

Index of International Prices
(1973 = 100)

1955	61.9	1970	78.5
1960	64.6	1971	85.1
1961	64.8	1972	90.0
1962	65.0	1973	100.0
1963	65.4	1974	105.8
1964	66.2	1975	110.2
1965	67.7	1976	114.3
1966	69.0	1977	118.3
1967	69.4	1978	122.4
1968	69.6	1979	126.7
1969	73.5	1980	131.2

(Source: IBRD, IMF)

II. Having completed section I, you are now asked to:

(a) project cotton world market prices in 1976 constant prices
(f.o.b. East Coast U.S.A.) for the years 1980-2020.

   i. plot your observations both in observed and constant
      terms;

   ii. fit a trend by least squares (should the data be smooth-
       ed beforehand – if so why?);

   iii. calculate the goodness of fit (R^2) and the standard er-
        ror associated with the slope coefficient (S_β).

(b) Calculate the 68% and 95% confidence intervals for projected
prices of cotton (1975 prices) in the years 1980, 1990, 2000,
2010 and 2020.

Answer Set III

2. Initial outlay (year 0) = $1500

   Expected annual net revenue

   (a) Mode:

   Years 1 to 4 = $150; years 5 to 10 = $200

   $\text{NPV}_{(0.05)}$ = -$1500 + $150(3.45) + $200(5.08)(0.82)

   $\qquad$ = -$1500 + $531 + $833

   $\qquad$ = -$136

   (b) Arithmetic mean:

   Years 1 to 4 = ($100 + $120 + $150 + $200 + $250) ÷ 5

   $\qquad$ = $164

   Years 5 to 10 = ($150 + $175 + $200 + $250 + $300) ÷ 5

   $\qquad$ = $215

   $\text{NPV}_{(0.05)}$ = -$1500 + $164(3.54) + $215(5.08)(0.82)

   $\qquad$ = -$1500 + $581 + $896

   $\qquad$ = $23

   (c) Expected value:

   Years 1 to 4 = $100(0.10) + $120(0.2) + $150(0.3) + $200(0.25) +
                   $250(0.15)

   $\qquad$ = $10 + $24 + $45 + $50 + $37.5

   $\qquad$ = $166.5

   Years 5 to 10 = $150(0.05) + $175(0.10) + $200(0.40) + $250(0.35)
                    + $300(0.10)

   $\qquad$ = $7.5 + $17.5 + $80 + $87.5 + $30

   $\qquad$ = $222.5

   $\text{NPV}_{(0.05)}$ = -$1500 + $1665(3.54) + $222.5(5.08)(0.82)

   $\qquad$ = -$1500 + $589 + $927

   $\qquad$ = $16

4. Initial outlay (year 0) = $2000

   Expected annual returns (years 1-5)

   (a) Expected annual yield (tons) = 0.0(25) + 0.15(75) + 0.2(90) +

   $$0.35(100) + 0.15(80) + 0.1(50) +$$

   $$0.05(10)$$

   $$= 0 + 11.25 + 18 + 35 + 12 + 5 + 0.5$$

   $$= 81.75 \text{ tons}$$

   (b) Expected annual returns = expected yield x price

   $$= 81.75 \times \$10$$

   $$= \$817.5$$

   Expected annual costs (years 1-5)

   (a) 3 point triangular method: $\bar{x} = \dfrac{0 + 2E + P}{4}$

   $$= \frac{200 + 2(300) + 350}{4}$$

   $$= \frac{1150}{4}$$

   $$= \$287.5$$

   (b) Beta method: $\bar{x} = \dfrac{0 + 4E + P}{6}$

   $$= \frac{200 + 4(300) + 350}{6}$$

   $$= \frac{1750}{6}$$

   $$= \$291.7$$

   Expected annual net revenue (years 1-5)

   Expected net revenue = expected returns - expected costs

   (a) = $817.5 - $287.5

        = $530

   or (b) = $817.5 - $291.7

        = $525.8

   Expected NPV (4%)

   (a) E (NPV) = - 2000 + 530(4.452)

              = - 2000 + 2359.6

              = $359.6

or (b) E (NPV) = - 2000 + 525.8(4.452)

$$= - 2000 + 2340.9$$

$$= \$340.9$$

Therefore, irrespective of the method used for calculating expected annual costs, the project's expected NPV is positive.

6. From Table 2, the expected values for the ten inputs are as follows:

i. $W = \$2$

ii. $Z_1 = \$3$

iii. $Z_3 = \$5$

iv. $X_2 = 50$ tons

v. $X_3 = 20$ tons

vi. $B_1 = \$2000$

vii. $n = 10$ years

viii. $b = 0.10$

ix. $e_1 = 0$

x. $e_2 = \$0$

Substituting these values into the equations in Table 1, the values of the remaining inputs can be calculated.

i. $A = 10 - 2$

$$= 8$$

ii. $Y = 10 - 2(2)$

$$= 6$$

iii. $X_1 = 8(6) + 0$

$$= 48$$

iv. $Z_2 = 10 - 0.1(50) + 0$

$$= 5$$

Expected annual gross revenue

i. Crop 1 $(S_1) = \$3(48)$

$$= \$144$$

ii. Crop 2 $(S_2) = \$5(50)$

$$= \$250$$

iii. Crop 3 $(S_3) = \$5(20)$

$$= \$100$$

$S_1 + S_2 + S_3 = \$144 + \$250 + \$100$

$$= \$494$$

Expected annual net revenue (B)

$B = (S_1 + S_2 + S_3) - \$70$

$\quad = \$494 - \$70$

$\quad = \$424$

Expected net present value

Expected initial outlay $(B_1) = \$2000$

Expected life of project $(n) = 10$ years

Discount rate $(i) = 8\%$

$E(NPV)_{0.08} = -\$2000 + \$424(6.71)$

$\quad\quad\quad\quad = -\$2000 + \$2845$

$\quad\quad\quad\quad = \$845$

8. (a) A compulsive gambler might adopt a 'maximax' returns decision rule and therefore select project B which gives the highest possible value in terms of NPB; i.e. 15.

   (b) A highly risk adverse decision-maker might adopt a 'maximin' returns decision rule and select project A which gives the highest value in terms of NPV if the worst outcome occurs; i.e. 7.

   (c) A thoughtfully cautious decision-maker might adopt a 'maximax risk' decision rule and select project A which minimises the degree of error he might make; i.e. by selecting A his maximum potential loss is 3, but by selecting B his maximum potential loss is 4. You might also have interpreted this as minimising 'regret' (Savage) and shown how a 'regret matrix' could be derived, or even gone on to discuss more sophisticated approaches such as Hurwicz's 'index of pessimism'.

Question Set IV: *Efficiency Pricing of Traded Goods and the SER*
                  (Based on Chapters 4 and 5)

1. The gains from autarky are greater than the gains from following comparative advantage in trade. Discuss.

2. The Little-Mirrlees and UNIDO methods differ only with respect to
   choice of the *numeraire*; systematically applied, the methods yield
   equivalent results. Comment.

3. Why is it necessary to use a 'shadow exchange rate' (SER) to value
   foreign exchange when using the UNIDO method? What are the main difficulties one is likely to encounter in estimating this?

* 4. You are supplied with the following data for a hypothetical five-good
   economy:

Good	Units imported/ exported	Domestic price per unit (pesos)	Accounting ratio $\{ P_w(\$) / P_d(P.) \}$
Food (export)	2000	200	1.0
Minerals (export)	500	250	1.0
Capital goods (import)	750	400	0.75
Consumer durables (import)	300	200	0.50
Textiles and clothing (import)	250	100	0.80

The official rate of exchange (OER) is $1 = 1 Peso (P).

Calculate the following:

(a) The 'border price' or foreign exchange equivalent for each good
    expressed in the domestic currency (P).

(b) The total value of exports minus imports at 'border prices' expressed in:

   i. foreign currency ($); and

   ii. domestic currency (P).

(c) The 'shadow exchange rate' (SER) for the economy, assuming that the marginal composition of exports and imports is equal to their average composition.

(d) The total value of exports minus imports using domestic consumption as the numeraire.

(e) The 'summary conversion factor' (SCF).

*5. Repeat the above exercise assuming an OER of $1 = P. 1.5.

*6. In relation to the evaluation of a project designed to expand the coffee industry in a Latin American country you have been provided with the following information:

(a) Each unit of coffee produced requires 25 man-days of unskilled labour, 10 man-days of skilled labour and 0.5 units of capital equipment.

(b) Daily wage rates are:

   i. unskilled labour, P. 4

   ii. skilled labour, P. 10

(c) Unskilled workers spend 90 percent of their wage on consumer non-durables and 10 percent on consumer durables.

(d) Skilled workers spend 30 percent of their wage on consumer non-durables and 70 percent on durables.

(e) The economy exports coffee (domestic price = P. 600/unit), and consumer non-durables (domestic price = P. 450/unit); and imports capital goods (world price = $800/unit), and consumer durables (world price = $500/unit).

(f) The official rate of exchange is $1 = P. 1.

(g) Tariff protection on imports: capital goods, 100%; consumer dur-
    ables, 300%.

You are required to calculate the net benefit (per unit) of expanding coffee production in terms of:

   a. domestic prices (P)
   b. impact on foreign exchange, using as the numeraire:
      i. foreign exchange (LMST method);
      ii. domestic consumption (UNIDO method).

*7. If a 25 percent tariff is imposed on the import of textiles and a 50
    percent tariff on the import of cotton, what is the effective rate of
    protection on textiles if cotton inputs are 60 percent of total inputs
    in textile production?

8. To use world prices for valuing traded goods, the price elasticity of
   import supply and export demand must be perfectly elastic. Explain
   this and discuss the implication of less than infinite price elasticities for the Little-Mirrlees approach.

*9. Calculate the domestic prices and accounting ratios (AR) for the fol-
    lowing traded goods:

    (a) Imported goods

Good	c.i.f. Price (P)	Duty (P)
Textiles	100	20
Clothing	120	40
Oil	300	30
Steel	500	75

(b) Exported goods

Good	f.o.b. Price (P)	Export Tax (P)
Tea	200	50
Sugar	750	250
Rice	450	50
Coffee	1250	250

*10. Calculate the accounting ratios for the following traded goods.

Good	Domestic price (R.)	c.i.f/f.o.b price (R.)	e_s / e_d^+
(a) import	100	75	1.5
(b) export	80	80	– 4.0
(c) import	36	40	10.0
(d) import	120	80	2.0
(e) export	75	60	– 5.0
(f) export	50	60	– 1.0

$^+ e_s$ and e_d are the price elasticities of supply and demand respectively. (Note that export demand elasticities are always negative.)

Answer Set IV

4.

Good	Domestic Price(P)	A.R.	World/Border Price $	World/Border Price P.	Tariff	F.E. value of trade $(10^3)	P(10^3)	SER/OER (=SER)	Domestic consumption value P(10^3)
	1	2	3(a)	3(b)	4	5(a)	5(b)	6	7
Food (export)	200	1.0	200	200	–	+400	+400	1.14	+456
Minerals (export)	250	1.0	250	250	–	+125	+125	1.14	+142.5
Capital goods (import)	400	0.75	300	300	33.3%	–225	–225	1.14	–256.5
Durables (import)	200	0.50	100	100	100%	– 30	– 30	1.14	– 34.2
Textiles and cloth (import)	100	0.80	80	80	25%	– 20	– 20	1.14	– 22.8
T o t a l	–	–	–	–	–	+250	+250	1.14	+285

Part:

(a) To calculate the world or border price of each good in terms of the domestic currency, the world price in $ (column 3(a)) is first calculated by multiplying the domestic price (column 1) by the accounting ratio (column 2).[†] World prices in $ are then converted to world prices in the domestic currency (column 3(b)) using the official rate of exchange (OER); $1 = P. 1.

(b) The value of exports/imports of each good at world prices is found by multiplying the number of units traded by: (i) the world price in $ (column 3(a)); and, (ii) the world price in Pesos (column 3(b)), to arrive at a figure for the net value of trade expressed in $ (column 5(a)) and Pesos (column 5(b)) respectively.

(c) On the assumption that the average composition of exports and imports gives an accurate indication of the marginal trade bill, the ratio SER/OER is calculated using the formula:

$$\sum_{i}^{n} f_i \left(Pd_i \Big/ Pw_i \right) + \sum_{j}^{m} x_j \left(Pd_j \Big/ Pw_j \right)$$

where: f_i = fraction of marginal foreign exchange spent on the ith import;

x_j = fraction of marginal foreign exchange earned on the jth export;

Pd_i = domestic price of the ith import expressed in domestic currency;

Pd_j = domestic price of the jth export expressed in domestic currency;

[†]Note that it is assumed here that the unit of account is $ and therefore $AR = \dfrac{Pw\ (\$)}{Pd\ (P)}$. If one makes the more common assumption that the domestic currency (P) is the unit account, the $AR = \dfrac{Pw\ (P)}{Pd\ (P)}$ which implies different results when $1 \neq P. 1$.

Pw_i = world price of the ith import expressed in *domestic* currency;

Pw_j = world price of the jth export expressed in *domestic* currency.

Therefore, SER/OER =

Food	+	Minerals	+	Capital goods	+	Durables	+	Textiles and cloth

$$\frac{400}{800} \cdot \frac{200}{200} + \frac{125}{800} \cdot \frac{250}{250} + \frac{225}{800} \cdot \frac{400}{300} + \frac{30}{800} \cdot \frac{200}{100} + \frac{20}{800} \cdot \frac{100}{80}$$

$$= \ 0.50 + 0.16 + 0.37 + 0.08 + 0.03$$

$$= \ 1.14$$

SER = 1.14 (OER)

  = 1.14(1)

  = 1.14

(d) To convert the value of goods traded from foreign exchange values into domestic consumption values (column 7) two procedures are possible:

  i. the foreign exchange value in \$ (column 5(a)) is multiplied by the SER (1.14);

  ii. the foreign exchange value in Pesos (column 5(b)) is multiplied by the ratio SER/OER (1.14).

  Both methods yield the same result.

  (Note in this case that as \$1 = 1 P., column 5(a) is the same as column 5(b), and SER/OER = SER.)

(e) If the summary conversion factor is defined as the reciprocal of the SER then:

  SCF = 1/SER = 1/1.14 = 0.88

5.

Good	1 Domestic Price (P)	2 A.R.	3(a) World Price $	3(b) World Price P.	4 Tariff	5(a) F.E. Value of trade $(10^3)	5(b) F.E. Value of trade P.(10^3)	6(a) SER	6(b) SER/OER	7 Domestic Consumption Value P.(10^3)
Food (export)	200	1.0	200	300	−33.3%	+400	·+600	1.14	0.76	+456.0
Minerals (export)	250	1.0	150	375	−33.3%	+125	+187.5	1.14	0.76	+142.5
Capital goods (import)	400	0.75	300	450	−11.1%	−225	−337.5	1.14	0.76	−256.5
Durables (import)	200	0.50	100	150	−33.3%	− 30	− 45	1.14	0.76	− 34.2
Textiles and cloth (import)	100	0.80	80	120	−16.7%	− 20	− 30	1.14	0.76	− 22.8
Total	−	−	−	−	−	+250	+375	1.14	0.76	+285.0

Repeating the exercise with a new OER of $1 = P. 1.5 involves the
identical calculations to those outlined in the answer to Question
4. In comparing the results note that:

(a) As the domestic prices (column 1) and accounting ratios (column
    2) of the goods are unchanged, the world prices expressed in $
    (column 3(a)) are also unchanged, but because the OER is now $1 =
    P. 1.5, the world prices expressed in Pesos (column 3(b)) have
    changed.

(b) As the world prices in $ are unchanged, the foreign exchange val-
    ue of imports and exports expressed in $ (column 5(a)) is also
    unchanged, but as the OER has changed the F.E. values expressed
    in the domestic currency (column 5(b)) have also changed; i.e.
    increased by 50%.

(c) As the ratios of domestic to world price of the goods *expressed
    in Pesos* have changed, the ratio of SER/OER (column 6(b)) has
    also changed, but as their foreign exchange values expressed in
    $ (column 5(a)), and the ratio of domestic price (column 1) to
    world price in $ (column 3(a) are unchanged, the SER is still
    1.14 (column 6(a)). (Note that SER = SER/OER x OER = 0.76 x 1.5
    = 1.14.)

(d) Following either of the procedures for converting foreign exchange
    values to domestic consumption values outlined in the answer to
    question 4(e) above [i.e. {column 5(a)} x {column 6(a)} *or* {col-
    umn 5(b)} x {column 6(b)}], the net domestic consumption value
    is derived (column 7) which, it should be noted, is unchanged.

(e) It follows that the SCF is also unchanged.

5. *Working Tables*

   Step 1: From parts (e), (f) and (g) of the information provided con-
           struct a table showing the protective structure of the econ-
           omy. (The bracketed figures are those that are provided in
           the question.)

		1	2	3(a)	3(b)	4	5
Good	Abrev.	Domestic price(P)	Tariff	World price P.	World price $	A.R.	Pd/Pw (P)
Coffee (export)	C	(600)	–	600	600	1	1
Non-durables (export)	N.D.	(450)	–	450	450	1	1
Capital goods (import)	K	1600	(100%)	800	(800)	0.5	2
Durables (import)	D	2000	(300%)	500	(500)	0.25	4

(a) The world prices of coffee (C) and non-durables (N.D.) expressed in P. (column 3(a)) are calculated by subtracting from their domestic prices (column 1), the tariff (column 2). As this is zero, domestic and world prices expressed in P. are equal. These are then converted to world prices expressed in $ (column 3(b)) using the OER, $1 = P. 1.

(b) Conversely the world prices of capital goods and durables expressed in $ (column 3(b)) are converted to world prices in P. using the OER, and then into domestic prices (column 1) by adding to these the respective tariffs (column 2).

(c) The accounting ratios (AR) (column 4) are found by dividing the world price of each good (column 3) by its domestic price (column 1).

(d) The ratio of domestic to world price of each good expressed in the domestic currency; i.e. (column 1) ÷ (column 3(a)) is calculated (column 5) to facilitate the calculation of SER/OER at a later stage (see explanatory note to column 9 below).

Step 2: Using information provided in parts (a) - (d) of the question construct a table showing the unit returns and costs of coffee production in terms of domestic prices, and the decomposition of these into their foreign exchange equivalents.

Item	6 Domestic returns/costs P.	7(a) Direct	7(b) Indirect	7(c) Total	8 F.E. impact P.	9 SER/OER (=SER)	10 Domestic consumption value P.
		Foreign exchange impact ($)					
Returns/unit:							
Coffee	600	+600		+600	+600	1.41	+846
Costs/unit:							
Capital goods	800	-400		-400	-400	1.41	-564
(Labour)							
(Unskilled - L_u)	(200)	–					
	(100)	–					
(Skilled - L_s)	(100)	–					
Non-durables	120		-120	-120	-120	1.41	-169.2
Durables	80		- 20	- 20	- 20	1.41	- 28.2
Net benefit	-400	-200	-140	+ 60	+ 60	1.41	+ 84.6

Explanatory Notes:

Column 6:   (a) Given the production function $1C = 25L_u + 10L_s + 0.5K$
and the wage rates for unskilled and skilled labour, the
returns and unit factor costs (capital and labour) are derived (column 6).   (b) Unit labour costs, shown in brackets,
are then decomposed into traded goods (non-durables and durables) on the basis of the consumption data provided in
parts (c) and (d) of the question.

Column 7(a): The return on coffee and the cost of capital inputs are
expressed in terms of world prices ($) using the A.R. cal-
culated in column 4 of the previous table.

Column 7(b): The cost of labour inputs, decomposed into traded goods,
are similarly expressed in world prices ($) using the A.R.'s
for non-durables and durables (from column 4).

Column 7(c): Columns 7(a) and 7(b) are combined to derive the total
foreign exchange impact per unit of coffee production, expressed in $.

Column 8:   The total foreign exchange impact is expressed in domestic
currency (P) using the OER.

Column 9:   If the marginal trade bill is defined, for the purpose of
calculating a SER, as the trade bill of the project as a
whole:

$$\text{SER/OER} = \underset{\text{Coffee}}{\frac{600}{1140}(1)} \; + \; \underset{\substack{\text{Capital}\\\text{goods}}}{\frac{400}{1140}(2)} \; + \; \underset{\substack{\text{Non-}\\\text{durables}}}{\frac{120}{1140}(1)} \; + \; \underset{\text{Durables}}{\frac{20}{1140}(4)}$$

$$= 0.53 + 0.70 + 0.11 + 0.07$$

$$= 1.41$$

Therefore, SER = 1.41(OER)

$$= 1.41(1)$$

$$= 1.41$$

Column 10: Foreign exchange values; (i) expressed in $ (column 7(c))
          are converted into domestic consumption values (column 10)
          using the SER (column 9); or (ii) expressed in P. (column
          8) are converted into domestic consumption values (column
          10) using the ratio SER/OER (column 9). (As OER is $1 = P.1
          these are identical.)

Answer

   Net benefit/unit of coffee: (a) in domestic (financial) prices is
   -P. 400 (column 6); (b) in terms of foreign exchange impact using
   as the numéraire, (i) foreign exchange values, is $60 *or* P. 60;
   (ii) domestic consumption values, is P. 84.6.

7. The effective rate of protection (ERP) measures the percentage by
   which actual domestic value added in the industry in question (V')
   exceeds the value added in that industry when all inputs and outputs are valued at world prices (V), i.e.:

$$ERP = \frac{V' - V}{V} \cdot 100$$

   Without any further information concerning the composition of the
   other inputs (apart from cotton) into textile production, and the
   tariffs on these, it is not possible to calculate the ERP.

   If it is assumed, however, that cotton is the only intermediate input, and the remaining 40 percent is made up entirely of value added
   it is possible to calculate the ERP as follows:

   Let the domestic price of textiles be 100:

	Domestic price	Tariff	World price
Textiles	100	25%	80
Cotton	60	50%	40
Value added	40	–	40

$$ERP = \frac{40 - 40}{40} \cdot 100$$

$$= 0\%$$

9. (a) Imported goods

	1	2	3 (=1+2)	4 (=1÷3)
Good	Price (P)	Duty (P)	Domestic Price (P)	A.R.
Textiles	100	20	120	0.833
Clothing	120	40	160	0.750
Oil	300	30	330	0.909
Steel	500	75	575	0.870

(b) Exported goods

	1	2	3 (=1-2)	4 (=1÷3)
Good	f.o.b. Price (P)	Export tax(P)	Domestic Price (P)	A.R.
Tea	200	50	150	1.333
Sugar	750	250	500	1.500
Rice	450	50	400	1.125
Coffee	1250	250	1000	1.250

10. As the price elasticities of supply and demand for these goods are less than infinity, it is necessary to calculate their marginal import costs (imports) and marginal export revenues (exports) in terms of the formulae:

$$MC = P_{cif}(1 + 1/e_s) \; ; \text{ and}$$

$$MR = P_{fob}(1 + 1/e_d).$$

The accounting ratios (AR) can then be calculated by dividing the marginal import cost (MC) or marginal export revenue (MR) of the good by its domestic price.

(a) MC_a = $75(1 + \frac{1}{1.5})$ AR_a = $\frac{125}{100}$

       = 125 = 1.25

(b) MR_b = $80(1 - \frac{1}{4.0})$ AR_b = $\frac{60}{80}$

       = 60 = 0.75

(c) MC_c = $40(1 + \frac{1}{10})$ AR_c = $\frac{44}{36}$

       = 44 = 1.22

(d) MC_d = $80(1 + \frac{1}{2.0})$ AR_d = $\frac{120}{120}$

       = 120 = 1.0

(e) MR_e = $60(1 - \frac{1}{5.0})$ AR_e = $\frac{48}{75}$

       = 48 = 0.64

(f) MR_f = $60(1 - \frac{1}{1})$ AR_f = $\frac{0}{50}$

       = 0 = 0

Question Set V: ARs for Traded and Non-Traded Goods, Labour's Con-
sumption and the FTER (Based on Chapter 6)

1. Explain why the AR for the c.i.f. or f.o.b. component of the price
   of a traded good is always unity while the duty or tax element is
   always zero.

2. Compare and contrast the definitions of 'traded', 'potentially
   traded' and 'non-traded' goods adopted in the earlier OECD (1968)
   manual with the more recent LM (1974) manual, and discuss the data
   sources which might be relevant for determining the category to
   which a project's inputs and outputs belong.

*3. You are required to calculate the AR for an *imported* piece of machinery from the information provided in the table below:

Component	Cost (P)	A.R.
c.i.f. price	1200	1.0
Duty	600	0.0
Handling	150	0.8
Transport	300	0.9
Distribution	750	0.6
Domestic price	3000	AR_m

*4. (a) You are required to calculate the AR for a certain *export* good
   from the information provided in the table below:

Component	Cost (P)	A.R.
f.o.b. price	+600	1.00
Export tax	− 60	0.00
Handling	− 80	0.95
Transport	−100	0.84
Storage	− 40	0.70
Insurance	− 20	0.60
Distribution	−100	0.80
Producer subsidy	+200	0.00
Domestic price	400	AR_x

(b) If the export tax and producer subsidy were abolished, what would be the value of the AR? Would the accounting price of the good also change?

5. Compare and contrast the problems of valuing non-traded goods as project inputs and as project outputs. What implications might such difficulties have for the view that adopting the LMST approach avoids the problem of measuring 'consumer willingness to pay'?

6. A hypothetical country has an electricity generating capacity of 750 megawatts (MW), produced by three thermal stations located in different regions A, B and C, and with capacities of 375 MW, 300 MW and 75 MW respectively.

From the information given in the table below you are required to calculate the average unit (Kwh) cost of electricity as an input, at economic prices.

Cost per Kwh supplied –
5-year average at market prices (K)

Cost component	A	B	C	A.R.
Coal imports c.i.f	13.28	9.72	19.50	1.00
Import duty	1.76	1.44	2.35	0.00
Depreciation	3.32	2.85	5.70	0.95
Maintenance	3.32	2.37	4.75	0.95
Salaries and wages	6.00	2.65	5.70	0.60
Social security	0.32	0.24	0.50	0.00
Other materials	1.68	1.20	2.40	0.90
Transportation	1.32	0.72	1.45	0.80
Transmission	3.32	2.61	5.25	0.75
Administrative overheads	1.68	1.20	2.40	0.80
Total cost/Kwh	36.00	25.00	50.00	

*7. In order to calculate the AR for coal (a traded good) you require
    the AR for electricity (a non-traded input into coal production).
    However, in order to calculate the AR for electricity, you require
    the AR for coal (a traded input into electricity production).

    (a) Show how the AR's for both coal and electricity can be derived
        simultaneously from the information provided below:

Component	Coal price(P)	Electricity price(P)	A.R.
c.i.f.	126	–	1.00
Tax	14	10	0.00
Electricity	50	–	AR_e?
Coal	–	300	AR_c?
Labour	10	90	0.80
Domestic price	200	400	

    (b) What are the accounting prices of coal and electricity?

    (c) Now start by assigning arbitrary values to AR_e and AR_c and
        solve by successive iteration.

*8. (a) You are required to calculate the AR for labour's marginal con-
        sumption from the information given in the table below.

Good	Average consumption (%)	Income elasticity	A.R.
Food	70	0.90	1.00
Clothing	15	0.80	0.83
Appliances	10	1.25	0.40
Transport	05	2.50	0.80
T o t a l	100	–	AR_w

    (b) What are the possible effects on the AR for labour's consumption
        of a reduction of import duties on appliances?

9. Estimate the income elasticities of demand for the goods for which
   cross-section income and consumption data appears in the table below:

Income	Consumption	(Dinars)		
(Dinars)	Food	Clothing	Appliances	Services
4000	2500	200	100	150
8000	4000	300	220	375
12000	5200	375	352	656
16000	6240	437	493	984
20000	7176	492	641	1353

10. Under what circumstances will the imposition of import duties improve a country's terms of trade?

*11. The Planning Office in the Republic of Uhuria has been concerned with working out a shadow exchange rate (SER) for project appraisal. The official rate is 1 Kobo to 1 Dollar, a rate which most officials privately consider to overvalue the Kobo by anything between 20 and 50 percent. Although trade is presently in balance, this has been achieved by heavily protecting consumer goods imports which have a high price elasticity of demand -- Uhurians do not yet consider cars and televisions to be 'essential' possessions.

You have been given the following information. Imports consist of consumer goods and capital goods; exports consist of raw materials. Capital goods account for 30% of the value of imports, have a demand elasticity of 1, and are unprotected. Consumer goods account for 70% of imports, have an elasticity of 3, and enjoy effective protection of 50%. Raw materials carry an export tax of 10% and have a supply elasticity of 1. At the margin, it is estimated that an extra unit of foreign exchange will be spent·entirely on the purchase of extra imports (capital and consumer goods) in the above indicated proportions. Determine:

(a) the SER if present policies are unchanged;
(b) the SER if protection is entirely removed and trade balance is achieved by devaluation;

(c) explain briefly the circumstances under which you would con-
    sider it desirable to remove protection, the circumstances
    under which you would maintain present policies, and explain
    what alternative policies you might also consider.

3. Imported goods

Component	1 Cost (P)	2 % Final Price	3 A.R.	4 (=2x3) Accounting cost/unit
c.i.f. price	1200	0.40	1.0	0.40
Duty	600	0.20	0.0	0.00
Handling	150	0.05	0.8	0.04
Transport	300	0.10	0.9	0.09
Distribution	750	0.25	0.6	0.15
Domestic price	3000	1.00	-	0.68

$AR_m = 0.68$

Accounting price = AR_m x Domestic Price

= 0.68 x P. 3000

= P. 2040

4. Exported good

(a) With export tax and producer subsidy:

Component	1 Cost (P)	2 % Final Price	3 A.R.	4 (=2x3) Accounting cost/unit
f.o.b. price	+600	+1.50	1.00	+1.50
Export tax	- 60	-0.15	0.00	0.00
Handling	- 80	-0.20	0.95	-0.19
Transport	-100	-0.25	0.84	-0.21
Storage	- 40	-0.10	0.70	-0.07
Insurance	- 20	-0.05	0.60	-0.03
Distribution	-100	-0.25	0.80	-0.20
Producer's subsidy	+200	+0.50	0.00	0.00
Domestic price	400	1.00		+0.80

$AR_x = 0.80$

Accounting price = AR_x x Domestic Price

$\qquad\qquad\qquad$ = 0.80 x P. 400

$\qquad\qquad\qquad$ = P. 320

(b) Without export tax and producer's subsidy:

Component	Cost (P)	% Final Price	A.R.	Accounting cost/unit
	1	2	3	4 (= 2x3)
f.o.b. price	+600	+2.308	1.00	+2.308
Handling	- 80	-0.308	0.95	-0.293
Transport	-100	-0.385	0.84	-0.323
Storage	- 40	-0.154	0.70	-0.108
Insurance	- 20	-0.077	0.60	-0.046
Distribution	-100	-0.385	0.80	-0.308
Domestic price	260	1.000	-	+1.23

$AR_x = +1.23$

Accounting price = AR_x x Domestic Price

$\qquad\qquad\qquad$ = 1.23 x P. 260

$\qquad\qquad\qquad$ = p. 320

(Note that without the export tax and producer's subsidy, the domestic price and AR are different but the accounting *price* remains
the same.)

7. (a) *Simultaneous derivation of ARs for traded and non-traded goods*

Component	1(a) Coal Price (P)	1(b) % Final price	2(a) Electricity Price (P)	2(b) % Final price	3 A.R.	4(a) (=1bx3) Coal	4(b) (=2bx3) Electricity
						Accounting price/unit	
c.i.f price	126	0.63	-	-	1.00	0.63	-
Duty/tax	14	0.07	10	0.025	0.00	0.00	0.00
Electricity	50	0.25	-	-	AR_e ?	0.25(AR_e)	-
Coal	-	-	300	0.750	AR_c ?	-	0.75(AR_c)
Labour	10	0.05	90	0.225	0.80	0.04	0.18
Domestic price	200	1.00	400	1.000	-		

AR_c = 0.63 + 0.00 + 0.25(AR_e) + 0.04 .... 1.

AR_e = 0.00 + 0.75(AR_c) + 0.18 .... 2.

AR_c = 0.67 + 0.25(0.75AR_c + 0.18)   (substituting 2 into 1)

     = 0.67 + 0.1875AR_c + 0.045

     = 0.715 + 0.1875AR_c

AR_c - 0.1875AR_c = 0.715

0.8125AR_c = 0.715

AR_c = $\dfrac{0.715}{0.8125}$

     = 0.88

AR_e = 0.75(AR_c) + 0.18

     = 0.75(0.88) + 0.18

     = 0.84

(b) *Derivation of accounting prices*

     Accounting price of coal = AR_c x Domestic price of coal

                     = 0.88 x P. 200 = P. 176

     Accounting price of electricity = AR_e x Domestic price of electricity

                     = 0.84 x P. 400 = P. 366

(c) Whatever the values initially chosen, 3 iterations should suffice to arrive at estimates similar to those shown above.

8. (a)   Food   Clothing   Appliances

     AR_w = (0.7 x 0.9 x 1.0) + (0.15 x 0.8 x 0.83) + (0.1 x 1.25 x 0.4)

           Transport

        + (0.05 x 2.5 x 0.8)

      = 0.63 + 0.10 + 0.05 + 0.10

      = 0.88

11.

	% of M or X	Elasticity	Protection
(X) Raw material	100%	1	+10%
(M) Capital goods	30%	1	-
(M) Consumer goods	70%	3	+50%

(a) *SER under present policies:*

If protection remains, there is no need to know elasticies; SER would be given by:

$$SER = \frac{X(1 - tx) + M(1 + tm)}{X + M}$$

But since all foreign exchange is spent on imports (M), the export side of the expression is dropped and we get:

$$\frac{SER}{OER} = \frac{M(1 + tm)}{M} = \frac{30(1 + 0) + 70(1 + .50)}{30 + 70}$$

$$= \frac{145}{100}$$

$$= 1.45$$

SER is $1 = K 1.45

(b) *SER under new policies (Free Trade Exchange Rate):*

The above expression becomes:

$$\frac{FTER}{OER} = \frac{X_e(1 - t_x) + M_n(1 + t_m)}{X_e + M_n}$$

In this case foreign exchange is valued both according to X and M effects. Substituting we get:

$$\frac{FTER}{OER} = \frac{100 \times 1(1 - .10) + 30 \times 1(1 + 0) + 70 \times 3(1 + .5)}{(100 \times 1) + (30 \times 1) + (70 \times 3)}$$

$$= \frac{435}{340}$$

$$= 1.28$$

FTER is $1 = K 1.28

*Question Set VI: Economic Pricing of Factors, Distributional Objectives
and Social Pricing (Based on Chapters 7 and 8)*

1. Define the concept of 'opportunity cost' and contrast the principles
   involved in measuring the opportunity cost of labour, land and capital.

*2. An agricultural project has been proposed for a particular rural
   region. It involves an initial outlay of K. 300 per acre, is expected
   to have a 10-year life and to increase net output by K. 50 per acre
   during this period. Without the project annual net output is expected
   to remain at K. 100 per acre for the next 20 years at least.

   Assuming a discount rate of 4% p.a., you are required to calculate
   the opportunity cost (in domestic prices) of:

   (a) not undertaking the project at all; and
   (b) posponing the project for five years.

3. What is meant by the term 'accounting rate of interest' and how is
   it determined in practice?

4. Discuss the view that it is sometimes cheaper to finance projects
   through commercial borrowing than through aid.

*5. Using a 10 percent discount rate, rank the following loan offers in
   order of preference:

   (a) a 20-year loan with a five-year grace period, at 7 percent, tied
       to a source of supply with prices 26 percent higher than the mar-
       ket price;
   (b) a 10-year loan with no grace period, at 3 percent, tied to a
       source of supply with prices 37 percent higher than the market
       price;
   (c) an untied five-year loan with no grace period, at 10 percent.

6. In passing from 'economic' to 'social' cost benefit analysis the project analyst is required to make a series of value judgements about
   aggregate social parameters which are essentially arbitrary in nature.
   Discuss this statement distinguishing carefully between 'economic'
   and 'social' pricing.

7. Calculate the economic and social wage rates in each of the three
   cases below:

	$m(=C_i)$	AR_m	W_i	AR_c	$\overline{C}$	C_{cr}	n
(a)	400	0.85	500	0.8	800	700	0.5
(b)	1000	0.70	1200	0.6	900	600	1.0
(c)	600	0.90	700	0.7	600	450	2.0

*8. As a member of a team of project analysts responsible for the evalu-
    ation of a number of potential public sector projects in the 'modern'
    sector of the economy of Ainaza, you have been asked to calculate the
    'economic' and 'social' wage rates for unskilled labour. You are pro-
    vided with the following information:

   (a) It has been estimated from migration studies that for every un-
       skilled job opportunity created in the modern sector, 1.20 wor-
       kers will migrate from the rural to the modern sector.

   (b) The average per capita income of rural workers is estimated at
       1000 Zanas (Z) *per annum*.

   (c) The composition of marginal rural production and the correspon-
       ding accounting ratios (AR's) have already been estimated and
       are provided in the table below.

Component	% of total	AR
Beef	50%	0.90
Maize	20%	0.75
Sorghum	15%	1.00
Dairy products	10%	1.10
Textiles	5%	0.80
T o t a l	100%	

(d) The modern sector wage rate for unskilled labour is fixed at
Z. 100 *per month*.

(e) The mean per capita consumption level ($\overline{C}$) is Z. 2500 *per annum*,
the government considers Z. 2000 per annum to be the 'critical'
consumption level (C^*), and the value of 'n' is 1.

(f) The composition of unskilled labour's *average* consumption and
income elasticities of demand for various consumption goods have
been estimated from household budget surveys. These estimates
and the corresponding AR's are provided in the table below.

Good	% of Average Consumption	Income Elasticity	A.R.
Food	60%	0.83	0.90
Clothing	25%	1.00	0.80
Appliances	10%	1.60	0.50
Services	5%	1.84	0.55
T o t a l	100%	–	–

Calculate *both* the economic wage rate (EWR) and the social wage
rate (SWR) for unskilled labour in accordance with the LMST methodology.

N.B.: Make any further assumptions *explicit*.

*9. You have been supplied with three estimates for the marginal product
of investment (q), (8%, 9% and 10%), and with two estimates of the
consumption rate of interest (CRI), (5% and 7%). What are the possible
values that the parameter 'V' could take if the marginal propensity
to save is 0.20?

*10. From the 1973 household consumption data for Yugoslavia given in the
table below, you are required to calculate the distributional weights
($\frac{d_i}{v}$) for a marginal increase in consumption accruing to an individual
in each of the consumption groups. Assume that the value of 'n' is
2.0 and that the government's critical per capita consumption level
is D. 4500 per annum.

YUGOSLAVIA: HOUSEHOLD CONSUMPTION LEVELS 1973 (Dinars)

% Population	Average household consumption level	Average size of household
0.91	3727	1.6
3.49	8156	2.0
7.00	13114	2.8
10.88	17892	3.4
12.48	22811	3.9
12.62	29667	4.2
16.13	38348	4.4
10.94	46853	4.6
6.06	54663	4.6
3.86	63101	4.8
5.55	77884	5.4

Source: Survey of Available Resources and Expenditures of Households,
          1973, reprinted in S.C. Yang (1975).

*11. From the information provided below you are required to calculate
     the NPV of a project's benefits, expressed in terms of base year
     (year 0) prices.

	Year 0	Year 1
Net foreign exchange benefits (in current prices)	P. 250	P. 1000
Consumer price index	100	150
Tariff rate	25%	50%
Base level income	P. 2000	P. 3090

The ARI is given by the formula $r = ng + p$ where; $n = 1$, $p = 2\%$,
and g is the annual percentage increase in base level income.

Answer Set VI

2. (a) NPV of cost of not undertaking project.

	Net benefit stream per acre (K)	
Years	0	1–10
(i) with project	−300	+150
(ii) without project	0	+100
(i) − (ii)	−300	+ 50

$$
\begin{aligned}
\text{NPV}_{(0.04)} &= -300(1.0) + 50(8.11) \\
&= -300 + 405.5 \\
&= 105.5
\end{aligned}
$$

Therefore, the opportunity cost of not undertaking the project is K. 105.5 per acre.

(b) NPV of cost of postponing the project for five years

Net Benefit Stream Per Acre (K)

Year	(i) Not postponed	(ii) Postponed	(i) − (ii)
0	−300	−	−300
1	+150	+100	+50
2	+150	+100	+50
3	+150	+100	+50
4	+150	+100	+50
5	+150	−200	+350
6	+150	+150	−
7	+150	+150	−
8	+150	+150	−
9	+150	+150	−
10	+150	+150	−
11	+100	+150	−50
12	+100	+150	−50
13	+100	+150	−50
14	+100	+150	−50
15	+100	+150	−50

$$NPV_{(0.04)} = -300(1.0) + 50(3.63) + 350(0.82) - 50(4.45)(0.68)$$
$$= -300 + 181.5 + 287.0 - 151.3$$
$$= 17.2$$

Therefore, the opportunity cost of postponing the project for five years is K. 17.2 per acre.

5. For convenience, let the amount of loan 1 be \$150 and of loan 2 be \$100. The NPV of the cost of each loan is then calculated by discounting their principal repayments (P) and interest charges (i) to the present, at 10 percent.

		L o a n	1 (\$)	At 10% to year 0		L o a n	2 (\$)	At 10% to year 0
	P	i	Total		P	i	Total	
1		10.5	10.5	9.55	10	3.0	13.0	11.82
2		10.5	10.5	8.67	10	2.7	12.7	10.50
3		10.5	10.5	7.89	10	2.4	12.4	9.32
4		10.5	10.5	7.17	10	2.1	12.1	8.26
5		10.5	10.5	6.52	10	1.8	11.8	7.33
6	10	10.5	20.5	11.56	10	1.5	11.5	6.49
7	10	9.8	19.8	10.16	10	1.2	11.2	5.75
8	10	9.1	19.1	8.92	10	0.9	10.9	5.08
9	10	8.4	18.4	7.80	10	0.6	10.6	4.50
10	10	7.7	17.7	6.83	10	0.3	10.3	3.97
11	10	7.0	17.0	5.95				
12	10	6.3	16.3	5.20				
13	10	5.6	15.6	4.52				
14	10	4.9	14.9	3.92				
15	10	4.2	14.2	3.39				
16	10	3.5	13.5	2.94				
17	10	2.8	12.8	2.53				
18	10	2.1	12.1	2.18				
19	10	1.4	11.4	1.87				
20	10	0.7	10.7	1.59				
Total				119.16				73.02

The payment equivalent (PE) for each loan is found by dividing the
NPV of the loan's cost by the amount of the loan.

P.E.

Loan 1: $119.16/$150 = 0.7944

Loan 2: $73.02/$100 = 0.7302

Loan 3: $x/$x = 1.0000

To buy $100 worth of goods costs:

(a) Loan 1:

   $100(1.26) x 0.7944 = $100.1

(b) Loan 2:

   $100(1.37) x 0.7302 = $100

(c) Loan 3:

   $100(1.0) x 1.0 = $100

Therefore the three loan offers are indistinguishable.

8. (i) $EWR = m.AR_m$

   where, m = marginal output foregone

   AR_m = accounting ratio for marginal output foregone

   Derivation of m

   $m = mp_1 \cdot r$

   where, mp_1 = marginal product of labour in rural sector

   r = rate of migration in response to creation of 1
       urban job

   On the assumption that average per capita income in rural sector
   is equal to marginal product of labour (must be made explicit):

   M = Z1000 x 1.20

     = Z1200

Derivation of AR_m

Beef	0.50 x 0.90 = 0.45
Maize	0.20 x 0.75 = 0.15
Sorghum	0.15 x 1.00 = 0.15
Dairy products	0.10 x 1.10 = 0.11
Textiles	0.05 x 0.80 = 0.04
T o t a l	0.90

AR_m = 0.90

EWR = Z1200 x 0.90

    = Z1080

(ii) SWR = EWR + { (w − m) − (w − m) $\frac{d_i}{v}$ } AR_c

where, w = urban wage rate

    $\frac{d_i}{v}$ = distributional weight

    AR_c = accounting ratio for labour's marginal consumption

w = Z100 x 12

  = Z. 1200

m = Z. 1000

$d_i = (\frac{\bar{C}}{C})^n$

where, $\bar{C}$ = mean consumption level

    C = labour's previous consumption level

    n = the elasticity of utility with respect to a marginal increase in consumption.

On the assumption that labour's marginal propensity to save is zero:

$$\left(\frac{\bar{C}}{C}\right)^n = \left(\frac{2500}{1000}\right)^1$$

$$= (2.5)^1$$

$$= 2.5$$

$$V = \left(\frac{\overline{C}}{C*}\right)^{n}$$

where, V = the value of public income

$\overline{C}$ = the mean consumption level

$C*$ = the government's critical consumption level

$$V = \left(\frac{2500}{2000}\right)^{1}$$

$$= 1.25$$

Derivation of AR_c

Food	$0.60 \times 0.83 \times 0.90 = 0.45$	
Clothing	$0.25 \times 1.00 \times 0.80 = 0.20$	
Appliances	$0.10 \times 1.60 \times 0.50 = 0.08$	
Services	$0.05 \times 1.84 \times 0.55 = 0.05$	
	$\overline{\qquad\qquad}$	
	0.78	
	$====$	

$AR_c = 0.78$

$SWR = Z1080 + \{(Z1200 - Z1000) - (Z1200 - Z1000)\frac{2.5}{1.25}\} \, 0.78$

$= Z1080 + \{(Z200) - (Z200)2\} \, 0.78$

$= Z1080 + \{-Z200\} \, 0.78$

$= Z1080 - Z156$

$= Z924$

9. Given the formula $v = (q - sq)/(CRI - sq)$:

CRI	0.08	q 0.09	0.10
0.05	(1.88)	(2.25)	(2.67)
0.07	(1.18)	(1.38)	(1.60)

(The figures enclosed in brackets are the values of the parameter 'v' corresponding to each combination of 'q' and 'CRI'.)

10. To calculate the distributional weights for each consumption group, two sets of calculations are necessary. Firstly, the per capita con--sumption level of each household group is calculated by dividing the household consumption level by the average household size (column 1). Secondly, the distributional weights for each consumption level (d_i/v) are calculated by applying the formula $(C^*/C_i)^n$.

Note that it is unnecessary to calculate the mean consumption level $(\bar{C})$ as $d_i/v = (\bar{C}/C_i)^n \div (\bar{C}/C^*)^n = (\frac{C^*}{C_i})^n$.

1	2
Per capita consumption level (Dinars)	d_i/v
2329	3.73
4078	1.22
4684	0.92
5262	0.73
5849	0.59
7064	0.41
8715	0.27
10185	0.19
11883	0.14
13146	0.12
14423	0.10

11. To convert year 1 foreign exchange benefits two adjustments must be made, viz. for the change in the consumer price index and for the change in the tariff rate (accounting ratio).

The formula for the composite price index (P_i/P_o) is:

$$P_i/P_o = A_1/A_o \cdot C_1/C_o,$$

where, A is the accounting ratio;
       C is the consumer price index; and
       subscripts o and 1 denote the time period.

Therefore P_1/P_0 = (0.67/0.80)(150/100)

$\qquad\qquad$ = 1.256

To convert P. 1000 in year 1 to year 0 prices

$\qquad\qquad$ P. 1000 x 1/1.256 = P. 796.17

To calculate the ARI it is necessary to find the percentage annual increase in base level income. Year 1 base level income must be deflated by the percentage increase in the price level.

$\qquad\qquad$ P. 3090(100/150) = P. 2060

Therefore, $\quad$ g = (2060 - 2000)/2000 x 100

$\qquad\qquad$ = 3%

ARI = (1 x 3)+ 2

$\quad$ = 5%

$NPV_{(0.05)}$ = P. 250(1.0) + P. 796.17(0.952)

$\qquad\qquad$ = P. 250 + P. 758

$\qquad\qquad$ = P. 1008

APPENDIX B

The appendix which follows contains a summary set of discount tables. Table 1 gives the present value of £1 accruing in a single future year (n) for various discount rates. Table 2 shows the present value of a stream of £1 payments starting in year one and accruing over n successive years for various discount rates.

TABLE 1

Present Value of £1 at Rate i *Payable in* t *Years* $(1+i)^{-t}$

n	2%	3%	4%	5%	6%	7%
1	0.980	0.971	0.962	0.952	0.943	0.935
2	0.961	0.943	0.925	0.907	0.890	0.873
3	0.942	0.915	0.889	0.864	0.840	0.816
4	0.924	0.888	0.855	0.823	0.792	0.763
5	0.906	0.863	0.822	0.784	0.747	0.713
6	0.888	0.837	0.790	0.746	0.705	0.666
7	0.871	0.813	0.760	0.711	0.665	0.623
8	0.853	0.789	0.731	0.677	0.627	0.582
9	0.837	0.766	0.703	0.645	0.592	0.544
10	0.820	0.744	0.676	0.614	0.558	0.508
11	0.804	0.722	0.650	0.585	0.527	0.475
12	0.788	0.701	0.625	0.557	0.497	0.444
13	0.773	0.681	0.601	0.530	0.469	0.415
14	0.758	0.661	0.577	0.505	0.442	0.388
15	0.743	0.642	0.555	0.481	0.417	0.362
16	0.728	0.623	0.534	0.458	0.394	0.339
17	0.714	0.605	0.513	0.436	0.371	0.317
18	0.700	0.587	0.494	0.416	0.350	0.296
19	0.686	0.570	0.475	0.396	0.331	0.277
20	0.673	0.554	0.456	0.377	0.312	0.258
21	0.660	0.538	0.439	0.359	0.294	0.242
22	0.647	0.522	0.422	0.342	0.278	0.226
23	0.634	0.507	0.406	0.326	0.262	0.211
24	0.622	0.492	0.390	0.310	0.247	0.197
25	0.610	0.478	0.375	0.295	0.233	0.184
26	0.598	0.464	0.361	0.281	0.220	0.172
27	0.586	0.450	0.347	0.268	0.207	0.161
28	0.574	0.437	0.333	0.255	0.196	0.150
29	0.563	0.424	0.321	0.243	0.185	0.141
30	0.552	0.412	0.308	0.231	0.174	0.131
40	0.453	0.307	0.208	0.142	0.097	0.067
50	0.372	0.228	0.141	0.087	0.054	0.034

TABLE 1 (Cont.)

n \ i	8%	9%	10%	11%	12%	13%	14%
1	0.926	0.917	0.909	0.901	0.893	0.885	0.877
2	0.857	0.842	0.826	0.812	0.797	0.783	0.769
3	0.794	0.772	0.751	0.731	0.712	0.693	0.675
4	0.735	0.708	0.683	0.659	0.636	0.613	0.592
5	0.681	0.650	0.621	0.593	0.567	0.543	0.519
6	0.630	0.596	0.564	0.535	0.507	0.480	0.456
7	0.583	0.547	0.513	0.482	0.452	0.425	0.400
8	0.540	0.502	0.467	0.434	0.404	0.376	0.351
9	0.500	0.460	0.424	0.391	0.361	0.333	0.308
10	0.463	0.422	0.386	0.352	0.322	0.295	0.270
11	0.429	0.388	0.350	0.317	0.287	0.261	0.237
12	0.397	0.356	0.319	0.286	0.257	0.231	0.208
13	0.368	0.326	0.290	0.258	0.229	0.204	0.182
14	0.340	0.299	0.263	0.232	0.205	0.181	0.160
15	0.315	0.275	0.239	0.209	0.183	0.160	0.140
16	0.292	0.252	0.218	0.188	0.163	0.141	0.123
17	0.270	0.231	0.198	0.170	0.146	0.125	0.108
18	0.250	0.212	0.180	0.153	0.130	0.111	0.095
19	0.232	0.194	0.164	0.138	0.116	0.098	0.083
20	0.215	0.178	0.149	0.124	0.104	0.087	0.073
21	0.199	0.164	0.135	0.112	0.093	0.077	0.064
22	0.184	0.150	0.123	0.101	0.083	0.068	0.056
23	0.170	0.138	0.112	0.091	0.074	0.060	0.049
24	0.158	0.126	0.102	0.082	0.066	0.053	0.043
25	0.146	0.116	0.092	0.074	0.059	0.047	0.038
26	0.135	0.106	0.084	0.066	0.053	0.042	0.033
27	0.125	0.098	0.076	0.060	0.047	0.037	0.029
28	0.116	0.090	0.069	0.054	0.042	0.033	0.026
29	0.107	0.082	0.063	0.048	0.037	0.029	0.022
30	0.099	0.075	0.057	0.044	0.033	0.026	0.020
40	0.046	0.032	0.022	0.015	0.011	0.008	0.005
50	0.021	0.013	0.009	0.005	0.003	0.002	0.001

TABLE 1 (Cont.)

n \ i	15%	16%	18%	20%	25%	30%	40%
1	0.870	0.862	0.847	0.833	0.800	0.769	0.714
2	0.756	0.743	0.718	0.694	0.640	0.592	0.510
3	0.658	0.641	0.609	0.579	0.512	0.455	0.364
4	0.572	0.552	0.516	0.482	0.410	0.350	0.260
5	0.497	0.476	0.437	0.402	0.328	0.269	0.186
6	0.432	0.410	0.370	0.335	0.262	0.207	0.133
7	0.376	0.354	0.314	0.279	0.210	0.159	0.095
8	0.327	0.305	0.266	0.233	0.168	0.123	0.068
9	0.284	0.263	0.225	0.194	0.134	0.094	0.048
10	0.247	0.227	0.191	0.162	0.107	0.073	0.036
11	0.215	0.195	0.162	0.135	0.086	0.056	0.025
12	0.187	0.168	0.137	0.112	0.069	0.043	0.018
13	0.163	0.145	0.116	0.093	0.055	0.033	0.013
14	0.141	0.125	0.099	0.078	0.044	0.025	0.009
15	0.123	0.108	0.084	0.065	0.035	0.020	0.006
16	0.107	0.093	0.071	0.054	0.028	0.015	0.005
17	0.093	0.080	0.060	0.045	0.023	0.012	0.003
18	0.081	0.069	0.051	0.038	0.018	0.009	0.002
19	0.070	0.060	0.043	0.031	0.014	0.007	0.002
20	0.061	0.051	0.037	0.026	0.012	0.005	0.001
21	0.053	0.044	0.031	0.022	0.009	0.004	0.001
22	0.046	0.038	0.026	0.018	0.007	0.003	0.001
23	0.040	0.033	0.022	0.015	0.006	0.002	
24	0.035	0.028	0.019	0.013	0.005	0.002	
25	0.030	0.024	0.016	0.010	0.004	0.001	
26	0.026	0.021	0.014	0.009	0.003	0.001	
27	0.023	0.018	0.011	0.007	0.002	0.001	
28	0.020	0.016	0.010	0.006	0.002	0.001	
29	0.017	0.014	0.008	0.005	0.002		
30	0.015	0.012	0.007	0.004	0.001		
40	0.004	0.003	0.001	0.001			
50	0.001	0.001					

TABLE 2

Present Value at Rate i of the Sum of N Annual

Instalments of £1 Payable at End of Year:

$$\sum_{t=1}^{n} (1+i)^{-t} = \frac{(1+i)^{n} - 1}{i(1+1)^{n}}$$

n \ i	2%	3%	4%	5%	6%	7%
1	0.980	0.971	0.962	0.952	0.943	0.935
2	1.942	1.913	1.886	1.859	1.833	1.808
3	2.884	2.829	2.775	2.723	2.673	2.624
4	3.808	3.717	3.630	3.546	3.465	3.387
5	4.713	4.580	4.452	4.329	4.212	4.100
6	5.601	5.417	5.242	5.076	4.917	4.767
7	6.472	6.230	6.002	5.786	5.582	5.389
8	7.325	7.020	6.733	6.463	6.210	5.971
9	8.162	7.786	7.435	7.108	6.802	6.515
10	8.983	8.530	8.111	7.722	7.360	7.024
11	9.787	9.253	8.760	8.306	7.887	7.499
12	10.575	9.954	9.385	8.863	8.384	7.943
13	11.348	10.635	9.986	9.394	8.853	8.358
14	12.106	11.296	10.563	9.899	9.295	8.745
15	12.849	11.938	11.118	10.380	9.712	9.108
16	13.578	12.561	11.652	10.838	10.106	9.447
17	14.292	13.166	12.166	11.274	10.477	9.763
18	14.992	13.753	12.659	11.690	10.828	10.059
19	15.678	14.324	13.134	12.085	11.158	10.336
20	16.351	14.877	13.590	12.462	11.470	10.594
21	17.011	15.415	14.029	12.821	11.764	10.836
22	17.658	15.937	14.451	13.163	12.042	11.061
23	18.292	16.444	14.857	13.489	12.303	11.272
24	18.914	16.936	15.247	13.799	12.550	11.469
25	19.523	17.413	15.622	14.094	12.783	11.654
26	20.121	17.877	15.983	14.375	13.003	11.826
27	20.707	18.327	16.330	14.643	13.211	11.987
28	21.281	18.764	16.663	14.898	13.406	12.137
29	21.844	19.188	16.984	15.141	13.591	12.278
30	22.396	19.600	17.292	15.372	13.765	12.409
40	27.355	23.115	19.793	17.159	15.046	13.332
50	31.424	25.730	21.482	18.256	15.762	13.801

TABLE 2 (Cont.)

n \ i	8%	9%	10%	11%	12%	13%	14%
1	0.926	0.917	0.909	0.901	0.893	0.885	0.877
2	1.783	1.759	1.736	1.713	1.690	1.668	1.647
3	2.577	2.531	2.487	2.444	2.402	2.361	2.322
4	3.312	3.240	3.170	3.102	3.037	2.974	2.914
5	3.993	3.890	3.791	3.696	3.605	3.517	3.433
6	4.623	4.486	4.355	4.231	4.111	3.998	3.889
7	5.206	5.033	4.868	4.712	4.564	4.423	4.288
8	5.747	5.535	5.335	5.146	4.968	4.799	4.639
9	6.247	5.995	5.759	5.537	5.328	5.132	4.946
10	6.710	6.418	6.145	5.889	5.650	5.426	5.216
11	7.139	6.805	6.495	6.207	5.938	5.687	5.453
12	7.536	7.161	6.814	6.492	6.194	5.918	5.660
13	7.904	7.487	7.103	6.750	6.424	6.122	5.842
14	8.244	7.786	7.367	6.982	6.628	6.302	6.002
15	8.559	8.061	7.606	7.191	6.811	6.462	6.142
16	8.851	8.313	7.824	7.379	6.974	6.604	6.265
17	9.122	8.544	8.022	7.549	7.120	6.729	6.373
18	9.372	8.756	8.201	7.702	7.250	6.840	6.467
19	9.604	8.950	8.365	7.839	7.366	6.938	6.550
20	9.818	9.129	8.514	7.963	7.469	7.025	6.623
21	10.017	9.292	8.649	8.075	7.562	7.102	6.687
22	10.201	9.442	8.772	8.176	7.645	7.170	6.743
23	10.371	9.580	8.883	8.266	7.718	7.230	6.792
24	10.529	9.707	8.985	8.348	7.784	7.283	6.835
25	10.675	9.823	9.077	8.422	7.843	7.330	6.873
26	10.810	9.929	9.161	8.488	7.896	7.372	6.906
27	10.935	10.027	9.237	8.548	7.943	7.409	6.935
28	11.051	10.116	9.307	8.602	7.984	7.441	6.961
29	11.158	10.198	9.370	8.650	8.022	7.470	6.983
30	11.258	10.274	9.427	8.694	8.055	7.496	7.003
40	11.925	10.757	9.779	8.951	8.244	7.634	7.105
50	12.234	10.962	9.915	9.042	8.304	7.675	7.133

TABLE 2 (Cont.)

n\i	15%	16%	18%	20%	25%	30%	40%
1	0.870	0.862	0.847	0.833	0.800	0.769	0.714
2	1.626	1.605	1.566	1.528	1.440	1.361	1.225
3	2.283	2.246	2.174	2.106	1.952	1.816	1.589
4	2.855	2.798	2.690	2.589	2.362	2.166	1.849
5	3.352	3.274	3.127	2.991	2.689	2.436	2.035
6	3.784	3.685	3.498	3.326	2.951	2.643	2.168
7	4.160	4.039	3.812	3.605	3.161	2.802	2.263
8	4.487	4.344	4.078	3.837	3.329	2.925	2.331
9	4.772	4.607	4.303	4.031	3.463	3.019	2.379
10	5.019	4.833	4.494	4.192	3.571	3.092	2.414
11	5.234	5.029	4.656	4.327	3.656	3.147	2.438
12	5.421	5.197	4.793	4.439	3.725	3.190	2.456
13	5.583	5.342	4.910	4.533	3.780	3.223	2.469
14	5.724	5.468	5.008	4.611	3.824	3.249	2.478
15	5.847	5.575	5.092	4.675	3.859	3.268	2.484
16	5.954	5.669	5.162	4.730	3.887	3.283	2.489
17	6.047	5.749	5.222	4.775	3.910	3.295	2.492
18	6.128	5.818	5.273	4.812	3.928	3.304	2.494
19	6.198	5.877	5.316	4.844	3.942	3.311	2.496
20	6.259	5.929	5.353	4.870	3.954	3.316	2.497
21	6.312	5.973	5.384	4.891	3.963	3.320	2.498
22	6.359	6.011	5.410	4.909	3.970	3.323	2.499
23	6.399	6.044	5.432	4.925	3.976	3.325	2.499
24	6.434	6.073	5.451	4.937	3.981	3.327	2.499
25	6.464	6.097	5.467	4.948	3.985	3.329	2.499
26	6.491	6.118	5.480	4.956	3.988	3.330	2.500
27	6.514	6.136	5.492	4.964	3.990	3.331	2.500
28	6.534	6.152	5.502	4.970	3.992	3.331	2.500
29	6.551	6.166	5.510	4.975	3.994	3.332	2.500
30	6.566	6.177	5.517	4.979	3.995	3.332	2.500
40	6.642	6.234	5.548	4.997	3.999	3.333	2.500
50	6.661	6.246	5.554	4.999	4.000	3.333	2.500

BIBLIOGRAPHY

Arrow, K.J.
  1963   *Social Choice and Individual Values* (2nd edition, Yale, 1963).
Arrow, K.J., and M. Kurz
  1970   *Public Investment, the Rate of Return and Optimal Fiscal Policy* (Johns Hopkins, 1970).
Bacha, E., and L. Taylor
  1971   'Foreign Exchange Shadow Price; a Critical Review of Current Theories', *Q.J.E.* (May 1971).
Balassa, B.
  1974   'Estimating the Shadow Price of Foreign Exchange in Project Evaluation', *O.E.P.* (July 1974).
Balassa, B., and Associates
  1971   *The Structure of Protection in Developing Countries* (Baltimore, 1971).
Balassa, B., and D. Schydlowsky
  1968   'Effective Tariffs, Domestic Cost of Foreign Exchange and the Equilibrium Exchange Rate', *J.P.E.* (May-June 1968).
Batra, R., and S. Guisinger
  1974   'A New Approach to the Estimation of the Shadow Exchange Rate in Evaluating Development Projects in Less Developed Countries', *O.E.P.*, Vol 26 (July 1974).
Bauer, P.T.
  1966   'Foreign Aid: an Instrument for Progress?' in B. Ward and P.T. Bauer, *Two Views on Aid to Developing Countries* (Institute of Economic Affairs, 1966).
Baumol, W.J.
  1968   'On the Social Rate of Discount', *A.E.R.*, Vol. 58 (1968).
  1972   *Economic Theory and Operations Analysis* (3rd edition, Prentice Hall, 1972).
Bienefeld, M.
  1975   Review of Roads and Redistribution, *I.D.S. Bulletin* (August 1975).
Bierman, H., and S. Smidt
  1971   *The Capital Budgeting Decision; Economic Analysis and Financing of Investment Projects* (Macmillan, 1971).
Blaug, M. (ed)
  1968   *The Economics of Education* (Penguin, 1968).
Boeke, J.H.
  1954   *Economics and Economic Policy of Dual Societies* (New York, 1954).
Bruce, C.
  1976   *Social Cost Benefit Analysis: A Guide for Country and Project Economists to the Derivation and Application of Economic and Social Accounting Prices* (World Bank Staff Working Paper No. 239, Washington, 1976).
Bruno, M.
  1967   'The Optimal Selection of Export Promoting and Import Substituting Projects' in *Planning the External Sector; Techniques, Problems and Policies* (United Nations, N.Y., 1967).
Byres, T.J. (ed)
  1972   *Foreign Resources and Economic Development* (Frank Cass, London, 1972).
Castro Tato, M.
  1972   *Análisis de Algunos Aspectos Metodológicos Sobre la Programación de las Inversiones en Cuba* (Pueblo y Educación, La Habana, 1972).
Chenery, H.B.
  1953   'The Application of Investment Criteria', *Q.J.E.* (February 1953).

Chenery, H., and A. Strout
1966   'Development Alternatives in an Open Economy', *A.E.R.* (September 1966).
Chenery, H. *et al*
1974   *Redistribution With Growth* (O.U.P., 1974).
Corden, W.M.
1971   *The Theory of Protection* (Clarendon Press, 1971).
Dasgupta, A. K., and D. W. Pearce,
1972   *Cost Benefit Analysis; Theory and Practice* (Macmillan, 1972).
Dasgupta, P.
1972   'A Comparative Analysis of the UNIDO Guidelines and the OECD Manual',
        B.O.U.I.E.S. (February 1972).
Diamond, P., and J. Mirrlees
1971   'On Optimal Taxation and Public Production, I and II', *A.E.R.*, Vol. 60
        (1971).
Dixit, A.K.
1971   'Short-run Equilibrium and Shadow Prices in the Dual Economy', *O.E.P.*
        (November 1971).
Dobb, M.
1960   *An Essay on Economic Growth and Planning* (Routledge and Kegan Paul,
        London, 1960).
1969   *Welfare Economics and the Economics of Socialism* (C.U.P., 1969).
Dorfman, R.
1962   'Basic Economic and Technological Concepts; a General Statement', in A.
        Maass *et al, Design of Water Resource Systems* (Harvard, 1972); reprinted in
        R. Layard (ed), *Cost Benefit Analysis* (Penguin, 1972).
Eckstein, O.
1958   *Water Resource Development; The Economics of Project Evaluation* (Harvard,
        1958).
Ellman, H.
1972   *Soviet Planning Today* (C.U.P., 1972).
Emmanuel, A.
1972   *Unequal Exchange* (New Left Books, 1972).
Federal Inter-Agency River Basin Committee
1950   Sub-committee on Benefits and Costs, *Proposed Practices for Economic
        Analysis of River Basin Projects* (Washington, 1950).
Feldstein, M.S.
1964   'The Social Time Preference Discount Rate in Cost Benefit Analysis', *E.J.*,
        Vol. 74 (1964).
1973   'The Inadequacy of Weighted Discount Rates', reprinted in R. Layard, *Cost
        Benefit Analysis* (Penguin, 1972).
Feldstein, M.S., and J.S. Flemming
1964   'The Problem of Time Stream Evaluation; Present Value versus Internal Rate
        of Return Rules', *B.O.U.I.E.S.*, Vol. 26 (1964).
Fellner, W.
1967   'Operational Utility: the Theoretical Background and Measurement', in Fellner
        et al, Ten Economic Studies in the Tradition of Irving Fisher (Wiley, New
        York, 1967).
Ferber, R., and P.J. Verdoorn
1969   *Research Methods in Economics and Business* (Macmillan, 1969).

Fisher, I.
  1930   *The Theory of Interest* (Macmillan, 1930).
FitzGerald, E.V.K.
  1976a   *Public Sector Investment Planning for Developing Countries* (Overseas Study
           Committee, University of Cambridge, 1976).
  1976b   'The Urban Service Sector, the Supply of Wagegoods and the Shadow Wage
           Rate', *O.E.P.* (March 1976).
  1976c   *The State and Economic Development; Peru since 1968* (C.U.P., 1976).
  1977   'The Public Investment Criterion and the Role of the State', *J.D.S.*, Vol. 13
           (1977).
Foster, C.D.
  1966   'Social Welfare Functions in Cost-Benefit Analysis' in M. Lawrence (ed), *Oper-
           ational Research in the Social Sciences* (London, 1966).
Galenson, W., and H. Leibenstein
  1955   'Investment Criteria, Productivity and Economic Development', *Q.J.E.*
           (August 1955)
Georgescu-Roegen, N.
  1963   'Economic Theory and Agrarian Economics', *O.E.P.* (February 1963).
Graaff, J. de V.
  1971   *Theoretical Welfare Economics* (C.U.P., 1971).
Griffin, K.
  1970   'Foreign Capital, Domestic Savings and Economic Development', *B.O.U.I.E.S.*,
           Vol. 32 (May 1970).
Guisinger, S., and D. Papageorgiou
  1976   'The Selection of Appropriate Border Prices in Project Evaluation',
           B.O.U.I.E.S. (May 1976).
Hansen, J.R.
  1975   'A Guide to the UNIDO Guidelines' (IBRD, July 1975).
ul Haq, M.
  1967   'Tied Credits; a Quantitative Analysis', in J.H. Adler and D.W. Kuznets (eds),
           Capital Movements in Economic Development (Macmillan, 1967).
Harberger, A.C.
  1969   'The Opportunity Costs of Public Investment Financed by Borrowing', re-
           printed in R. Layard, *Cost Benefit Analysis* (Penguin, 1972).
  1971   'On Measuring the Social Opportunity Cost of Labour', *International Labour
           Review* (1971).
  1972   *Project Evaluation* (Macmillan, 1972).
Harcourt, G.C., and N.G. Laing
  1971   *Capital and Growth* (Penguin, 1971).
Harris, J.R., and M.P. Todaro
  1970   'Migration, Unemployment and Development; a two sector analysis', *A.E.R.*,
           Vol. 60 (March 1970).
Harrison, A.J., and D.A. Quarmby
  1969   'The Value of Time in Transport Planning, a Review' reprinted in R. Layard,
           Cost Benefit Analysis (Penguin, 1972).
Henderson, P.D.
  1968   'Investment Criteria for Public Enterprises' in R. Turvey (ed), *Public Enter-
           prise* (Penguin, 1968).

Hirschman, A.O.
1967   *Development Projects Observed* (Brookings, Washington, 1967).
1969   'How to Divest in Latin America and Why?' in *Princeton Essays in International Finance*, No. 76 (Princeton, 1969).
Hirshleifer, J.
1958   'On the Theory of the Optimal Investment Decision', *J.P.E.* (August 1958).
Hoel, P.G.
1965   *Introduction to Mathematical Statistics* (Wiley, 1965).
I.B.R.D.
1974   *Economic Analysis of Projects* (Development Research Center; staff review, mimeo, June 1974).
I.L.P.E.S.
1973   *Guia Para la Presentación de Proyectos* (Siglo XXI, Mexico, 1973).
Irvin, G.W.
1975a   *Roads and Redistribution* (I.L.O. Geneva, 1975).
1975b   'Rural Savings, Wage Remittance Effects and Real Industrial Wage Determination', *Development and Change* (October 1975).
Jolly, R.
1975   'Redistribution with Growth – a Reply', *I.D.S. Bulletin*, Vol. 7 (August 1975).
Joshi, H.
1972   'World Prices as Shadow Prices: A Critique', *B.O.U.I.E.S.* (February 1972).
Joy, J.L.
1968   'What an Economist Wants to Know about Dams' (IDS Reprint Series, Sussex, 1968).
Kahn, A.E.
1951   'Investment Criteria in Development Programs', *Q.J.E.* (February 1951).
Kao, H., K. Anschel and C. Eicher
1964   'Disguised Unemployment in Agriculture – a Survey' in C. Eicher and L. Witt, *Agriculture in Economic Development* (McGraw-Hill, 1964).
Kantarovich, L.V.
1965   *The Best Use of Economic Resources* (Oxford, 1965).
Kindleberger, C.P.
1969   *International Trade* (Irwin, 1969).
King, J.A.
1967   *Economic Development Projects and their Appraisal* (Johns Hopkins, Baltimore, 1967).
Knight, F.H.
1921   *Risk, Uncertainty and Profit* (Houghton Mifflin, Boston, 1921).
Kornai, J.
1967   *Mathematical Planning of Structural Decisions* (North Holland, 1967).
Kruger, A.O.
1966   'Some Economic Costs of Exchange Control: the Turkish Case', *J.P.E.*, LXXIV (1966).
Krutilla, J., and O. Eckstein
1958   *Multiple Purpose River Basin Development* (Johns Hopkins, 1958).
Labys, W.C. (ed)
1975   *Quantitative Models of Commodity Markets* (Ballinger, Cambridge, Mass., 1975).

Lal, D.
  1972a   *Wells and Welfare* (OECD, Paris, 1972).
  1972b   *On Estimating Income Distribution Weights for Project Analysis* (IBRD Econo-
          mic Staff Working Paper No. 130, March 1972).
  1973   'Disutility of Effort, Migration and the Shadow Wage Rate', *O.E.P.*, Vol. 25
          (March 1973).
  1974a   *Methods of Project Appraisal; a Review* (Johns Hopkins, 1974).
  1974b   'Adjustments for Trade Distortions in Project Analysis', *J.D.S.*, Vol. II, No. 1
          (1974).
  1976   'The Evaluation of Aid and Foreign Investment Inflows' in H. Neunteufel and
          T. Sener, *Manual*, Vols. I and II (Conference on Financing and Appraisal of In-
          vestment Projects, Istanbul, 1976).
Lange, O.
  1938   'On the Economic Theory of Socialism', in B. Lippincot (ed), *On the Econ-
          omic Theory of Socialism* (Minnesota, 1938).
  1973   'Planning Economic Development' in H. Bernstein (ed), *Underdevelopment
          and Development* (Penguin, 1973).
Lawson, G.H. and D.W. Windle
  1974   *Tables for Discounted Cash Flow* (Longman, 1974).
Layard, R. (ed)
  1972   *Cost Benefit Analysis* (Penguin, 1972).
Leibenstein, H.W.
  1957   'The Theory of Unemployment in Backward Economies', *J.P.E.* (April 1957).
Lerner, A.
  1944   *The Economics of Control* (New York, 1944).
Lewis, W.A.
  1954   'Economic Development with Unlimited Supplies of Labour', *Journal of the
          Manchester School* (May 1954).
Leys, C.
  1975   'The Politics of Redistribution with Growth', *I.D.S. Bulletin*, Vol. 7 (August
          1975).
Liberman, E.G.
  1964   Article in *Kommunist* No. 5 (1964).
Lind, R.C.
  1964   'The Social Rate of Discount and the Optimal Rate of Investment; Further
          Comment', *Q.J.E.*, Vol. 78 (1964).
Linn, J.F.
  1976   'Economics and Social Analysis of Projects in the World Bank; Principles and
          Application', paper presented at *International Conference on Financing and
          Appraisal of Investment Projects* (Istanbul, June 1976).
Little, I.M.D.
  1950   *A Critique of Welfare Economics* (O.U.P., 1950).
Little, I.M.D., and J.A. Mirrlees
  1974   *Project Appraisal and Planning for Developing Countries* (Heinemann, 1974).
Little, I.M.D., T. Scitovsky and M.FG. Scott
  1970   *Industry and Trade in Some Developing Countries* (O.U.P., 1970).
Little, I.M.D., and M.FG. Scott (eds)
  1976   *Using Shadow Prices* (Heinemann, 1976).
Little, I.M.D., and D.G. Tipping
  1972   *A Social Cost Benefit Analysis of the Kulai Oil Palm Estate* (OECD Develop-
          ment Centre, Paris, 1972).

Marglin, S.A.
1963a 'The Social Rate of Discount and the Optimum Rate of Investment', *Q.J.E.*, Vol. 77 (1963).
1963b 'The Opportunity Cost of Public Investment', *Q.J.E.*, Vol. 77 (1963).
1967 *Public Investment Criteria* (Allen and Unwin, 1967).
1976 *Value and Price in the Labour Surplus Economy* (O.U.P., 1976).
Mayston, D.J.
1974 *The Idea of Social Choice* (Macmillan, 1974).
Mazumdar, D.
1965 'The Theory of Urban Underemployment in Less Developed Economies' (L.S.E.; mimeo, 1965).
McGuire, M., and H. Garn
1969 'The Integration of Equity and Efficiency Criteria in Public Project Selection', *E.J.* (December 1969).
Mellor, J.W., and R.D. Stevens
1956 'The Average and Marginal Product of Farm Labor in Underdeveloped Economies', *J.F.E.* (August 1956).
Merret, A.J., and A. Sykes
1966 *Capital Budgeting and Company Finance* (Longman, 1966).
Mikesell, R.F.
1968 *The Economics of Foreign Aid* (Weidenfeld and Nicholson, 1968).
Mishan, E.J.
1971 'Evaluation of Life and Limb; a Theoretical Approach', *J.P.E.*, Vol. 79 (1971).
1972 *Elements of Cost Benefit Analysis* (Allen and Unwin, 1972).
Moroney, M.J.
1962 *Facts from Figures* (Penguin, 1962).
Musgrave, R.
1969 'Cost Benefit Analysis and the Theory of Public Finance', *Journal of Economic Literature* (1969).
Nash, C., D. Pearce and J. Stanley
1975 'An Evaluation of Cost Benefit Analysis Criteria', *S.J.P.E.* (June 1975).
Novozhilov, V.V.
1970 *Problems of Cost Benefit Analysis in Optimal Planning* (International Arts and Science Press, New York, 1970).
Nurkse, R.
1957 'Excess Population and Capital Construction', *Malayan Economic Review* (October 1957).
O.D.M.
1972 *A Guide to Project Appraisal in Developing Countries* (H.M.S.O., 1972).
O.E.C.D.
1968 *Manual of Industrial Project Analysis*, Vols I and II (Paris, 1968).
1973 *Methods of Project Appraisal in Developing Countries* (Paris, 1973).
Packard, P.C.
1974 *Project Appraisal for Development Administration* (Mouton, 1974).
Pearce, D.W.
1971 *Cost Benefit Analysis* (Macmillan, 1971).
Pigou, A.C.
1920 *The Economics of Welfare* (London, 1920).
Pouliquen, L.Y.
1970 *Risk Analysis in Project Appraisal* (IBRD, Johns Hopkins, 1970).

Powell, K.A.
  1970   *Practical Accounting* (Intertext Books, London, 1970).
Powelson, J.P.
  1968   'An Integrated Documentation System for Development Banks', *International Development* (1968).
Prest, A.R., and R. Turvey
  1965   'Cost Benefit Analysis; a Survey', *E.J.*, Vol. 75 (1965).
Price Gittinger, J.
  1972   *Economic Analysis of Agricultural Projects* (Johns Hopkins, 1972).
Qayum, A.
  1966   *Numerical Models of Economic Development* (Rotterdam, 1966).
Raiffa, H.
  1970   *Decision Analysis* (Addison-Wesley, 1970).
Raj, K.N., and A.K. Sen
  1961   'Alternative Patterns of Growth under Conditions of Stagnant Export Earnings', *O.E.P.* (February 1961).
Rawls, J.
  1972   *A Theory of Justice* (Clarendon, 1972).
Reutlinger, S.
  1970   *Techniques for Project Appraisal under Uncertainty* (IBRD, Johns Hopkins, 1970).
Robbins, L.
  1938   'Interpersonal Comparisons of Utility', *E.J.* (December 1938).
Robinson, J.
  1936   'Disguised Unemployment', *E.J.* (June 1936).
  1951   'The Pure Theory of International Trade' in J. Robinson, *Collected Economic Papers* (Oxford, 1951).
Rosenstein-Rodan, P.
  1957   'Disguised Unemployment and Underemployment in Agriculture', *F.A.O. Monthly Bulletin* (July-August 1957).
Ruffing, K.
  1972   *Application of Social Cost Benefit Analysis to the Problem of Choosing Among Alternative Technologies, A Survey* (ILPES, Santiago, August 1972).
Sachs, I.
  1964   *Patterns of Public Sector in Underdeveloped Economies* (Asia Publishing House, Bombay 1964).
Schultz, T.W.
  1964   *Transforming Traditional Agriculture* (New Haven, 1964).
Schydlowsky, D.M.
  1968   'On the Choice of a Shadow Price for Foreign Exchange', Economic Development Report No. 108, *D.A.S.* (Harvard, 1968).
Scott, M.FG.
  1974   'How to Use and Estimate Shadow Exchange Rates', *O.E.P.* (July 1974).
  1977   'The Test Rate of Discount and Changes in Base Level Income in the U.K.', *E.J.* (June 1977).
Scott, M.FG., J. MacArthur and D.M.G. Newbery
  1976   *Project Appraisal in Practice: The Little-Mirrlees Method Applied in Kenya* (Heinemann, 1976).
Self, P.
  1975   *Econocrats and the Policy Process; the Politics and Philosophy of Cost Benefit Analysis* (Macmillan, London, 1975).

Sen, A.K.
1960   *Choice of Techniques* (Blackwell, 1960).
1966   'Peasants and Dualism with and without Surplus Labour', *J.P.E.*, Vol. 74 (October 1966).
1967   'Isolation, Assurance, and the Social Rate of Discount', *Q.J.E.* (February 1967).
1970   *Collective Choice and Social Welfare* (London, 1970).
1971   *Growth Economics* (ed) (Penguin, 1971).
1972   'Control Areas and Accounting Prices, an Approach to Economic Evaluation', *E.J.*, Vol. 82 (1972).
1973   *On Economic Inequality* (O.U.P., 1973).
Seton, F.
1972   *Shadow Wages in the Chilean Economy* (OECD, Paris, 1972).
Soligo, R., and J.J. Stern
1965   'Tariff Protection, Import Substitution and Investment Efficiency', *Pakistan Development Review* (Summer 1965).
Squire, L., and H.G. van der Tak
1975   *Economic Analysis of Projects* (Johns Hopkins, 1975).
Stewart, F.
1975   'A Note on Social Cost Benefit Analysis and Class Conflict in LDCs', *World Development* (January 1975).
Stewart, F., and P. Streeten
1971   'Conflicts between Output and Employment Objectives' in R. Robinson and P. Johnson (eds), *Prospects for Employment Opportunities in the 1970s* (H.M.S.O., London, 1971).
Stiglitz, J.
1974   'Alternative Theories of Wage Determination and Unemployment in Less Developed Countries, I, II and III', *Q.J.E.* (1973 and 1974).
Streeten, P.P.
1968   *The Crisis in Indian·Planning* (Oxford, 1968).
Streeten, P.P., and F. Stewart
1972   'Little-Mirrlees Methods and Project Appraisal', *B.O.U.I.E.S.* (February 1972).
Tinbergen, J.
1956   'The Optimal Rate of Savings', *E.J.*, Vol. 66 (1956).
Todaro, M.P.
1969   'A Model of Labour Migration and Urban Unemployment in Less Developed Countries', *A.E.R.* (March 1969).
Toye, J.
1976   'Review of Little and Mirrlees (1974)', Book Reviews, *J.D.S.*, Vol. 12 (April 1976), pp. 293-295.
Trotsky, L.
1926   *Towards Socialism or Capitalism* (Methuen, London, 1926).
U.N.I.D.O.
1972   *Guidelines for Project Evaluation* (United Nations, New York, 1972).
U.N.O.
1958   *Manual on Economic Development Projects* (United Nations, New York, 1958).
Waterston, A.
1965   *Development Planning: The Lessons of Experience* (Baltimore, 1965).
Weisbrod, B.A.
1968   'Deriving an Implicit Set of Governmental Weights for Income Classes' in R. Layard (ed), *Cost Benefit Analysis* (Penguin, 1972).

White, J.
   1974   *The Politics of Foreign Aid* (Bodley Head, 1974).
Wonnacott, T., and R. Wonnacott
   1972   *Introductory Statistics for Business and Economics* (Wiley, New York, 1972).
Yamane, T.
   1964   *Statistics, an Introductory Analysis* (New York, 1964).
Yang, S.C.
   1975   *Social Rate of Return for Project Evaluation; an Estimate for Yugoslavia*
            (World Bank Staff Working Paper No. 205, Washington, June 1975).
Yeomans, K.A.
   1968   *Applied Statistics; Statistics for the Social Scientist*, Vol. II (Penguin, 1968).

INDEX

Page numbers in italics refer to text-figures, often with text on the same page